Ed veen,

Sow soylley jee!
(Enjoy!)

James Franklin

A Guide to the Folklore Sites of the Isle of Man

A Guide to the Folklore Sites of the Isle of Man
by James Franklin, Sam Hudson and Katie Newton

First edition 2023
Second (revised) edition 2024
© Culture Vannin

Culture Vannin
Fairfield House
Main Road
St John's
IM4 3NA

www.culturevannin.im

Culture Vannin is the trading name for the Manx Heritage Foundation,
registered charity 333 in the Isle of Man

Front cover photograph by Brook Wassall
brookwassall.com

Design by Kim Gee Studio
kimgeestudio.com

All Rights Reserved

ISBN 978-1-912668-12-0

Contents

"...there is not a creek or cranny in this Island, but what is haunted, either with fairies or ghosts."

George Waldron, *A Description of the Isle of Man* (1731)

~

Introduction

The Isle of Man is full of folklore. There is barely a road, farm, glen or hilltop in this Island without a tale of fairies, bugganes, ghosts or similar.

Folklore provides much more than merely entertaining stories to tell one another. It offers us a deeper appreciation of the landscape and the lives of those who have lived here before us. It gives an insight into people's experiences in these spaces and it tells us something of who they are through the activities, concerns and interests expressed within these tales. Folklore unites us, offering us the chance to share tales together and make connections, empowering us to feel like we belong here, in this space, in this Island.

This book began in 2018 as simply a good idea, but it is only now, as we look back, that we can fully appreciate the journey.

These pages are the fruits of years of work, trawling through thousands of pages of books, journals and manuscripts, as well as undertaking hundreds of trips into the field. We do not pretend to have gathered and located all possible historical sources, and we have barely scratched the surface of what might be available to be collected today. We very much view this book as a first volume, and we look forward to improving and expanding the project in the future.

In working to uncover, explore and locate these tales over the past five years, we have come to a deeper appreciation of the Island and the people who live and have lived here for centuries. It has been a privilege and a joy to be immersed in these stories for so long and to explore our Island through them.

We hope that this book will offer a similar experience to the reader.

Notes for the reader

This book is not an attempt to present a complete account of Manx folklore. Rather, it is an overview of many of the tales that can be located in the Isle of Man.

Full **references** have been included here, offering complete transparency and openness of our sources. We do not wish to be the gatekeepers of knowledge, but instead to hand it back into popular currency. We hope that many readers will be inspired to read the original works referenced here, both to bypass our editorial hand and its inevitable errors, and to enjoy the originals in their own telling, many of which offer a detail and vividness not possible to reproduce here. Great efforts have been made to remove errors wherever possible, but undoubtedly some will remain, and for which we take responsibility.

Sources vary in quality and attitude, with some even openly mocking of, or hostile to, the material they cover. Any attempt to impose our judgment of these sources, or to pass on their own judgement, was not felt to be appropriate here. This publication therefore faithfully retains the repetition, confusion and conflict of the originals. Theories attempting to dismiss or debunk tales have been omitted here unless they form a relevant or integral part of the tale itself. Accounts from history or archaeology which do not reference the folklore have been omitted as beyond the scope of the current project, even in instances where they appear to conflict with the folklore material. Some sources are derivative of others and are included here to show the development or popularity of a tale. However, sources which merely reproduce earlier works are omitted, with the exception of A. W. Moore's *Folk-lore of the Isle of Man*, because of its established place in Manx Studies and easy availability. Where variant versions of a story are available, the fullest or best-known version has been chosen to lead the entry, with variants coming after.

Every effort has been made to give **placenames** correctly. We have used the names in the original texts wherever possible, but we have deferred to George Broderick's seven-volume study, *Placenames of the Isle of Man*, whenever conflicts have arisen. We have also tried to respect current usage of placenames wherever possible and appropriate. We ask for the reader's understanding and forgiveness where the placenames vary from what they hold as correct. An added benefit of this project is to be returning into use a number of little-known or long-forgotten placenames.

All **Manx language** has been kept as in the original sources wherever appropriate. However, modernisation of spelling has been undertaken in a very small number of places, with the awareness that the written sources are only representations of what would have been the original spoken form. Readers will also find it useful to note that lenition or mutation occurs in Manx at the start of words in many situations. For example, when 'mooinjer veggey' (little people) follows 'moghrey mie' (good morning), it becomes 'vooinjer veggey.'

Please read and respect all **access notes**. Our attitude has been one of openness, supported by the fact that the information herein is already publicly available in the original sources or else could be otherwise easily obtained.

The **coordinates** for the sites are accurate to the site only when they can be visited. At times this is very specific to a particular location or object, but at other times it is unfortunate that specific co-ordinates relate to only a vague area. For view-only sites, the co-ordinates are for the location from which the site can be viewed, rather than the site itself. The co-ordinates should always be intelligently interpreted by the reader in relation to the story to which it connects.

The **site information** and **accessibility** has been assembled to the best of our ability and in good faith. It follows the same model as that established by the publication, *A Guide to the Archaeological Sites of the Isle of Man*. We offer the site and accessibility information here as a guide to help the reader to go out and visit the sites for themselves, but it should be treated as such, with individuals making assessments that are appropriate to them. Please read the Country Code included here and use the information within this book in conjunction with up-to-date maps and weather forecasts if you intend to visit any of the sites.

Further details of the access information used for the sites is as follows:

Access only   There is not an official Right of Way, but a temporary access route has been agreed with the landowner.

Public   Public access. The site can be reached by, or viewed from, a public footpath. Please note that a site being on public land does not mean that it is actually accessible in practice.

Public ram   Public ramblage. Land available to open public access by foot. Certain restrictions might apply. Please see Isle of Man Government, Department of Infrastructure for further information.

PROW   Public Rights of Way. Routes where the public has a right to pass and re-pass. Certain restrictions might apply. Please see Isle of Man Government, Department of Infrastructure for further information.

Private   The site is in private ownership. There is no right of access. Photographs are printed in this book with the landowner's permission.

Private land –   The site is in private ownership. There is no right of access. However, the
View only   site can be viewed from a footpath or road.

Thanks

This book has only been possible thanks to the generous help and kindness of so many landowners and custodians of our Island's memories. Perhaps the chief privilege and pleasure of this project has been in sharing in their knowledge of and respect for our Island.

There have been innumerable scholars and experts of Manx folklore and landscape without whom this project would not have been possible. In need of special mention is Stephen Miller RBV, whose *Manx Notes* and other works have been a constant source of information and inspiration.

The expertise of a number of people has been essential in the production of this book. These include John Quirk, Paul Quayle, Ffinlo Williams, Rob Clynes, Graeme Watson and Shaun Murphy.

On a more personal note, James wishes to thank Finn, Orry and Oshin for sharing the adventure of exploring these sites together, and Cori, always.

Sam would like to thank William Cowell, Patricia Newton, David Martin, Ber Weyde, Marinda Fargher, Helen Mason, the staff of the Manx Museum Library and others who have helped in the research. He gives special thanks to his wonderful friend, Anne-Marie Robinson, for accompanying him on so many adventures and in offering her wisdom in helping to find and rediscover some forgotten places.

Katie is grateful that this project has allowed her to share so many experiences with her family. Her father, Malcolm, who she sadly lost in February 2020, was very excited by the project and would be so proud of this finished book. It was his fascination with the Manx landscape and history which set her off on this journey many years ago. She also wishes to thank the many wonderful landowners and tenants met during the last few years, many of whom have since become friends. She would also like to thank the staff at the Manx National Heritage Library – Wendy, Sarah, Kim and Suzi – for their patience and encouragement. Also, all those who wrote down the stories over the years and kept them from being forgotten.

This book has seen in love, death, the birth of two children, a global pandemic, one house burnt, three homes bought, and much else besides. To all who have helped on the journey, gura mie eu.

The Country Code

You are requested to observe the following code to protect yourselves, the wildlife and farm animals, and to preserve the natural beauty of the Manx countryside.

Please do...

- Keep to paths across farmland
- Close all gates unless it is obvious that they are intended to stay open
- Keep dogs under control at all times and especially around farm animals. Please make sure that dogs do not foul footpaths or public open spaces.
- Clear up your litter, particularly glass

Please do not...

- Disturb livestock
- Drop cigarette ends
- Pick wild flowers
- Disturb birds' nests
- Damage walls or fences
- Trespass on private property
- Foul pools or streams
- Damage crops
- Camp, light fires, have barbecues or use a naked flame stove, except in designated areas
- Park across gateways
- Disturb ruins or historic sites (digging or metal detecting requires a licence from Manx National Heritage)

Personal safety

Please do...

- Refer to up-to-date maps or guidebooks
- Check weather forecasts before you leave, and be prepared to turn back if the weather worsens
- Let someone else know where you are going and when you expect to return
- Get to know the signs and symbols used in the countryside to show paths and open countryside
- Take extra care if you are walking near cliffs, mines or quarries – especially with children and the less agile
- Remember to take your mobile phone

Please do not...

- Forget that you are responsible for your own safety and for others in your care, so be prepared for changes in weather and other events

- Assume that your mobile phone will work everywhere – it won't

Other points to remember

Events, road closures, land management operations or other such activities might interrupt access to the sites in this book. Please check relevant Government websites before visiting.

Unlike Scotland there is no concept of 'Free Public Ramblage' in the Isle of Man. Unlike England and Wales there are no areas of 'Open Access.' However, a large amount of the hill land of the Isle of Man is Government-owned and much of it is officially designated as 'Areas of Public Ramblage.' You will need to look at the 1:25,000 Outdoor Leisure Map issued by the Department of Infrastructure or the 1:30,000 Harvey Superwalker map. Both are readily available.

Parishes

Andreas

The folklore of Andreas is dominated by the Teares of Ballawhane. Undoubtedly the best-known practitioners of charms and traditional cures in Manx history, the wealth of stories that feature them demonstrates the extent to which Manx imagination has been excited by this family at Gat y Whing. It is perhaps under their influence that a large proportion of the other folklore in the parish concerns charming in some form or other.

1. Dropping iron in a grave

2. The three-headed giant

3. The burnt witch's broom

4. The bleeding stone of Guilcagh

5. Two ghosts drifting up out of the grave

6. The evil eye at Ballachurry

7. The witch doctor of Keeillthustag

8. The charmer's shipwreck

- Jim Crellin, the blood-charmer [private land]

9. The fear of Smeale mound

- Lag ny Ferrishyn [private land]

- Gat y Whing, home of the Teares of Ballawhane [private land]

10. Leodest

11. Cashtal Ree Gorree

12. The curse of the stolen keeill font

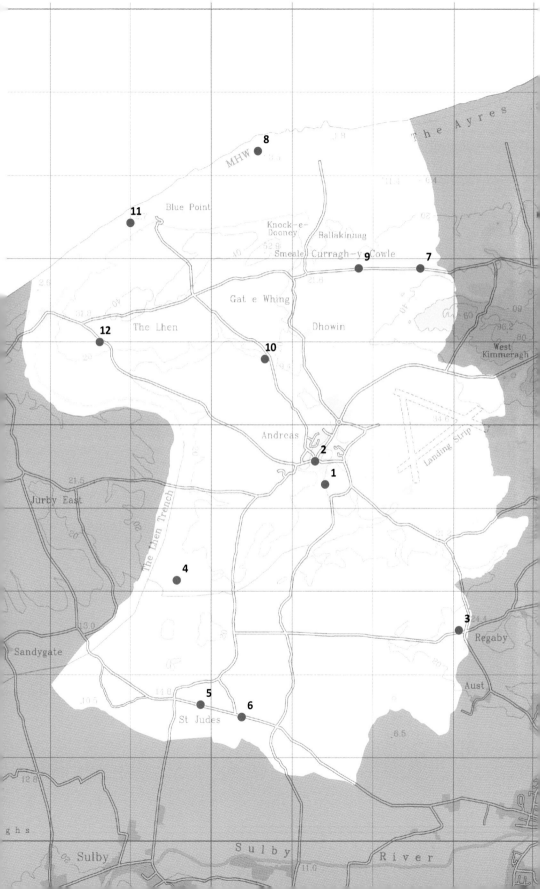

Dropping iron in a grave

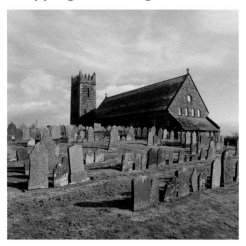

Open during daylight hours | Level access to church, uneven ground in graveyard | SC 4149 9928 | 54.364272, -4.441214 | The church of Kirk Andreas is on the south-east side of Andreas village.

At a burial here at Kirk Andreas in 1628 a man named Philip Crebbin was fearful that the spirit of the deceased person would return to haunt him. So, he dropped a piece of iron into the partly filled grave, hoping to ensure that the spirit would not be able to leave. However, despite his best efforts to conceal his action, Crebbin was spotted and he was obliged to do penance for this apparent attempt to carry out witchcraft.

DC-MI 26

The three-headed giant

Private land – view only | Viewable from pavement beside a road | SC 4136 9955 | 54.366731, -4.443293 | The old rectory is in Andreas village, north of the church. Its main gate comes off Andreas Road, the main road through the village.

When a band of Norsemen landed at the Lhen they brought with them a three-headed giant to act as their parson. When they settled here, the giant was appointed to the rectory in Andreas, but he did not deal with his parishioners fairly as he exhorted all the tithes he could from them. However, despite this, the people got used to the giant's ways and soon they came to like him. It was because of this that, for a long time after, the parson of Andreas was paid three times more than in other parishes.

AWM-FIOM 64–65 | WWG-MS3 226

The burnt witch's broom

Public | Pavement beside main road | SC 4314 9752 | 54.349025, -4.414827 | The Regaby crossroads is roughly halfway between Ramsey and Andreas. It is the meeting of the Andreas Road with Regaby West Road and Nassau Road. Modern changes to the road layout have disjointed what used to be a perfect cross of the roads.

A man came across a woman carrying out witchcraft three or four times and eventually threatened her with a kick if he found her doing it again. When he was returning home from courting very early one morning, he saw her at this crossroads sweeping a circle round her as large as that made by horses when threshing. The man kicked her and took her besom (broom) from her. This besom was remarkable for having 'seventeen sorts of knots,' and he hid it until midday, when he built a bonfire of dry gorse and put the besom on top. As it burned, the besom made explosions like gun shots so loud they could be heard as far away as Kirk Andreas. The old woman did not survive long after the destruction of the besom.

AWM-FIOM 91 | JR-MFS 2.292–293

The bleeding stone of Guilcagh

Private land – view only | Rough and uneven public footpath | SC 3965 9812 | 54.353328, -4.468813 | Guilcagh is a private farm on a footpath, a little under a mile south-west of Andreas village along St Jude's Road.

A large stone used to stand on the top of a tumulus here at Guilcagh. This was known as the bleeding stone, owing to the red liquid that oozed from it. However, when a man named Arthur Cottier came to own the farm, he set dynamite around it and blew the thing to pieces. He used a larger piece of the debris as a corner stone at the farm, but once it was there the stone gave them no rest as there was a constant 'rumpus' in the farm street. Eventually Cottier was forced to take the stone out and return it to the tumulus.

FLS C/43-A

Two ghosts drifting up out of the grave

Open during daylight hours | Uneven ground | SC 3995 9662 | 54.339985, -4.463483 | The church of St Jude's is 400 metres east of the St Jude's crossroads along the Jurby Road. The grave of the Misses Murray is the cross standing immediately under the eastern window of the church.

In about 1900 the slab over the grave of the Misses Murray was taken away to reveal the two coffins within. The spirits of the two women floated out of the grave, much to the amazement of those who were stood by watching.

CV-OH-JC

The evil eye at Ballachurry

Private land – view only | Visible from road | SC 4045 9649 | 54.338888, -4.455686 | A little over half a mile east of St Jude's along the Jurby Road towards Ramsey. The private house is on the northern side of the road.

In December 1896 a calf at Ballachurry that had previously been fine began to bellow loudly, rush around its stall wildly with wide eyes and generally behave 'almost as though possessed.' Within an hour it was dead. When the farmer, named Crellin, was discussing this later with a neighbour, he was able to identify it as resulting from the evil eye. The neighbour explained that the same had happened to one of his calves but that he had cured it by sweeping up the dust from the road outside the cowhouse and sprinkling it over the animal. Crellin was sorry not to have known this before his calf fell ill.

YLM 3.6.286–287

The witch doctor of Keeillthustag

Private land – view only | Visible from road | NX 4266 0187 | 54.387924, -4.424609 | Keeillthustag is a private farmhouse on the north side of the Coast Road about half a mile west of the Thurot Cottage Road.

Two Maughold fishermen were on the way to their boat when they met a woman known to be a witch. It was after this that the boat failed to catch anything at all on the first two or three nights at sea and the meeting with the witch was identified as the cause. The skipper told the men to go to Keeillthustag, where a renowned witch doctor was living at that time. When they arrived at Keeillthustag the man gave them some herbs to return their luck. He also told them to return to the witch with a pair of scissors and cut off a piece of her skirt or shawl when she was not looking. This piece of the witch's clothing was then to be stitched into their own clothing. When they did this, they not only got plenty of fish from then on, but the witch was unable to harm them again due to the piece of her clothing stitched among their own clothes.

WWG-MS3 336–337

The charmer's shipwreck

Public | Sand and rocks, tidal | NX 4066 0328 | 54.399970, -4.456160 | Rue Point is a point of the coastline about halfway between Jurby and the Point of Ayre.

The Teares of Ballawhane gained their legendary knowledge of charms and cures from a mysterious book of charms and remedies that was handed down through the family. The book first arrived on the Isle of Man at Rue Point, when a French ship was shipwrecked and its survivors came ashore here. At their own personal risk, the Teares rescued some of the crew and cared for them in their home. It was in thanks for this that the captain of the ship left with them this important manuscript that enabled them to gain their amazing powers and ability.

MD-EVAF 32–33 | WH-MM1 182 | WWG-MS3 314–315

Jim Crellin, the blood-charmer

Private | Smeale Farm is on the seaward side of the Coast Road, between Smeale Road and Thurot Cottage Road. The original farmhouse at Smeale today functions as a garage/workshop.

Perhaps the most celebrated blood-charmer of the north of the Island was a Primitive Methodist preacher from Baldromma, Maughold, named Jim Crellin. An amazing example of his charming happened here at Smeale when a bad castration of a bull left blood audibly pouring onto the straw beneath the animal. The bull was on a clear course towards death and so someone was swiftly dispatched to Jim Crellin. When the charmer said a charm while still at his home some six miles away in Maughold, the bleeding here in Smeale miraculously stopped instantly.

WWG-MS2 191 | WWG-MS3 323–324

The fear of Smeale mound

Private land – view only | Visible from road | NX 4190 0188 | 54.387767, -4.436288 | The tall hedge opposite the entrance to Smeale Farm, on the landward side of the Coast Road, between Smeale Road and Thurot Cottage Road. A mound forms into the hedge here but the rear of the mound can be seen from over the gate a little further east down the road.

Bad occurrences are known to hound those who disturb ancient burial mounds. The fear of this used to be so prevalent that when the road was widened here in the nineteenth century and an ancient burial urn was discovered, the workers swiftly reburied it close by, in fear of the possible repercussions. Nothing is recorded of whether anything happened to these workers, though the urn was rediscovered by archaeologists in 1928.

AJAF-ASG 40–41 | JMM 1.16.221

Lag ny Ferrishyn

Private | Lag ny Ferrishyn is along a private track coming off eastwards from the Leodest Road.

A small dip along the track here is known as Lag ny Ferrishyn (Hollow of the Fairies). No specific story of the fairies is recorded here, but the name is possibly linked to Gat y Whing, the home of the famous Teares Ballawhane, which lies a short distance further along the track.

WWG-MS3 214

Gat y Whing, home of the Teares of Ballawhane

Private | Gat y Whing today used to lie to the west of the Leodest Road, though nothing remains of the house today.

Gat y Whing was once the home of the most famous family of charmers in the Isle of Man, the Teares of Ballawhane. Their skill was so renowned that even the chief magistrate of Castletown knew of it and admitted to Chalse Teare that, 'I know that by probing the secret springs of nature you can accelerate, return or turn aside, at pleasure, the natural course of events.' Chalse Teare travelled all over the Island on his ambling little Manx pony, dressed all in clothes of loaghtan wool and wearing his broad-brimmed hat too large for his head. He spoke with 'pithy quaintness' and was fond of using 'idiomatic proverbialisms.' When people visited for help, they were to neither eat nor drink on the way and they were to tell no one of the cause of their journey.

The stories of the Teares are wonderous and plentiful. As well as what follows here, other stories of them appear elsewhere at other locations.

JT-HSA 2.160–162 | WL-DPG 15–16 | WWG-MS2 181–182 | YLM 1.9.291

The sparrows

Chalse Teare's ability to help with crops was so renowned that farmers would delay sowing their seeds until he had blessed the seed. A story relating to this comes from July 1883 when he visited Laxey and met an innkeeper named Fargher, who was complaining of the sparrows eating the grain from his field. Teare first chastised him for not having called him in before sowing and then he went to banish the sparrows with a charm of some sort. After this the neighbours were amazed that, although the sparrows still flocked to the edge of the field, none dared to go in to take the grain.

Another time, the Manx potato crop did not seed properly because of a disease. Teare diagnosed this as the work of the fairies, as the potatoes he had attended alone flourished that year.

AWM-FIOM 95–96 | JT-HSA 2.160 | WL-DPG 15–16 | YLM 1.9.291

The boy who ate ashes

A woman once grew envious of another woman's pretty child and she put the evil eye on the child just by looking at him. The child then began to eat ashes, and this was only halted when the boy's parents came to Teare for herbs with which to cure him.

N-IOME-03091898

The boy who lay in the gooseberry bushes

A twelve-year-old boy from Maughold became ill immediately after falling asleep amongst some gooseberry bushes near his home. The boy's father did not believe in Teare and so refused to send for him. However, a neighbour went in secret to Teare and obtained herbs for the boy's mother to secretly make a drink from and give it to the boy. After this, the boy made a complete recovery. Teare recognised that the boy had been lying where he should not have been and so told the parents to never let him lie amongst the gooseberry bushes again.

WWG-MS3 317

The buitched Sunday school girls

Six or seven young girls were returning from Sunday school when they all fell ill as they passed a particular house. Their parents sent for a doctor but without effect, so they came to consult Chalse Teare. He explained that the woman in the house had begrudged the girls the pretty dresses that they were wearing and so had brought about their illness through witchcraft. He got a herb and began to pound it, at which point the woman soon appeared, having been drawn there by a stinging sensation as he prepared the herb. At this the girls began to make a speedy recovery.

YLM 3.4.163

Rolling in the herbs

The power of the Teares of Ballawhane attracted such reverence that fishermen were known to sneak into the garden at Gat y Whing so that they could roll in the herbs that the Teares grew for charms. The hope was that they would thereby take their luck with them to sea.

WWG-MS2 179

Boiling the purse in tea

The reverence shown to Teare was so remarkable that when he forgot his purse on a boat in Peel, the fishermen cut it up into as many pieces as there were men on the boat, then boiled it in their tea, drank it, and threw the remainder over their nets for luck.

AELM-MY 176 | WWG-MS3 318

Retribution for mockery

Charles Teare was once abused and accused of deceiving people when he visited a public house in Maughold. Before he left, Charles announced that, 'there's more than one of you fellows won't get home tonight.' Indeed, two of the men fell asleep at the roadside and awoke in directions the wrong way for their homes, but, more seriously, the third man fell into a hole and broke his neck.

On a separate occasion some time before 1883, the young fishermen of Peel 'showed rudeness and ill-nature' towards Teare, and so in retribution he 'cut the fish off' for them.

WWG-MS3 317–318 | YLM 1.9.291

Cure for stroke

Chalse Teare is credited with many wonderous cures, including righting the effects of a stroke suffered by a man named Tom Kermode. Having woken one morning with his mouth all twisted, Kermode's wife got some herbs from Teare, boiled or simmered them, and then gave them to Kermode to drink. After this he made a complete recovery.

WWG-MS3 316–317

The fairy doctor

As well as his gift with cures and charms, Chalse Teare was also known for his closeness with the fairies. One time a tailor visited him just before Chalse was due out to a feast with the fairies. Chalse invited him along but the tailor pointed out that he did not have a horse to ride. Chalse took a board from the parlour and went outside. When the tailor joined him, he was amazed to find a horse there waiting for him. Chalse warned the tailor not to say a word, under any circumstances, and then they set off at great speed to ride fearlessly over hedges and ditches. The tailor was amazed, especially when they came to a great jump, when he let out the cry, 'Oh, Lord, what a jump!' At this, his horse turned back into the lapboard and the tailor landed in a bog.

SM-MFT 40–44

Leodest

Private land – view only | Visible from road | NX 4073 0078 | 54.377522, -4.453723 | A private farm about halfway down Leodest Road, which runs between the Coast Road and Andreas village.

Charley Chalse cures the bellowing cow

A cow at Leodest had been standing, bellowing and refusing food and water for days. They went for Charley Chalse, one of the legendary Teares of Ballawhane, and although they found him half-drunk, Charley Chalse cut some herbs from his garden and came here to Leodest. He rubbed the herbs along the cow's back and then threw them down beside and before her. The cow gave one final bellow and then at last began to eat and drink again.

Another account of this gives the cause of the cow's ailment not as witchcraft but rather a piece of turnip stuck in its throat. However, Teare's mysterious method of curing the cow's problem was not questioned.

WWG-MS2 180–181 | WWG-MS3 318

The blood-charmer at the operation

Jack Corlett, commonly known as 'Jack-o'-me-onny,' was a man from Ramsey famed for his ability to stop bleeding merely by speaking a charm. Because this skill extended to animals, he was frequently asked to be present at operations on farms. Once, near Leodest, a farrier refused to begin his operation until Corlett arrived, after which the farrier cut out a tumour from the vaginal passage of a cow. After the work was done, Corlett uttered the charm and the bleeding stopped immediately.

WWG-MS3 322–323

Cashtal Ree Gorree

Private land – view only | Visible from car park | NX 3907 0242 | 54.391752, -4.480036 | The earthwork of Cashtal Ree Gorree sits below the brooghs at Blue Point, just south of the Blue Point car park.

The Manx name, Cashtal Ree Gorree, translates as King Orry's Castle. This site would be an appropriate site for the legendary Norse King to have a stronghold, as it was close to here that he first landed on the Isle of Man.

This is also known to be the site of battles between the Manx and the Norse invaders, as was confirmed by the waking visions of a man known as Juan Gob y Gorum, who saw a crowd of big men landing from long boats here and marching inland.

This spot was also known as a gathering place for the fairies, who enter the earth here and travel underground to emerge in Maughold churchyard.

HIJ-JG 206 | JJK-PN 586 | WWG-MS1 198 | WWG-MS3 228–229

The curse of the stolen keeill font

Private land – view only | Visible from road | NX 3869 0099 | 54.378781, -4.485216 | A keeill which used to stand in a field beside the Kiondroghad Road, which leaves the Coast Road landwards about a quarter of a mile east of the bridge over the Lhen Trench. No trace of the keeill remains today but it stood roughly in the centre of the field behind Ballacomaish.

When a ruined keeill still stood here a fisherman removed the font from the ruins, looking to use it as a barking-pot (a container in which to treat fishing gear). However, it was because of this disrespect of the religious site that the next time he went to sea, the boat would not hold him and so they had no choice but to turn back and put him ashore.

JJK-PN 578–579

Arbory

Arbory is perhaps best-known for its folklore around St Catherine. With her dedication on a holy well, a cursed keeill and a curious custom involving the mock funeral of a dead hen, the area along the bottom of Ballakilpheric Road is rich in St Catherine folklore specific to the parish.

Less well-known today is another centre of folklore at Ballachrink, where an association with the glashtyn was once legendary. The rest of the parish enjoys a wide range of strange tales, including a buggane cat, a White Lady and a headless donkey with eyes in its neck.

1. The White Lady of Balladoole
2. Two ladies dressed in black
-   Death follows tampering with a burial mound [private land]
3. The witch-seeking fire at Ballabeg
4. Kirk Arbory
5. Being dragged by an unseen hand
6. Gathering the dust from the crossroads
7. Laa'l Catreeney
8. The curse of Keeill Catreeney
9. Chibbyr Catreeney
10. Colby Glen Road
11. The glashtyns of Ballachrink
12. Ballakindrey Road
13. The stones of Cabbal Dreem Ruy
14. The Death Coach of the Whallag ford
15. Cronk Fedjag

The White Lady of Balladoole

Private land – view only | Visible from pavement beside a main road | SC 2557 6833 | 54.081237, -4.667943 | The gates to Balladoole are just outside the western edge of Castletown, 90 metres beyond Arbory Road.

Balladoole is haunted by a White Lady and she is often seen or experienced by those passing by the gates on the road here. She is sometimes seen along the avenue towards the house, but her presence can be felt without actually seeing her. People walking along the main road, distracted in thought, have been known to be overcome with panic when coming across her presence here, such that they are compelled to run away down the road.

A moddey doo is also known to haunt the grounds of Balladoole, but no detailed accounts of it are recorded.

EK-CC 364 | MT 33 | WWG-MS1 325

Two ladies dressed in black

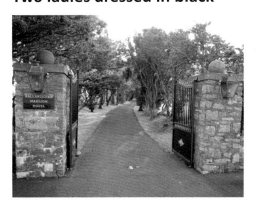

Private land – view only | Visible from pavement beside a main road | SC 2538 6846 | 54.082356, -4.670920 | Ballakeigan Mansion House is to the west of Castletown. It is the first property on the north side of the main road towards Port Erin, about 300 metres after the junction with Arbory Road.

Two ladies dressed in black are known to haunt Ballakeigan and are often seen or experienced by those passing by the gates on the road here. The apparitions are sometimes seen along the avenue towards the house, but their presence can also be felt without them actually being seen. People walking along the main road, distracted in thought, have been known to be overcome with panic when they encounter them here, such that they are compelled to run away down the road. The black clothing of these ghostly women has led some to suggest that they might be nuns.

MT 33 | WWG-MS1 325

Death follows tampering with a burial mound

Private land | A field on the private land of Ballacross.

The great collector of Manx music and folklore, Dr John Clague, was involved in an archaeological dig of what was believed to be an ancient burial site at here at the end of May 1908. His sudden and unexpected death in August that year was later attributed by some to his having disturbed this ancient site.

WWG-MS2 140

The witch-seeking fire at Ballabeg

Public | Visible from pavement beside a road | SC 2492 7049 | 54.100460, -4.679090 | Ballabeg is in the middle of the parish, between Colby and Ballasalla.

If a person has made you ill through witchcraft, their power can be undone if you light a bonfire over their footsteps, and the person who has done the witchcraft will be impelled to come and present themselves. So it was in 1713 when the wife of the Captain of the Parish in Arbory lit a bonfire in the main road in Ballabeg.

The fire was sufficiently large that it burned for more than a day, causing much annoyance to the Arbory community. The Church took a dim view of such practices and so she was brought to the ecclesiastical courts on the charge of witchcraft. However, the case was adjourned indefinitely, partly owing to her position in society but also owing to the difficulty of finding evidence since no incantations or the like were said upon lighting the fire.

DC-MI 27

Kirk Arbory

Open during daylight hours | Level access | SC 2472 7052 | 54.100649, -4.682164 | The church of Kirk Arbory is in Ballabeg, on the north side of the road on the Colby side of the village.

The giant's skull

Sometime before the early eighteenth century, an enormous human skull was uncovered when they were digging a new grave at Kirk Arbory. The skull was reported to be of such a 'monstrous circumference that a bushel would hardly cover it.' Other bones true to that size of person were reported as being frequently found here at Arbory at that time, supporting the belief, once widely held, that the Isle of Man was originally the home of giants.

GW-DIM 61–62

The light in the window

One night in December 1897 a woman saw a light in the window of Kirk Arbory. She went inside the church to investigate but found no light nor anything that could explain it. She thought that perhaps the mysterious light was somehow the sexton there late and so she asked him in the morning if he had been in his seat by the organ the night before. He replied that he had not and, upon hearing her explain what she had seen, he realised what it meant and replied that, 'that was my sign, M'm.' He was dead and buried within a fortnight.

WWG-MS2 65

The spinning woman in white

Two men were walking past Kirk Arbory one night when they saw a woman dressed all in white standing in the angle of the wall opposite the church gate. They went across to speak to her but she grabbed hold of one of the men by his arms and spun him around. This went on until he grew so dizzy that he almost fell to the ground when she eventually let him go. The marks of this strange woman's hands remained on his biceps for the rest of his life.

WWG-MS3 358

Being dragged by an unseen hand

Public | Pavement beside a main road | SC 2435 7026 | 54.098169, -4.687732 | Outside Ballabeg, westwards on the main road towards Colby.

One night a man was walking towards his home in Surby but when he was not far out of Ballabeg he was suddenly gripped by the arm. He turned to see who it was, but he could not see anyone. He was dragged forcibly for about 200 metres down the road, back towards Ballabeg, and then he was left unconscious. In the morning he was found and taken into a house close by. Here the black imprint of four fingers and a thumb were discovered at the top of his arm. These marks were to remain with the man for the rest of his life.

WWG-MS1 158

Gathering the dust from the crossroads

Public | Pavement beside a main road | SC 2315 7007 | 54.096087, -4.705852 | The crossroads at the centre of Colby, the meeting of the main road, the Colby Glen Road and Station Road by the Methodist Hall.

The dust gathered from a crossroad is effective at undoing witchcraft. An example of this being done here was when the woman of Ballachrink would come to sweep up the dust from this crossroads with a goose wing. She then took this dust home in her apron and sprinkled it on her husband, who was lying sick because of the evil eye.

JC-MR 170–171

Laa'l Catreeney

Private land – view only | Visible from pavement beside a main road | SC 2284 7003 | 54.095570, -4.710618 | The fair field is at the corner of the main road through Colby and Ballakilpheric Road on the north-west side, over the stream.

A fair used to be held here on Laa'l Catreeney (St Catherine's Day, 6 December) in honour of the saint to whom a keeill nearby was dedicated. The young men from the neighbourhood would walk around this fair with a dead hen solemnly held between them. During this mock funeral procession, they would sing:

Kiark Catreeney marroo,	Catherine's hen is dead,
Gow's y kione,	You take the head,
As goyms ny cassyn,	And I'll take the feet,
As ver mayd ee fo'n thalloo.	And we'll put her under the ground.

They then cut off and buried the hen's head and feet, and retired to the local inn to consume a large amount of ale.

If anyone got drunk at the fair, they were said to have 'plucked a feather of the hen' ('T'eh er goaill fedjag ass y chiark').

It has been thought by some that this procession of the dead hen might be one of the oldest Manx customs.

AWM-FIOM 126–127 | EK-CC 125–127 | EK-CC 240–241 | JC-MR 42-45 | JR-MFS 3.77 | JRB-AS6 38 | MNHL 09702 | N-IOME-29051909 | PIOMNHAS 3.1.78 | YLM 3.4.189

The curse of Keeill Catreeney

Private land – view only | Visible from road | SC 2279 7016 | 54.096749, -4.711478 | The site of the keeill is beside the Ballakilpheric Road just north-west of Colby. Nothing remains of the keeill today, but it is thought to have once stood close to the southern end of the plateau which lies over the river opposite Bell Abbey.

An evangelic Protestant Irishman named Bell bought this land in the seventeenth century and took offence to the ancient keeill which was here. He rooted out the remains of the building and so brought about the curse that the land should never be inherited by a male heir of the same name. This was recorded as having remained true in the 1890s, and previous owners of the farm report that it has remained true to the present time also.

AWM-MN 223 | JJK-PN 70 | JRB-AS6 37 | N-IOME-15091939 | YLM 3.9.446 | Add

Chibbyr Catreeney

Private land – view only | Visible from road | SC 2276 7022 | 54.097225, -4.712023 | Chibbyr Catreeney is opposite Bell Abbey on the Ballakilpheric Road. It sits on private land below the downstream side of a small bridge over the river.

It is said that whoever drinks from this holy well will have an unquenchable thirst forever more, unless they leave some metal here (presumably in the form of coins or something else appropriate as an offering).

JRB-AS6 38 | WWG-MS1 26

Colby Glen Road

Public | Road without pavement | SC 2316 7087 | 54.103238, -4.706312 | Colby Glen Road runs beside the glen itself, heading north from the village of Colby.

The growing dog

A man named John Costain was walking here one night when he came across a mysterious brown dog. He was horrified as he watched it growing bigger and bigger until eventually reaching the size of a calf. Costain grew so frightened that he ran more than a mile up the road to the Round Table Inn at Ronague, where he woke the owner, who let him in all white and trembling.

FLS CC-B

The buggane growing from a cat

Two men were going up Colby Glen Road towards Ballachrink when they met a cat in the road. One of the men went to kick it, but the cat then grew to the size of a horse. The men quickly leapt into a ploughed field, which the buggane could not enter, and so the buggane watched them closely as it followed them from along the road. When the men got to the road again, they called out at the buggane, 'Ayns ennym Chris' my Chiarn, as my Yee; cretoor, chass ersooyl!' ('In the name of Christ my Lord and God; creature, turn away!') At this the buggane went away and the men were able to escape.

Other versions of this tale have the men dashing across the road chased by the buggane and one of them calling out the Lord's name upon almost being caught.

YLM 3.4.141–142

The glashtyns of Ballachrink

Private land – view only | Visible from rough and uneven footpath | SC 2329 7111 | 54.105404, -4.704376 | North of Colby along the Colby Glen Road, Ballachrink is on the north side of the road at the point where it emerges from the trees turning away from running beside the glen. A public footpath runs through the farm street.

Ballachrink used to be famous for its glashtyns, as it was said that the farm was 'thick' with them. The glashtyns were enormously strong giant-like men who did not wear clothes but were instead covered in hair.

The glashtyns emerged at night to do work around the farm. For example, whenever corn was left out loose in the barn, they would come and thresh it during the night so that the famer found the work completed when he came in the morning.

Once the farmer called upon a glashtyn to get his sheep in from the mountain ahead of a storm. The glashtyn set out and by early morning he returned to say he had done the task, though he had to chase one lamb around South Barrule before it was caught. When the farmer went out to check on the sheep, he found that it was a hare there in their midst.

Another group of glashtyns once came close to the land here and so the Ballachrink glashtyns went and drove them off, telling them to go elsewhere. As these glashtyns left they called out, 'If this place is thine, Glen Reagh Rushen (merry Glen Rushen) is not yet thine.'

There are two stories of what eventually happened to the glashtyns here, the first of which came when the farmer went to the barn to see who was doing the work at night. When he saw these enormous naked beings doing the hard work, he thought he would thank them by having clothes made for them. However, when the glashtyns saw these gifts of clothes they took offence and remarked, 'Though this place is thine, the great Glen Rushen is not.' At this they all left and were never again seen at Ballachrink.

A very different story of how they went tells of a glashtyn being tricked into being castrated. A man named Costain lived at Ballachrink and one day met a glashtyn while he was out ploughing. The glashtyn asked how his horses were so well built and Costain replied that it was because they had been castrated and recommended it to the glashtyn. The glashtyn was initially unsure but then agreed to Costain doing the operation on him after Costain had assured him that he would allow the glashtyn to do the same to him in return later. So Costain got out his knife and performed the operation, after which the glashtyn went off in great pain and he was not seen for months. However, when planting time came around Costain was too frightened to go out in case the glashtyn returned to fulfil his half of the bargain. So his clever wife got dressed up as Costain and went out with the horses in his stead. The glashtyn appeared and came over with the intention of returning the castration, but the wife said that she had already done the job. When he doubted her, she lowered her trousers and showed him. The glashtyn was aghast, thinking that she had done the job even more severely than he had. The glashtyn left Costain alone after that and the glashtyns were soon no longer seen at all, presumably due to Costain's operation.

In addition to these tales reminiscent of the better-known phynnodderee, there is a more sinister story of a glashtyn at Ballachrink. The woman of the farm once heard a voice crying over and over, 'The pee veg is in the renniagh' ('The young calves are in the fern'). She went out to see what the matter was and as she got down to the river something caught hold of her by the apron strings. It was the glashtyn, who had been lying behind a rock in wait for her, but the woman reacted quickly, untied the apron and ran away.

A variant of this story has the woman successfully caught by the glashtyn. Claiming her as his own, he took her to a secluded spot along the river, where he held tight to her apron strings but allowed himself to fall asleep. The woman then untied her apron and made her escape. When the glashtyn awoke with only the apron he said, 'Cha nel veg faagit aym agh sambyl' ('I have nothing left but a sample').

EF-MSR 175–176 | EK-CC 354–355 | FLS C16-A | FLS W/003-A | JJK-PN 84 | JR-MFS 2.286 | KR-MNQ 105 | WWG-MS1 201 | YLM 3.4.138–139

Ballakindrey Road

PROW | A quiet road and a narrow, rough and uneven footpath | SC 2362 7104 | 54.104950, -4.699250 | Ballakindrey Road is a small road and footpath north of Colby. Beyond the Ballachrink estate at the top of Colby Glen, the main road takes a right-angled turn northwards. Ballakindrey Road comes off at the corner here, heading east towards Ballakelly and Ballaoates Farm, but turning into a footpath as it turns off south towards Ballakindrey itself.

Tom Stych's coffin

Three men were walking from Colby when they heard a great screaming and shouting from Ballakindrey Road. After running here over the fields, they found three boys of about 13 years old crouched down by the gorse hedge crying and sobbing in shock at having seen the coffin of a man named Tom Stych going up the road but without anyone carrying it. It had been that day that Tom Stych had been buried and the men took the boys as simply being foolish. However, when the episode was mentioned to Tom Stych's widow, she did not think it so ridiculous, as she had seen the coffin up on its trestles in her own parlour in the moonlight the night before.

FLS CC-B

The headless donkey

A donkey with no head and with eyes in its neck used to be seen walking along Ballakindrey Road. This was reported independently by a number of people from Colby at the start of the twentieth century. One person who saw it wisely called out, 'Shee Jee y marym!' ('Peace of God be with me!') to protect herself from this unnatural thing.

FLS CC-B

The stones of Cabbal Dreem Ruy

Private land – view only | Visible from uneven ground | SC 2502 7384 | 54.130529, -4.679598 | The remains of Cabbal Dreem Ruy are in a field 200 metres below the Cringle Plantation. Between the Cringle Reservoir to the east and the small car park inset into the plantation to the west, take the track marked as a footpath southwards from the Corlea Road. Turn off west after around 200 metres, following the footpath into the field, where the keeill is to be found.

In around the 1820s someone removed some of the large stones which used to circle the keeill here at Cabbal Dreem Ruy. Their intention was to use the stones for building materials but their cattle soon started to fall ill and die. It was recognised that this was caused by the damage the person had done to the keeill, and so no more stones were ever taken away from the site.

JRB-AS6 33

The Death Coach of the Whallag ford

Public | Public road | SC 2532 7432 | 54.134959, -4.675179 | The site of the Whallag Ford is today the bridge on the Corlea Road, below the Cringle Reservoir.

On dark nights the sound of the wheels of a horse and coach can be heard crunching and swishing through the stream here where the Whallag ford used to be. This is believed to be the invisible appearance of the Death Coach which has been sighted at Solomon's Corner and is piloted by a headless driver.

WWG-MS1 343–344

Cronk Fedjag

Public ram | Rough and uneven ground, or visible from the road | SC 2398 7498 | 54.140416, -4.696090 | Cronk Fedjag is the hill directly in front of the stile north-west of the road, about halfway between the Round Table crossroads and the ninety-degree turn at the foot of Cronk ny Arrey Laa. The hill is low, undefined and does not have a clear peak.

This hill is associated with the fairies through its name, which some take to contain a mutated form of 'Feathag,' an alternative word for the fairies. This would therefore mean that the hill's name translates as 'Fairy Hill.'

It was here that a man was digging turf when he met the White Lady of the Cronk, associated with Cronk ny Arrey Laa. He looked up from his work and saw a large grey cloud coming swiftly towards him as it changed into the shape of a caillagh 'with teeth as long as his forearm.' The man called out, 'What in God's name is this?' and, at the mention of God, the figure melted back into being a cloud again.

WWG-MS1 450-451

Ballaugh

Although Ballaugh's folklore is found all over the parish, the largest concentration is along Ballaugh Glen. The stretch of road above the village boasts a ghost, a moddey doo, the phynnodderee, the fairies and one of the oldest known detailed accounts of witchcraft.

1. Ballaugh Old Church
2. Giving bonnag to a fairy child
- The thumbs left after a fairy battle [private land]
- Brough Jairg [private land]
- The dust under the bride's chair [private land]
3. Ballaugh Bridge
4. The dead weasel hung in a pigsty
- The giant of Yn Cashtal [private land]
5. Scrundal
6. The house partly built by the phynnodderee
7. The mother's ghost tending to her children

Ballaugh Old Church

Open for services or by arrangement | Steps and uneven ground | SC 3406 9572 | 54.329939, -4.553471 | Ballaugh Old Church is at the Cronk, a little over a mile north of Ballaugh village.

A buitched cow saved by snow

One winter, a man in Ballaugh was visited by his neighbour who saw his cow in the cowhouse and commented, 'Fine cow that.' The two men then came here for a church service but when the man returned home afterwards, he found his wife greatly concerned about the cow, which had become sick and had not eaten since the neighbour spoke of it. The man immediately went out after the neighbour and gathered up a handful of snow from his footprints, which he then took home and sprinkled over the cow's food. The cow soon recovered and began to eat again, as the snow had been effective in undoing the evil eye put on the cow by the jealous neighbour.

YLM 1.6.170

The seller of love potions

At the start of the eighteenth century a woman named Alice Cowley lived in Ballaugh and was known for her charms. In 1713 she sold a charm to a young man for ninepence which she said would 'make a young woman fall in love with him.' The charm was to use a white powder which she gave to the man in some paper, though how he was to put it to use is not recorded. Cowley was brought to trial for this apparent witchcraft and sentenced to 30 days in prison, after which she had to stand for two hours at the market cross in each of the Island's four major towns wearing a white sheet, holding a white wand and with a sign hung upon her that said, 'for charming and sorcery.' After this she had to do penance here in her own parish church in Ballaugh.

Another account has this event taking place in 1735 rather than 1713.

YLM 1.7.191 | YLM 3.6.309–310

Giving bonnag to a fairy child

Public | Sand, tidal, or visible from car park | SC 3365 9606 | 54.332870, -4.559962| The site of the lime kilns was at the mouth of the Ballaugh River. The kilns eroded into the sea long ago, but their site was where the river today enters the sea, at Ballaugh Shore, north-west of Ballaugh Old Church and the Cronk.

Sometime before the 1890s a woman was baking bonnags by the limekilns here when a little child appeared. The woman gave the girl a bonnag but as soon as it touched her hand the girl disappeared.

YLM 1.8.223

The thumbs left after a fairy battle

Private | Ballakoig is a private farm off the Bollyn Road at the Cronk, north of Ballaugh village.

Ballakoig used to have a number of old tramman trees that were important for the fairies. When these trees were cut down great numbers of fairies came to where they used to stand, to weep and lament. But soon such crowds of them had gathered that a fight broke out and in the morning the farm street was found to be strewn with fairies' thumbs.

WWG-MS1 207 | YLM 1.8.223

Brough Jairg

Private | Brough Jairg is the first farm on the north side of the main road west of Ballaugh village. The farm track is a private road and the farm buildings are not visible from the main road.

A giant named 'Jiarg' used to rule over the people of Ballaugh. He arrived on the Island with King Orry and some accounts report him as having three heads. His name is remembered in the name of this farm, Brough Jairg.

AWM-FIOM 64–65 | WWG-MS3 226

The dust under the bride's chair

Private | Broughjiarg Beg is midway between Ballaugh village and Bollyn Road. It is on the north of Brough Jiarg road, which leaves Ballaugh village opposite the graveyard of St Mary's Church. The house is not visible from the public footpath.

At the wedding dinner of John and Katreena Corlett, held here at Broughjiarg Beg, Ealish Vrian and her sister took the dust from the threshold of the outer door and put it under the bride's chair at the feast. This act of witchcraft resulted in no child being born to the married couple for years after. Katreena eventually discovered the cause of their misfortune and so went and drew blood from the faces of each of the two women with a scratch 'above the breath' (on the face or head above the mouth). This successfully undid the witchcraft and she fell pregnant soon after.

DC-MI 25

Ballaugh Bridge

Public | Public road or visible from pavement | SC 3476 9343 | 54.309676, -4.541424 | Ballaugh Bridge is at the heart of Ballaugh village on the main road between Ramsey and Peel.

Gathering dust

A women was in danger of being kicked or crushed by her cow every time she milked it and so she had to tie its legs before starting. A neighbour advised her that it was witchcraft that had made her cow so troublesome and that it could be undone by coming to the bridge with a friend at one o'clock in the morning to sweep the dust from the road. She did this and she followed the further instructions to sprinkle the dust around the cow in the cowhouse. In the morning, when the woman went to milk the cow, it did not have to be restrained at all, and it remained calm and gentle from that day on.

YLM 1.6.172

Fairies drinking

A group of fairies were known to have Ballaugh Bridge as their home. The fairies of the north would meet and drink here at the start of the herring season when on their way to Peel. The fairies would also wait under the bridge for the farmers on their way to Peel for herring. After the farmers had gone 200 or 300 yards beyond the bridge, the fairies would pull them back towards the pub with a long, crooked stick. The fairies would then knock on the pub door crying out, 'We want some ale, we want some ale.' When the ale was served to the farmers the fairies took all the good part and left the men with only water.

GB-HBLSM 1.254–257 & 436 | N-MH-20011953

The dead weasel hung in a pigsty

Private land – view only | Visible from road | SC 3493 9301 | 54.305947, -4.538635 | Ballamoar is a private farm south-east of Ballaugh, which today incorporates a camp site. The pigsty stood on the side of Ballaugh Glen Road.

The earliest detailed case of apparent witchcraft in the Isle of Man concerned the farmer here at Ballamoar. In 1560 a man known as Juan Yernagh (John the Irishman) set up a pigsty on a pathway used regularly by the farmer of Ballamoar. In this he hung a dead weasel and connected his rival's fortunes to the weasel with some dust through which the Ballamoar man had walked. Juan Yernagh was brought to trial and found guilty of sorcery.

DC-MI 16 | N-RC-10111961

The giant of Yn Cashtal

Private | Cashtal Lajer is an earthwork on the hillside south-east of Ballaugh village.

Yn Cashtal (The Castle or Fort) was once the home of a giant. Sadly, no specific stories of this giant have been passed down to us.

WWG-MS3 240

Scrundal

Public | Public road | SC 3508 9233 | 54.299912, -4.535915 | Scrundal is the area around the site of the old mill on Ballaugh Glen Road. The remains of Scrundal mill are part of a private roadside garden on the west side of the road, about 250 metres down from the Druidale road.

The Scrundal fairies

The Scrundal mill that used to stand here was known as 'a great fairy place,' so much so that it was even said to be 'full of them.' The fairies would sit on the mill stone at night holding lights and singing sweetly while it turned. They would also sometimes be heard singing inside the house itself at night. They could also be heard singing in the hills over the glen here.

One particular tale was of the miller calling his daughter and another child down to the bottom of the garden one summer evening, where they saw the fairies walking along the wall of the tholtan there. The legs of fairies were visible but their bodies were obscured by the trees, though they appeared to be about two feet tall. The family came to learn that seeing or hearing the fairies near their house was a sign of coming trouble or even death.

It was also likely to be here that a woman and her brother were walking late one night when something brushed up against her. She touched her brother's arm to draw his attention to it, but he whispered to her to not say anything. They then saw a fairy wearing a red hat and a red jacket pass over the road in front of them and disappear into some old buildings.

WWG-MS1 208-209 | WWG-MS2 231-232 | YLM 1.8.223

The phynnodderee and the ghost
The phynnodderee used to live in the gorse and oak trees that used to surround the mill here. Also, in one of these oak trees lived the spirit of a dead man. It fled into the tree whenever it was seen. However, in the early nineteenth century these trees and the gorse were cut and cleared away, but the man responsible for the work fell ill and was in a bad way for a long time afterwards.

WWG-MS1 208–209

The moddey doo of Ballaugh Glen
A moddey doo used to haunt Ballaugh Glen. It would appear suddenly at your feet in the night-time along this road, between Scrundal and Ballathoar, and disappear in a similar manner. Although one man claimed to have proven the dog was fully mortal after he came across it at the gates of Ballathoar, he could not catch it and his story failed to convince many people.

As with other moddee doo, this creature here was held to be 'the incarnation of a lost soul.'

WWG-MS3 378

The house partly built by the phynnodderee

Private land – view only | Visible from road | SC 3511 9210 | 54.297862, -4.535360 | The Ballathoar farmhouse is on the corner of Ballaugh Glen Road and Druidale Road.

When the farmer of Ballathoar was building himself this house he set his sights on a particular boulder which he wanted for the foundations. However, it was on the shore and he had no way of getting it here to the site. But one morning he awoke to find that the phynnodderee had brought it in the night and set at the corner of the new building. The farmer then tried to give the phynnodderee some clothes in thanks, but this offended the phynnodderee so much that he left and was never seen here again.

WWG-MS1 212

The mother's ghost tending to her children

Public | Steep, rough and uneven footpath, a substantial walk | SC 3700 8976 | 54.277396, -4.504968 | The ruins of Sherragh Vane are today deep within Tholt y Will Plantation. From the converted chapel at Tholt y Will, follow the steep and rough track uphill. Go through the gate and follow this track past a prominent white boulder and twin wooden bridges, keeping to the uphill track, until you can see the ruins of Sherragh Vane in the trees on your left.

The woman who lived here at Sherragh Vane died when her children were still young. However, she continued to care for them by returning in a ghostly form to tuck them into their beds and keep them from the cold at night.

MJ 6.364

Braddan

Braddan has some of the Island's most important traditional folklore, including the Ballafletcher Cup taken from the tomb of St Olave, the holy well blessed by St Bridget, the ghostly Ben Veg Carraghan, and the Saddle Stone, which offers one of the Island's most well-formed stories of the fairies. Beyond these, the parish's wonderful variety of tales include mermaids, a curse from St Trinian's Chapel, a fairy fort, and 'the cursed stone of destiny' still on display at St Luke's.

1. Port Soderick
2. Bathing ground of the mermen
3. Fairy music in the river
4. The spectral congregation at the former chapel
- Chibbyr Vreeshey [private land]
5. The Fairy Bridge at Oakhill
6. Joney Lowney and the Ballaughton Mill
7. The Saddle Stone
- The Ballafletcher Cup [private land]
8. Old Kirk Braddan
9. The miraculous message found beneath a cross slab
10. The cursed tower of Kirk Braddan
11. The fairy fort
- Camlork keeill [private land]
12. St Luke's
- Oie'll Vreeshey at Earyween [private land]
13. The Phynnodderee's Track
14. Carraghan
15. Lhiaght y Kinry

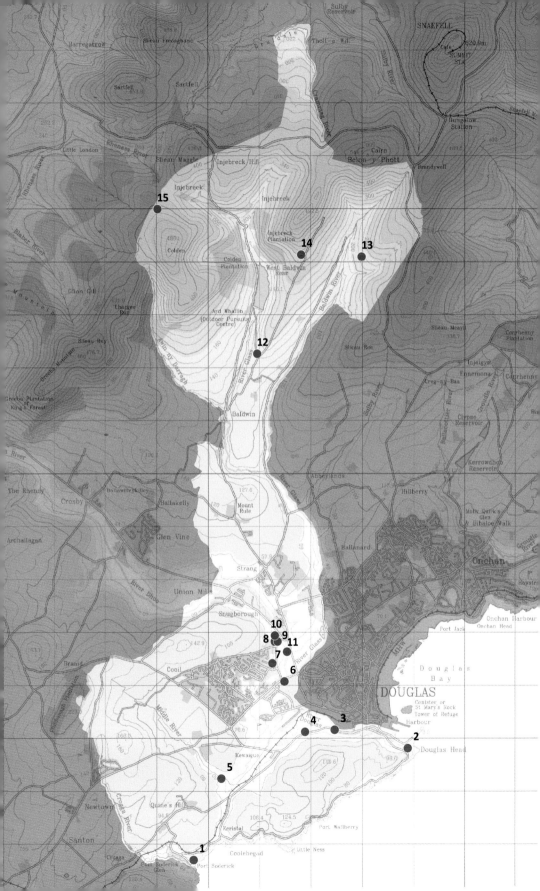

Port Soderick

Public | Uneven, rocky shore or visible from car park | SC 3466 7262 | 54.122769, -4.531448 | Port Soderick is a bay on the edge of the parish, roughly three miles below Douglas, accessed from the Old Castletown Road.

The enchanted island

There used to be a beautiful island off the coast from Port Soderick but the people there offended the great magician who lived in the Isle of Man at that time, and in punishment he transformed all its people into blocks of granite and submerged the island beneath the waves. This island returns to the surface of the water only once every seven years and only for half an hour at the end of September. However, if someone is able to place a bible on the ground there during the time that it is above the waves then the curse will be lifted and the island will never again disappear beneath the waves.

A woman named Nora Cain was once walking with her beloved close to here one fine moonlit night at just the time that the island appeared from beneath the waves. She rushed to get a bible but by the time she was back, she was too late and the island was returning below the waves. This failure resulted in her wasting away and dying, with her lover following soon afterwards from heartbreak, and the Isle of Man itself suffered also. Since then, none have dared try to lift the curse on the island.

In one version of this tale the magician who plunged the island beneath the waves was Finn MacCooil.

AWM-FIOM 87–88 | HIJ-JG 45 | JT-HSA 2.359–360 | PIOMNHAS 4.4.581 | WH-MM 250–251

A caught mermaid

Before the 1650s mermaids and mermen were regular night-time visitors to Manx shores. They combed their hair and amused themselves on the shore, but they would dive back into the water if any human ever came near. However, some people lay out a net here on Port Soderick shore and hid some distance away to watch as a mermaid came ashore and became caught in the net. The people picked her up and carried her to a house where they tried to care for her kindly, but without success, as she refused any food or drink and did not speak at all. After three days of this, they grew worried of what might happen if they allowed the mermaid to waste away in their care and so they opened the door to allow her to escape. The mermaid got up on her tail and 'glided with incredible swiftness' to the shore and plunged back into the sea. Upon the questioning of her friends, the mermaid reported that she had seen 'nothing very wonderful' on the land 'but they are so ignorant as to throw away the water in which they have boiled their eggs.'

HIJ-JG 44–45 | GW-DIM 54–55

Bathing ground of the mermen

Public | Steps and rocky shore | SC 3896 7480 | 54.143740, -4.466920 | Port Skillion is a small beach at the tip of Douglas Head. It is beyond Douglas harbour, by the lighthouse.

Port Skillion used to be famed as a place where mermen and mermaids were to be found. Even as late as the 1860s it was recorded that the place 'continues to be the favourite resort of the mermen of the present day.'

WH-DIM 122 #70

Fairy music in the river

Public | Visible from pavement | SC 3755 7515 | 54.146395, -4.488654 | The site of the old Douglas bridge is about 150 metres upstream from the modern bridge. It crossed the river opposite the set-back houses on the Old Castletown Road.

An English gentleman was riding his horse from Douglas and was obliged to cross the river above the old Douglas bridge due to the tide. In the middle of the river, he heard some music that was the finest he had ever heard. It was far more beautiful than any human could make and both he and his horse were mesmerised by it, remaining motionless in the river for around 45 minutes. It was only after the music had stopped that they were at last able to go on, leaving the man in no doubt that the music had been from the fairies.

AWM-FIOM 40 | GW-DIM 37 | JJK-PN 221

The spectral congregation at the former chapel

Private land – view only | Visible from pavement | SC 3697 7511 | 54.145907, -4.497526 | One of the four terraced houses named Park View, on the Old Castletown Road, close to the western entrance to the Nunnery.

An old Roman Catholic chapel used to stand on the site of these houses and the woman who lived here would often sit up waiting for her husband to return home until a very late hour. Every night when the clock struck twelve, she would hear the sound of many people entering the room where she was sitting. Then, after a period of silence, there was the sound of feet again. It was believed that this was the arrival of the worshippers for midnight mass and their departure from it.

AWM-FIOM 155

Chibbyr Vreeshey

Private | Chibbyr Vreeshey is a well close to the Nunnery.

Chibbyr Vreeshey is a holy well associated with St Bridget and its water has the power to cure your ailments if taken in the right way. It used to be venerated and its holy water was attributed with 'many occult properties.'

The origin of this well's dedication goes back to St Bridget herself, who came to the Isle of Man at the age of fourteen to receive the veil from St Maughold before staying to found and run the Nunnery. She eventually died here and was buried on the grounds, although few accounts hold that her body remains here, as most assert that her body was later removed to Ireland for their final interment.

Chibbyr Vreeshey is also associated with the fairies. One story is of its attendant, Old Mary, who had an encounter with the fairies shortly after giving birth to her first child. As she was lying-in she watched helplessly as a troop of fairies came into her home and began to eat the food and drink laid out on the table – bread, cheese, brandy, etc. As she lay trembling in fear and lamenting the loss of her food, the 'Queen of the Fairies' came to her and blew a powder in her face, which caused her to lose the sight in one eye. After that she would not go near the well, as she frequently heard beautiful music from it which she knew could only come from the fairies and she feared another encounter with them.

DR-TIOM 29 | DR-TIOM 117–118 | EK-CC 93 | HIJ-JG 31–32 | HL-CL 199 | JT-HSA 1.323 | JT-HSA 2.48 | JT-HSA 2.121 | KF-MR 16 | N-MS-26081865 | N-IOME-03091898 | WH-MM1 137 | WH-MM1 146 | WWG-MS1 74–75

The Fairy Bridge at Oakhill

Public | Rough and uneven track | SC 3534 7423 | 54.137480, -4.522030 | The Fairy Bridge lies between Kewaigue and the Old Castletown Road. A little up the hill from Kewaigue School, a track runs south past Middle Farm for about half a mile before dipping down to the river. Just before the ford, a path leads off upstream to this picturesque bridge.

There are a very small number of 'fairy bridges' in the Isle of Man, but only this one at Oakhill was sufficiently well known or established enough to be marked as 'Fairy Bridge' on the 1870 OS map. No specific stories are known today of the fairies here at the bridge. It is only in recent times that people have begun leaving notes and offerings for the fairies here.

OS-25-XIII.11 | Add

Joney Lowney and the Ballaughton Mill

Private land – view only | Visible from level path | SC 3656 7606 | 54.154286, -4.504302 | The Ballaughton Mill used to stand on the Dhoo river, on the opposite bank to the northern end of the National Sports Centre's running track.

A woman named Joney Lowney visited Ballaughton Mill in the 1710s in the hope of charity. However, the miller refused to give her anything at that time as the corn in the mill was producing flour too good to be given away in charity. Lowney complained that the poor should receive the best flour and then walked away. It was at this point that the mill stopped working, and it could not be brought to work again until the corn was changed. It was for this and other offences that Lowney was brought to trial for witchcraft in 1717.

DC-MI 18

The Saddle Stone

Public | Pavement beside main road | SC 3632 7641 | 54.157290, -4.508146 | A remarkable saddle-shaped rock built into the wall halfway along Saddle Road, a short distance to the north of Ballaughton Manor Hill.

The vicar of Braddan was concerned about finding his horse exhausted and covered in sweat every morning. He did not know what was causing this until he returned early one morning from attending to a sick parishioner and saw a little man in a green jacket turning his horse loose into the field. When the little man turned and saw the vicar, he vanished, and the saddle turned to stone where it lay on the ground nearby. From here the saddle was later moved to its current position in the wall.

This is not the only instance of this use of the stone as a saddle, as it was widely known in the early eighteenth century that the fairies used it at night when riding the horses of the local gentry and farmers.

From at least the 1870s, the Saddle Stone has been recognised as a good place to sit and make a wish. Since the mid-twentieth century, the practice observed by many has been to sit on the seat, make a wish with your eyes closed, and then spit into the small hole in the stone.

In the 1890s it was also believed that women could increase their chances of becoming pregnant by straddling the Saddle Stone. It is also thought to once have acted as a penitent's seat.

AWM-FIOM 38–39 | AWM-MN 223 | GW-DIM 65 | N-IOMT-07061879 | N-MS-11021888 | N-IOMT-31101888 | WL-DPG 46–47 | WWG-MS1 214–215 | WWG-MS2 278 | Add

The Ballafletcher Cup

Private | Today known as Kirby, the estate of this large private residence lies between Saddle Road and Peel Road, and New Castletown Road and Old Kirk Braddan.

Passed down through the family at Ballafletcher was a small glass cup. This was brought to the Isle of Man by the Norse King Magnus Barelegs, who had taken it from the grave of St Olave. The cup was kept safe as it was said that, 'as long as he preserved it peace and plenty would follow; but woe to him who broke it, as he would surely be haunted by the lhiannan-shee.' The glass was only taken out at Christmas and Easter when the head of the household drank a glass of wine from it in honour of the lhiannan-shee and to gain her continued protection.

AWM-FIOM 49–50 | HIJ-JG 24–25 | HRO-VIMA 189–190 | JT-HSA 2.153–154 | SM-MFT 171-174 | WWG-MS2 242–243 | YLM 1.10.318–319

Old Kirk Braddan

Open during daylight hours | Uneven ground, steps | SC 3641 7681 | 54.160996, -4.506965 | On the south side of the Peel Road, heading west out of Douglas just past Braddan Bridge.

The giant's bone

Giants used to inhabit the Isle of Man before the arrival of humans. At the start of the eighteenth century the writer, George Waldron, was doubtful of this but was convinced otherwise when he was present at the digging of a new vault here at Kirk Braddan graveyard as they uncovered an enormous leg bone. Measuring around 120cm in length, it appeared to be a giant's shin bone. Waldron's amazement at the sight was apparently unmatched by those doing the digging, as they reported that bones similar to that were regularly found there.

GW-DIM 61

The skull charm on the beer

A man named William Kissack was the landlord of a pub on Douglas North Quay, and his wife sent their servant to get a skull from Kirk Braddan. The servant managed this by taking a skull from a newly opened grave and carrying it home in a basket, for which she received a new frock and apron as payment. Mrs Kissack then put the skull near the beer casks, in the belief that it would bring a larger demand for their drinks. However, the skull was discovered by a soldier and taken back to his barracks, to which the relatives of the deceased were invited to collect the skull.

N-IOME-01101898 | N-MA-13071826

The sieve and the shears

It used to be known that the guilt of criminals could be uncovered by using a sieve and some shears, but it was considered witchcraft by the Church and in 1733 James and Jane Kelley were brought to trial in Braddan for attempting it. They balanced the sieve on the point of the shears, supporting it upright with two fingers. They then spoke the names of people they suspected of stealing from them and watched to see the sieve turn upon the calling of the names of the guilty. Because of the Church's attitude to this practice, the Kelleys were found guilty of witchcraft and sent to St German's prison for a period, before having to do penance here at the parish church.

DC-MI 22

The miraculous message found beneath a cross slab

Open during daylight hours | Uneven ground, steps | SC 3641 7681 | 54.160996, -4.506965 | Cross no. 65, inside Old Kirk Braddan church, which is on the south side of the Peel Road, heading west out of Douglas just past Braddan Bridge.

This cross used to stand in a lonely barren field near Middle Farm. Many people had tried to remove it but without success. One day many people were there discussing how to get the cross out when an old man appeared and spoke to a boy of six or seven, telling him to go and lean against the stone. When the boy did this, the cross toppled over and revealed a piece of paper below, on which was written, 'Fear God, obey the priesthood, and do to your neighbour as you would have done to you.' When the people looked back, the old man had vanished. The message was copied and worn as a defence against 'witchcraft, evil tongues, and all efforts of the devil or his agents.'

AWM-FIOM 26–27 | GW-DIM 64–65 | PMCK-MAS 5.19–20

The cursed tower of Kirk Braddan

Open during daylight hours | Level access | SC 3639 7690 | 54.161771, -4.507403 | Kirk Braddan is on the south side of the Peel Road, on the corner of Saddle Road opposite Old Kirk Braddan.

Stones from St Trinian's Chapel in Marown were used in the building of the spire that was once on top of the tower of the new church here at Kirk Braddan. However, it was these stones which caused the tower to be blown down in a storm shortly after its consecration in 1876, and again when it was rebuilt within ten years later. The spire remains absent to this day.

FLS B1/A

The fairy fort

Private land – view only | Visible from car park | SC 3663 7664 | 54.159458, -4.503636 | The site of the earthwork stands on the small hill beside the entrance to Douglas Rugby Club, on Peel Road between Quarterbridge and Royal Oak roundabouts.

One suggestion for the name, Port e Chee, is that it comes from 'Purt ny Shee' or 'fort of the fairies.' This is likely to have referred to the ancient earthwork here on the brow of the hill, where we might suppose fairies used to be known.

JJK-PN 192

Camlork keeill

Private | The remains of Camlork keeill are in the private field on the north-east side of the Mount Rule Road, between The Strang and Ballamillaghyn.

Not long before the 1890s a farmer began levelling the keeill on Camlork farm, but he experienced a pain in his arm and was forced to give up the work. However, a few days later he felt better and, together with his wife and daughter, he returned to continue the task of clearing the keeill. It was a result of this that the two women were dead soon after and the man lost his mind and remained in that state until he himself met his death.

AWM-FIOM 154 | HIJ-JG 38–39

St Luke's

Open during daylight hours | Steps, or visible from road | SC 3603 8226 | 54.209745, -4.515877 | St Luke's Church is on the crest of the hill between East and West Baldwin, about half a mile south of the West Baldwin Reservoir. The stone sits above the window in the eastern external wall of the church.

The cursed stone of destiny

A farmer took this stone from the old Keeill Abban site to use it in his farmhouse. However, he and his household could then not sleep at night for the noises which sometimes resembled a calf bleating and at other times a cart of stones being upset. The stone was then moved from the house to be placed on a hedge of an adjoining field but the hedge would then never stand. The family's troubles only ceased when the stone was finally brought here to be built into the gable end of the church.

In one version of story, the stone is referred to as 'the cursed stone of destiny,' and the death of cattle was also suffered at the farm.

A similar story tells of how the owner of Algare, a farm about a quarter of a mile south of the church, foolishly used stones from Keeill Abban in building a part of the farm. However, as he lay in bed at night, he became aware of two men in his room discussing whether to kill him, but instead they decided merely to 'straake' (strike) him 'unmarciful.' After this the farmer became ill and he did not live long after that.

AWM-FIOM 154 | HIJ-JG 39 | HIJ-JG 41–42 | TC-BMV 49 | WWG-MS1 217 | YLM 1.7.123 | YLM 3.10.483

Burying the King of All Birds

St Luke's is one of the very few churches specifically mentioned as having the wren buried here at Hunt the Wren on 26 December. The people paraded the dead bird suspended in a wren pole around the village, singing their song about the 'King of All Birds' and giving out feathers for luck in exchange for money. They would then bring the bird here to be buried in a corner of the graveyard.

EK-CC 164 | JK-MD 'Baaltin'

Oie'll Vreeshey at Earyween

Private | Earyween is the final farm up the East Baldwin Road. The ruins of the old barn and other farm buildings are below the farmhouse towards the stream.

The woman here at Earyween was very good for keeping up the traditions of ending each day with blessing the fairies and at Oie'll Vreeshey she was sure to follow the old custom of making up a bed in the barn, laying out a fine feast on the table and calling out the invocation to St Breeshey at her doorstep before retiring to bed. However, a man named Juan Lewin was passing here one year late on Oie'll Vreeshey, having been out courting a woman, and he saw the barn prepared and so went in to eat the bread and cheese, drink the beer and have a quick sleep in the bed. However, he was gone before sunrise and so the woman of Earyween knew no better than to believe that it had been Breeshey herself who had paid her a visit. She lived out the rest of her life happy with this idea, believing that she had been blessed and it was only after her death that Juan Lewin spoke of how it actually happened.

EF-MSR 147–148

The Phynnodderee's Track

Public | Steep, rough and uneven track | SC 3807 8409 | 54.226843, -4.485608 | A public footpath between Windy Corner and East Baldwin. The lower entrance to the track is far up the East Baldwin Road, signposted on its eastern side just after the remains of the former East Baldwin Chapel.

This track is known as the Phynnodderree's Track because he placed the white stones here to mark the way. He put them here out of kindness for a woman of Glen Ruy who often had to use this track.

WWG-MS1 219

Carraghan

Private land – view only | Visible from steep, rough and uneven track, a substantial walk, or visible from road at a distance | SC 3689 8412 | 54.226778, -4.503625 | Carraghan is one of the Isle of Man's highest peaks. It stands over the Injebreck Reservoir in West Baldwin.

It is said that Carraghan takes its name from the great king who is buried at its peak. Rather than erecting a gravestone or other such monument, the mourners placed a great pile of stones over the tomb, to which people ever afterwards have contributed when visiting the site. Other such kings are buried at Snaefell and Barrule.

This is also the place to see Ben Veg Carraghan. She was a young woman from Maughold who made her living by going around the Island with her spinning wheel on her back and cheerfully doing work for people. However, it became thought that she was saving a lot of money from her work and so somebody murdered her for her riches. Following this her spirit has been seen between one and two o'clock in the afternoon on the side of Carraghan, with her spinning wheel on her shoulder, slumped down with her head on her arm as if in worry or woe. Seeing her is an omen of something bad happening in the near future.

Another version of this tale adds the curious detail that she is followed by a goose and that she can also be found spinning in a sheltered nook here.

Sometime around the 1860s a man came across the Ben Veg Carraghan here and determined to confront her, so he and some others approached her from different sides so she could not get away. The woman came close to one man and, as she did, his dogs began to tremble and even shed tears. She then moved towards a small gully and vanished. It was later discovered that she was seen on North Barrule at that precise moment heading towards Maughold Head. The man who got close to her immediately fell ill and was in a bad way for six months afterwards. It was said that Ben Ven Carraghan had not been seen again here at Carraghan after that time.

Another version of the tale has Ben Ven Carraghan spinning further southwards down the slope towards St Luke's, where she span the history of those being born in the Baldwin valleys. When the man came close to her, he found her silent but her lips were moving and 'her eyes were like stars.' The man ran home in fright and he and all his family died soon after.

AWM-FIOM 72–73 | GW-DIM 58 | HIJ JG 128–129 | PIOMNHAS 3.3.220–221 | WWG-MS1 217–218 | WWG-MS1 232

Lhiaght y Kinry

Public ram | Steep, rough and uneven ground, a committed walk | SC 3398 8508 | 54.2343899, -4.5487157 | Lhiaght y Kinry is a collection of rocks on the slopes of Colden. It is perhaps best accessed from Governor Loch's Road, a track heading south from the Sartfield Road, along the side of Slieau Maggle. Take the footpath off to the slopes of Colden, where Lhiaght y Kinry sits only a metre or two to the left of the path, about two thirds of the way up.

The Manx name, Lhiaght y Kinry, translates as 'Kinry's tomb.' It was here that a man named Kinry (or 'Harrison' in the English form) dropped down dead during a foolish attempt to run naked between Bishopscourt and Douglas one snowy winter's day for a bet. It was on the return leg of his journey that Kinry died and he was buried where he fell, here where these rocks now mark the spot. One account has Kinry as a king.

AWM-MN 100 | JF-TIOM 219 | JJK-PN 167 | PIOMNHAS 3.1.20–21 | YLM 2.30

Bride

Bride's folklore is remarkable for being predominantly about curses or bad luck resulting from disturbing ancient monuments of some sort. Unfortunately, many of these and other sites in the parish are not publicly accessible, but this is certainly preferable to the fate of at least one site in Bride which has been lost to coastal erosion.

1. A message from Cape Horn

2. The two dancing women

- Cabbal ny Chooilley [private land]

3. The Mheillea at Ballavair

- The Clagh Vedn cure [private land]

- Samson's Stone [private land]

- The pool of the dead [private land]

4. The ghostly figure by Kirk Bride

5. Cranstal

6. The Kerrowdhoo coach

7. The Point of Ayre

POINT OF AYRE

7

Sand and
Gravel Pit

MHW

The Ayres

Phurt

Lough
Cranstal

Ballaghennie

6

Cranstal **5**

Cowle

Glentruan

4

Bride

West
Kimmeragh

Shellag Point

Landing Strip

3

2

MHW

1

The Dog Mills

Regaby

Aust

A message from Cape Horn

Public | Public road | SC 4515 9780 | 54.352123, -4.384160 | The Dog Mills is a small cluster of houses along the Bride Road, 1½ miles north of the turning from the Andreas Road.

A woman was at home here at the Dog Mills when she inexplicably heard a favourite tune of her son's being hummed just as if he were there, even though he was far away at sea. She was so struck by this that she thought to make a note of the day and time at which it happened. Upon his return, her son reported that, at that time, he had been rounding Cape Horn in bad weather, when two men had been washed overboard and he was in great fear of his own life.

WWG-MS3 402

The two dancing women

Public | Public road | SC 4490 9893 | 54.362225, -4.388541 | Grenaby Road meets the main Ramsey to Bride road about three quarters of a mile north of the Dog Mills. No traces of the blacksmith building remain today.

A man was walking from Ramsey one night when he came across two young women near here. They asked him if he would like to go dancing and he felt like he was not able to refuse and so they led him to a large hall. Sweating and fearful of who these people he was with could be, the man took one end of the apron of one of the girls to wipe the sweat off his face and he said, 'O my God!' At that instant he found himself all alone in the roofless old smithy that stood here at the end of Grenaby Road.

FLS C/117

Cabbal ny Chooilley

Private | The keeill of Cabbal ny Chooilley is on the private land of Ballachrink.

The large stone on the top of this keeill was taken to be used as a gatepost on the nearby farm, Ballacamain. However, the man who took the stone got no sleep in the night and, understanding the stone as the cause, he returned it the following morning. The stone remains today where he returned it, laid on top of the keeill mound, next to a standing stone still in its original position.

WWG-MS3 189

The mheillea at Ballavair

Private land – view only | Visible from road | SC 4485 9919 | 54.364533, -4.389512 | On the seaward side of the main road from Ramsey to Bride, about 1¼ miles from Bride village.

The best record of the Manx harvest traditions of the mheillea comes from Ballavair in the 1850s. On the final day of gathering in the harvest, the last sheaf was left to be cut by an old woman. After games in the field, the plaited form of this last sheaf then took pride of place at the mheillea dinner before much dancing was done in the barn. The decoration of the last sheaf was elsewhere known as the Babban ny Mheillea (harvest baby), where it was given the form of a human figure. This was recorded normally as being kept on the mantelpiece for luck until the following year.

GQ-TMB | WWG-MS3 272–276

The Clagh Vedn cure

Private | A former well on the private land of Kionlough.

A young man was found unconscious after an encounter with the fairies near here one night. He was put to bed in a fever so bad he was unable to speak. Seeking a cure for the man, an older woman came here at night when the moon was at its highest. She filled a cup with water from this well three times, each time turning around and pouring it onto the ground. As she took the water she repeated the charm, 'Ping, ping, prash, cur un cadley-jiargan ass my chass' ('Penny, penny, brass, send the pins and needles from my foot'). She then made the sign of the cross with her right thumb, laid some luss ny chiolg over the cup and carried it back to the young man. After drinking some of this water the man immediately came round from his fever and in the morning he was out at work again.

N-MS-15031902 | WWG-MS3 328–329

Samson's Stone

Private | Samson's Stone was a large quartz boulder. seven feet high and five feet wide. that used to stand on the slope of Cronk ny Arrey Laa, on the private land of Ballavarkish.

A giant on North Barrule once saw an enemy's ship approaching the Manx coast so he picked up a massive quartz boulder and hurled it towards the ship, but it fell short and landed here on Cronk ny Arrey Laa. The marks of the giant's fingers could be seen on the rock, until the sea eroded the coastline back and the rock has been lost.

Another story has the Biblical figure of Samson as the person who threw the rock here from Maughold Head, and that it is his fingerprints that were imprinted on the rock.

PIOMNHAS 3.3.197 | WCR-KBM 55 | WWG-MS1 221 | WWG-MS3 188 | WWG-MS3 372 | YLM 1.7.181

The pool of the dead

Private | Dem ny Marroo is on the private land of Ballakilley, south of Bride village.

This dub stands on the ancient Bayr ny Merroo (Road of the Dead), along which funeral processions would always travel towards the church. The procession would only stop at determined points, including here at Dem ny Marroo (Pool of the Dead). The bearers would lay the bier on a stone and the mourners would gather round to say a prayer and call out the deceased's name as the chief mourner sprinkled a handful of water from the dub onto the body. It was only after this was completed that the procession continued to the church. It has been conjectured that this might relate to 'some association with an early Celtic Saint' or that perhaps it had been 'handed down from still earlier pagan times.'

JJK-PN 564 | N-RC-03081951 | PIOMNHAS 1.9.624–625 | PMKC-MAS3 35 | WWG-MS1 139

The ghostly figure by Kirk Bride

Open during daylight hours | Level access | NX 4492 0118 | 54.382387, -4.389482 | The road in front of the church in the middle of Bride village.

In the early twentieth century a ghostly figure was well-known around this church. It was frequently encountered approaching people outside the church, coming quite close but then turning and going away. The figure was encountered one night by a group of young men who were standing by the church. They saw the figure approach them but turn before it got too close and then it went away.

FLS C/135

Cranstal

Public | Public road | NX 4620 0233 | 54.393169, -4.370428 | Cranstal is a small community about a mile north-east of Bride village on the way to the Point of Ayre.

The witch of Cranstal

There used to be a person known as the 'Witch of Cranstal.' Little is known of her other than one occasion where she helped a farmer who needed a cow and hay in the same field. Having dipped her stick in 'some filthy mixture' she drew it across the field and made a divide that proved impossible for the cow to cross. The animal remained on one side as the hay grew on the other.

YLM 2.195–196

The ball of fire

In the first half of the twentieth century a man was cycling down the Cranstal road at night when he passed by a gate, out of which came a ball of fire which rolled down the road in front of him. Amazingly, no damage or anything further remarkable came of it.

FLS C/117

The Kerrowdhoo coach

Private land – view only | Visible from road | NX 4637 0260 | 54.395599, -4.367813 | Heading north-east out of Bride village, Kerrowdhoo is the last farm on the left before the road takes a sharp turn left onto Bayr ny Hayrey, which leads the final one and a half miles to the Point of Ayre.

A mysterious coach and horses, driven by a coachman and all lit up, used to be seen driving down the Cranstal road and in at the Kerrowdhoo gates here before going on across the fields towards the Ayres. The coach was never seen coming back and it was understood to be something supernatural.

It is possible that this is connected to a field on this land known as 'Baase Sleih.' Although authorities believe that the name is derived from 'Bayr Sloo' ('Smallest Road'), most records for this field name it as 'Baase Sleih' ('Death of People'). No record exists of how the field got this name.

FLS C/117 | WCR-KBM 12

The Point of Ayre

Public | Rocky and uneven shore, or visible from car park | NX 4672 0509 | 54.418080, -4.363798 | The most northern point of the Isle of Man.

The proposed bridge to Scotland

In the thirteenth century King Reginald had the intention to put a bridge between the Point of Ayre and the Mull of Galloway in Scotland. It is unclear in what context this intention arose, and no story has been passed down to us of it actually being attempted.

WWG-MS1 125

The sign of the end of the world

The Caillagh ny Ghueshag (old woman of the spells) was the Isle of Man's most famous prophet. One of her predictions was of the markers of the coming of the end of the world. One of these occurrences was the Point of Ayre coming so close to the Mull of Galloway that the Manx and Scottish could throw their beetles at one another.

Another telling of this has it as the prophecy of Caillagh ny Faashagh (the prophet wizard) who was in the form of a goat when they said that a sign of the end of the world will be when 'Mann and Scotland will come so close that two women, one standing in Mann and another in Scotland, will be able to wring a blanket between them.'

AWM-FIOM 89–90 | SM-MFT 190–191 | WH-MM1 36 | WH-MM2 196–197

German

Together with the neighbouring parish of Patrick, German enjoys the benefits of Sophia Morrison having carried out most of her collecting here. It is thanks to her that one of the Island's finest tales of the fairies was given its best-known form in 'The Lost Wife of Ballaleece.' Hers too are well-known versions of tales connected to St Patrick's Isle, including Manannan, St Patrick and perhaps the best-known of all Manx folk tales, the moddey doo of Peel Castle. Also remarkable in the parish are stories of giants, bugganes, the devil, and the legendary charmer, Nan Wade, as well as an unusually large number of stories relating to harm caused by destroying ancient monuments.

1. Eaoch's trial
2. The moddey doo of Peel Castle
3. Counting the pillars of the crypt
4. Fairies climbing the flagpole
5. The wishing stone of St Patrick's Isle
6. The bleeding skull
7. The giant of St Patrick's Isle
8. St Patrick's prayer
9. Peel harbour
10. Ghosts at Harbour Lights
11. The former Wesleyan chapel
12. Creg Malin rocks
13. Gef's visits to the bus driver's flat
14. Gef's visits to Peel bus depot
15. Swearing on a person's grave
16. The black dog's warning
17. A grave connected to Nan Wade
18. The lost wife of Ballaleece
19. The grey man of Ballaleece Bridge
20. Tynwald Hill
21. Giant's Grave
22. The cursed cross slab of Tynwald Chapel
23. Manannan's hill
24. The cabbyl ushtey of Kerroo ny Glough
25. The phynnodderee's round meadow
26. The fairies flee from the mill
27. Beary Mountain
28. Ballalough
29. Liaght ny Foawr
30. The crossroads fire on Bayr ny Staarvey
31. Manannan's Chair
32. A keeill made from the devil's timber
33. Fairy women at Glen Cam
34. Buggane Mooar
35. Meir ny Foawr
- Crosh Vooar [private land]
- The Devil's Altar [private land]

Eaoch's trial

Public, seasonal opening, admission fee applies | Steps, uneven surfaces | SC 2422 8455 | 54.226447, -4.698063 | Peel Castle, on St Patrick's Isle off the coast of Peel.

Kitterland close to the Calf of Man got its name during the Norse era when Earl Kitter drowned there in a storm raised by a witch named Ada. He had been racing back from the Calf when he saw his castle on the top of South Barrule on fire having been alerted to it by the loud call of his faithful cook, Eaoch, from the top of South Barrule. This led to the accusation that Eaoch had a hand in Kitter's death and so he was brought before King Olaf here in Peel Castle. The king decreed that he should be executed, but Eaoch used the Norse custom to choose his own method of execution, asking to be beheaded by the sword Macabuin whilst lying on the king's legs. This would mean certain death for the king as the sword would cut through everything in its path. However, the witch, Ada, was consulted and recommended nine times nine toad skins, rowan twigs and adders' eggs to be put between the king's legs and Eaoch's neck. This proved successful as Macabuin cut through Eaoch's neck and all the materials below except for the toad skin, thus saving King Olaf's life.

AWM-FIOM 27–28 | HIJ-JG 156–158 | JT-HSA 2.177–179 | KR-MNQ 231 | SM-MFT 109–111

The moddey doo of Peel Castle

Public, seasonal opening, admission fee applies | Steps, uneven surfaces | SC 2420 8450 | 54.225918, -4.698238 | The guardroom of Peel Castle is on the right-hand side just inside the entrance.

In the 1650s or 1660s, when soldiers were stationed in Peel Castle, a mysterious large black dog would appear from a passage off the guardroom. It would come in as night fell and lie by the fire through the night, only rising to return into the dark passage just before sunrise. The soldiers recognised this moddey doo as an evil spirit and they feared to be alone with it. However, one night a foolish man got drunk and bragged of how he was unafraid of the beast, boasting that he would go on his own through the passage to return the keys. The others tried to stop the man, but he would not listen and so he set off into the passageway. As he left the room, the moddey doo lumbered up from the fire and followed him. There was a pause, and then awful and unearthly screams flooded the room and struck horror into the remaining men. After silence returned, the foolish man got himself back into the room, with a face white and twisted with fear. He was unable to speak another word and he died in unnatural agony three days later.

An early account of this has the moddey doo seen in every room of the castle, but most frequently the guardroom. It was here accounted to be 'in the shape of a large black spaniel with curled shaggy hair.'

AWM-FIOM 61–62 | GW-DIM 12–13 | HAB-HIOM 364–365 | JT-HSA 1.300–302 | RJK-SIOM 32–34 | SM-MFT 136–139

Counting the pillars of the crypt

Public, seasonal opening, admission fee applies | Steep and narrow steps, uneven surfaces | SC 2422 8452 | 54.226152, -4.697965 | The crypt of Peel Castle is beneath the eastern end of the cathedral ruins.

During the time when this crypt was a prison, it was said that anyone who visited the place had to count its thirteen pillars or else they would be doomed to later return here as a prisoner. This superstition continued after the closure of the prison, with bad luck following anyone who fails to count the pillars.

GW-DIM 10 | WH-MM1 192

Fairies climbing the flagpole

Public, seasonal opening, admission fee applies | Steps, rough and uneven surfaces | SC 2415 8456 | 54.226508, -4.699050 | The flagpole in Peel Castle is obvious on a raised mound at the centre of the castle grounds.

The crew of a fishing boat leaving Peel was once surprised to see 'innumerable' fairies climbing up and down the flagpole here.

WWG-MS1 244

The wishing stone of St Patrick's Isle

Public, seasonal opening, admission fee applies | Steps, rough and uneven surfaces | SC 2414 8453 | 54.226246, -4.699246 | Inside Peel Castle, between the chapel close to the flagpole in the centre of the site, and the larger former church to the south. The stone is no longer to be found.

A wishing stone used to stand somewhere between the church and chapel, which had the power to grant wishes if someone spoke them whilst stood on the flat surface of the rock. This was recorded in the 1930s, but today the stone cannot be located.

WWG-MS3 288–289

The bleeding skull

Public | Steps | SC 2408 8457 | 54.226547, -4.700208 | The rocky edge of St Patrick's Isle outside the walls of Peel Castle below Fenella's Tower, which is on the side farthest from the town, by the sally port projecting out across the path.

Two lovers once fell into an argument when they were sat near here. She had been idly unearthing a nail from the ground when a comment of his caused her to impulsively use a stone to drive the nail into the back of his head. The blow killed him almost immediately. She panicked and pushed the body down a gully towards the sea to hide her crime. She left the Island early the next day, allowing people to assume that the two of them had eloped, and so no search was carried out. Years later, the woman returned to visit the Island and she took a tour around the castle. When the tour reached this point along the path outside the walls, a youth from the group, who had been clambering over the rocks below, uncovered a skull lodged in the gully. Weather-beaten and sea-aged, the skull had the appearance of being very old and so no one thought anything of passing it around the party. Not wanting to arouse suspicion, the woman took her turn to handle it but, in her hands, tiny drops of blood tellingly began to ooze from the base of the skull. However, no one in the party saw or had any suspicions, and so it was only on her deathbed that the woman spoke of this tale for the first time.

WWG-MS3 303–305

The giant of St Patrick's Isle

Public | Steps | SC 2419 8463 | 54.227120, -4.698572 | The Giant's Grave is a raised area of land on the far side of Peel Castle. The path goes over the Giant's Grave after it comes up the slope from the Breakwater, just as it levels off to run alongside the wall of the castle. It is about 2 metres wide and roughly 20 metres long.

Peel Castle is said to have originally been Manannan's home. This Celtic god and first ruler of the Isle of Man would protect the Island from invaders by hiding it in mist, but if the enemy got through to the Island, Manannan would make one man on the battlements of the castle appear as a thousand men. He would also throw woodchips in the River Neb and they would emerge from Peel harbour as fearsome battleships fit to scare off any potential invaders. Some say that it is Manannan who lies within the Giant's Grave outside the castle walls.

Another account tells of a three-legged giant who lived in Peel Castle during the time of St Patrick. He could leap between St Patrick's Isle and Peel Hill with ease, and he was known to throw rocks for fun, such as those that landed two miles away at Lhergydhoo. With his strength and ferocity, the giant terrorised the Island until St Patrick finally confronted him. The giant tried to kill the saint but St Patrick cursed him in the name of the Virgin and the giant was banished. It is perhaps only in death that he was returned here, as he is said to lie within this mound.

Some say that the two smaller mounds nearby are the burial places of the giant's wife and dog.

Although not directly linked to the grave, another account tells of giant fairies who were seen walking around the ruins of Peel Castle. It was one of these giants who cared for the fishermen of Peel by calling out warnings to them from this far side of St Patrick's Isle. On one occasion this giant called out a warning of an approaching storm as the Peel boats were about to head off to the Calf, but they ignored the call and all the boats were lost in the storm.

It was possibly also this protective giant that was seen in a harbour in Ireland by a Peel fisherman, although none of his Irish counterparts could see him.

AWM-FIOM 6 | HIJ-JG 171–172 | JT-HSA 2.96 | JT-HSA 2.174 | LT-SCI 188 | N-IOMT-11091886 | PIOMNHAS 3.3.229 | PIOMNHAS 3.4.351–352 | PIOMNHAS 4.2.165 | SM-MFT 179–183 | SM-MFT 203–208 | WC-WCF 20 | WC-WCF 47 | WWG-MS1 241 | WWG-MS1 243–244

St Patrick's prayer

Public | Steps and frequently slippery surfaces| SC 2422 8469 | 54.227646, -4.698096 | Horse Rock is the northern-most rocky tip of St Patrick's Isle, just behind the breakwater.

St Patrick's Isle took the name of the saint after he visited the Island to bring Christianity to the Manx. Standing here at the Horse Rock, St Patrick saw a boat in trouble out in a storm in the bay and so he raised his arm and the storm subsided, allowing the boat to return safely to harbour. Ever since that time, the Peel fishermen would take off their hats and put up a prayer when passing this part of St Patrick's Isle on the way out:

Parick Noo bannee yn Ellan ain,
Dy bannee eh shin as yn Baatey,
Goll magh dy mie, çheet stiagh ny share,
Lesh bio as marroo vaatey.

Which translates as:

St Patrick who blessed our Island
Bless us and our boat,
Going out well, coming in better,
With living and dead in the boat.

The dead they wished for here was fish.

A version of this was collected in the 1900s from a woman of nearly 100 who recalled that her grandfather's version of the prayer was not to the Christian saint, but to the Island's pre-Christian deity:

Manannan beg Mac-y-Lir, fer vannee yn Ellan,
Dy bannee shin as nyn maatey
Mie goll magh as ny share cheet stiagh
As bio as marroo 'sy vaatey.

Which translates as:

Manannan beg Mac y Lir, one who blessed the Island,
Bless us and our boats
Good going out, and better coming in,
And living and dead in the boat.

EW-FFCC 118 | PIOMNHAS 1.7.267 | SM-MFT 23–24 | SM-MFT 179–183 | VAMD 'Prar' | WC-WCF 35

Peel harbour

Public | Public road | SC 2419 8417 | 54.223026, -4.698242 | The harbour in Peel.

Manannan's fleet

Manannan was walking on South Barrule when he saw a fleet of Viking invaders heading towards Peel. He made himself into the shape of three legs and rolled like a wheel down to Peel harbour, where he put leaves into the river. When these emerged into the bay, they appeared to the attackers as great warships, frightening them so much that they rowed away as fast as they could.

SM-MFT 181–183 | WC-WCF 47 | YLM 3.4.135

Predicting disaster in a basin of water

Before the Peel fishing fleet set out on Laa Boaldyn (1 May), they called on a wise woman to tell them if luck would be with them for the season. They brought her a basin of water from a holy well and she looked in, reporting that:

> 'I'm seeing the wild waves lashed to foam away by great Bradda Head,
> I'm seeing the surge round the Chicken's Rock an' the breaker's lip is red;
> I'm seeing where corpses toss in the Sound, with nets an' gear an' spars,
> An' never a one of the Fishing Fleet is riding under the stars.'

The men thought this was ridiculous and scoffed at her words, setting off regardless. However, her prediction was proven right when a storm arose and destroyed the fleet. People then blamed the woman, claiming that she had not predicted the storm but actually caused it. They took her to Slieau Whallian and rolled her down in a spiked barrel.

SM-MFT 153–158 | WWG-MS1 243 | YLM1 1.9.290

Taking the luck from a boat

A boat was landing its successful catch of herring on the quay here when a man from another boat came by and lamented that he had not caught enough fish even for his breakfast. A man from the successful boat kindly gave him a half basket of fish but he foolishly did not salt it before passing it over and thereby gave away his boat's luck. They had no more good fishing from then on, until they went to the famous charmer of Poortown, Nan Wade. She gave them a bundle of herbs and directed them to boil them in water and then all drink, before sprinkling it on the nets and boat. Following her further instructions, they did not shoot their nets until it was dark. When they hauled in the full catch at daybreak the other man from earlier came alongside in his boat, as Nan Wade had predicted, and again asked for some fish. As Nan Wade had advised them, they refused his request this time and so regained their good luck.

FP-P1 26–27 | WWG-MS3 333–334

Boiling Chalse Teare's purse

The reverence shown to Chalse Teare, the famous charmer of Andreas, was so remarkable that when he mistakenly forgot his purse on a boat at Peel harbour, the crew cut it up into as many pieces as there were men on the boat, boiled it in their tea, drank the brew and then threw the remainder over their nets for luck.

AELM-MY 176 | JR-MFS 2.295–296 | WWG-MS3 318

Ghosts at Harbour Lights

Private land – view only | Visible from pavement beside road | SC 2440 8428 | 54.224086, -4.695095 | Harbour Lights is a restaurant and café on Peel Promenade, at the corner of Queen Street.

The end of the Harbour Lights building furthest from the harbour used to be the boathouse for the customs boat. At certain times the boat can still be heard scraping out over the stone floor that used to be here, though nothing can be seen.

A flagpole used to stand on the roof of this building and it was from here that a person hanged themselves. Ever since then heavy breathing can sometimes be heard near where the flagpole used to stand.

FP-P1 79

The former Wesleyan chapel

Private land – view only | Visible from public road | SC 2460 8425 | 54.223820, -4.692098 | The former Wesleyan chapel is today the Peel Youth Centre. It is located back from Peel Promenade, up a short alley between Stanley Road and Bridge Street.

The miraculous sovereign

This building was formerly the first Wesleyan chapel in the Isle of Man. After building work began in 1777, funds eventually ran out and the work was forced to come to a stop as they could not pay the workers. However, a prayer meeting was held to ask for divine help in their mission and then one of the congregation miraculously found a sovereign on the beach. This was enough to fund the completion of the building.

FP-P1 85

The preacher riding the devil

After leading a prayer meeting late into the evening here, a local preacher had to get his old white mare from the stalls in the dark. Having found his horse, he set off towards his home on the far side of Glen Maye but at the Creggans, just after Patrick, the mare began to be uncharacteristically restless until eventually it plunged through the bushes towards the cliffs. After the preacher failed to restrain the horse, he called out, 'Lord, help me!' At this, the mare made a sharp swerve and the preacher fell off safely onto the grass just before the horse plunged over the rocks towards the sea. Much disturbed by the experience, the preacher walked home only to find that his groom had forgotten to bring his horse to town, and that it had been safely in his stable all along. The preacher then understood that it was the devil he had ridden, and he took it as a sign that he was evidently doing good work for the Lord if the devil took such a keen personal interest in him.

MT 17–20 | WWG-MS1 492

Creg Malin rocks

Public | Level access with parking at the site | SC 2501 8447 | 54.225980, -4.685880 | The rock face at the north-eastern end of the promenade in Peel; the termination of Marine Parade.

It is a widely held practice among Peel people to 'kick the rock' at the cliff face. A century or so ago the belief was that unmarried people who failed to touch the cliff's rock when walking to this end of the promenade would be doomed to never marry. Today the tradition is carried out for luck, regardless of age or marital status.

Independently of this tradition, it was said that a giant woman built Peel Castle from rocks taken from here at Creg Malin. When she was carrying the rocks to St Patrick's Isle in her brat (apron), she dropped one of the rocks in Peel harbour, where it remained visible at low tide.

WC-WCF 20 | WWG-MS3 289 | Add

Gef's visits to the bus driver's flat

Private land – view only | Visible from pavement beside road | SC 2459 8412 | 54.222707, -4.692175 | Cowley's Pharmacy is in the heart of Peel, on the corner of Atholl Place and Atholl Street.

Gef, the Dalby Spook, made numerous trips away from his home at Doarlish Cashen. Some of these were inspired by his particular interest in John Cowley, one of the bus drivers on the Glen Maye to Peel route. Gef reported in great detail things such as the colour of his tea service or the interior of Cowley's flat in the upper rooms above Cowley's Pharmacy. When Cowley heard the report of Gef's descriptions, he became convinced of Gef's existence, going so far as to set up traps for him in the waiting room of the bus depot and underneath bus number 81.

CJ-GTM 229–230

Gef's visits to Peel bus depot

Private land – view only | Visible from pavement beside road | SC 2458 8410 | 54.222521, -4.692182 | The former bus depot is today a storage facility on Atholl Street, next to the Centenary Centre in Peel.

One of the most popular places for Gef, the Dalby Spook, to visit when on trips away from his home at Doarlish Cashen was the Peel bus depot. The talking mongoose regularly reported conversations he overheard here with such uncanny accuracy that the employees here had no doubt of Gef's existence. They set traps for him in the waiting room and under bus number 81 but inevitably Gef knew exactly where these traps were and easily avoided them. On one occasion Gef particularly annoyed a man named Jack Teare by stealing his sandwiches after slicing open their brown paper wrapping with some sharp point, be it a knife or a claw, and taking out the sandwiches.

CJ-GTM 229–231

Swearing on a person's grave

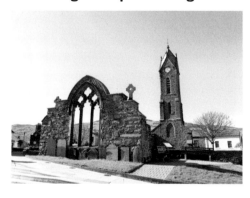

Public | Level access | SC 2433 8414 | 54.222803, -4.696152 | The remains of St Peter's church are at the clock tower at Market Place, on the corner of Castle Street in Peel.

Compurgation was a church practice officially outlawed in 1609 though it continued for decades after. To prove the truth of any claims in a case relating to a dead person, a person would go to their grave and lay down upon it on their back. An open bible was then put on their breast and around them knelt a number of 'compurgators' (witnesses) who were willing to swear to their integrity. The person then swore an oath in this position, assuring the truth of their claims relating to the dead person. A significant case of this was recorded in 1654 when a Mrs Radcliffe of Gordon carried out compurgation in St Peter's Church in the sight of six clergymen, two laymen and six women compurgators. Her innocence was thereby proven and her accuser was imprisoned in St German's prison within Peel Castle for fourteen days before having to do penance at the market crosses of Douglas, Castletown and Peel.

DC-MI 141–142

The black dog's warning

Public | Pavement beside road | SC 2429 8375 | 54.219289, -4.696536 | Glenfaba Road in Peel, the main road south out of the city towards Glen Maye and Dalby. The specific site would have been around the junction with North View.

One evening a fishing boat's captain was on his way to his boat in Peel harbour but here at what was then the edge of Peel he met a big black dog which would not let him pass. He went home for a stick and returned, but still the dog persisted in blocking his way. The man then tried to go round other ways but always the dog was there to block his path. At this the man recognised it as a sign and so he returned home, and the boat did not put out to sea that day. This saved the boat and its crew as a sudden storm came up later which would certainly have sunk the boat.

WWG-MS1 242–243

A grave connected to Nan Wade

Public | Rough and uneven ground | SC 2529 8314 | 54.214089, -4.680797 | The grave of Anne Boyde, the first grave in the north-west corner of Peel cemetery.

Although this is actually the grave of Nan Wade's daughter, this has been mistakenly identified as the resting place of Nan Wade herself, one the Isle of Man's most famous charmers. Whether through misidentification, or the daughter's inheritance of her mother's ability, this grave was renowned for those seeking charms. Fishermen would come here even into the 1930s to pluck leaves from the grave, which they would then keep on them for luck.

Nan Wade was described as a short plump woman normally wearing a sun bonnet and always to be found in a homespun skirt, checked apron and a red shawl. Her renown was Island-wide and there are many tales of her work.

A Manx boat fishing off Shetland was having such a bad time that they sent two half-crowns back to Nan Wade, who in return sent a bundle of herbs to bring the boat luck. After the crew boiled the herbs and put them on their nets and other gear, their next catch brought such a volume of fish that their nets broke under the load.

A different boat had their herbs tied in a packet to the nets but when it went missing one of the crew had to go to Nan Wade for more. She told the man that the previous herbs had been cut off and burned by one of the crew. The crew identified and confronted the unbeliever and he admitted that he had indeed done what Nan Wade said he had.

Another variation of a charm for fishermen from Nan Wade was to buy three paper rows of unused pins from the shop and boil them with some herbs that she gave them. The whole crew then very carefully drank a mouthful of the mixture and sprinkled the remainder on the nets.

A man unknown to Nan Wade visited her from Agneash in Lonan in the hope of discovering where his missing dog had gone. After retiring to the next room for a short time, Nan Wade returned to tell the man that the dog was dead but that its body could be found at the exact location she then described relative to the man's house. The man returned home and found the dog where she had said, hidden under a bush deep in brambles, where a vengeful neighbour had hidden it.

A woman from Arbory was suffering from witchcraft and so her brother came to consult Nan Wade. Following her advice, when he got home, the woman and her brother stuck pins in a pullet's liver and fried it in a pan. Great screams then began to be heard from outside as they fried the liver, as the person who had put the witchcraft on the sister began to burn as if the pins were in her own liver. After this the sister made a complete recovery.

Someone went to Nan Wade as they could not get butter from the churn. After giving the charmer a sixpence, she was told that it was the evil eye and that they could not only discover who had caused it but also undo the charm if they put red-hot tongs in the churn. They did this when they got home and in rushed a neighbour straight away to tell them that some of their clothes that had been out drying had blown into the road. They saw that this was not true but only a story to excuse their having been forced into the room by the charm. The butter came easily at their churning after that.

Someone went to Nan Wade about their horse that was sweating badly and not eating anything. Nan Wade's direction was: 'Go your ways to the cross of four roads and get some dust there, and throw it over the base, and then cover the craythur well up.' They did as instructed and by the morning the horse had recovered completely.

An old woman recalled the cure she received from Nan Wade when she visited her as a 'delicate' young girl. The charmer had everybody leave the room but for the girl, who was instructed to remain silent throughout what followed. First Nan Wade covered the silver she had received as payment with salt and threw it on something like pinjean. Then, with the girl standing on the earthen floor, Nan Wade rubbed the earth beneath her with her forefinger and then dipped it in the saucer. She then uttered a charm in Manx as she crossed the girl's forehead, chin, palms and the tip of her tongue with her wet finger. She did this two or three times before concluding the charm by throwing the saucer of salted pinjean-like substance into the fire.

Another example of one of Nan Wade's cures was when she treated an old woman for rheumatism. The charmer had fresh butter brought to her, which she cut into three pieces with a special knife she had with her. She uttered a charm in Manx and wiped the knife under her left foot at each cut. She did this three times before bringing out a parcel of finely chopped herbs. This she gave to the woman with the direction that she should pour boiling water over it and bathe in it. After the bath, the woman was then to pour the water away into a running stream at midnight.

Rather less mysterious was a cure Nan Wade gave to a woman whose young child would not stop screaming and crying. After discovering that the mother dried the family's clothes on the grass near their house, the charmer instructed her to instead dry them on a line. The child ceased crying almost as soon as this was done, evidently now free of a painful irritation caused by the clothes' contact with the soil.

Nan Wade was aware of her limitations, as was shown when a woman came to her for help with her ailing child. The charmer went out for some herbs in her garden but found a dead insect on the first one she lifted. This was a sure omen of the girl's doom and so Nan Wade returned to the woman and told her, 'I have got no herbs for you. Go home and look to her; she won't be long with you.' The child died very soon after that.

MD-EVAF 33 | N-IOME-24081951 | N-IOMT-03101936 | WH-MM1 182 | WWG-MS2 184–185 | WWG-MS2 192–194 | YLM 4.156–157

The lost wife of Ballaleece

Private land – view only | Visible from pavement beside road | SC 2725 8208 | 54.205281, -4.650119 | Ballaleece is west of St John's, just after the Peel road crosses over the river Neb.

The farmer here at Ballaleece married a beautiful young woman named Ellen, but she went missing shortly after their wedding day. After failing to find her anywhere on the Island, the farmer eventually gave up looking and, with regret, remarried. Not long after this the first wife appeared to him and told him that she had been taken by the fairies but that he had the chance to get her back that Friday night. She would be riding through the barn with the fairies and if he cleared the place entirely of straw then he would be able to grab hold of her as she rode past and save her.

So the man swept the barn clean of all the straw and hid in a corner. At midnight the fairies rode in on fine horses all dressed in green jackets and red caps and on the final horse the man saw his wife. He leapt out to take hold of her but he found it impossible to keep hold of her, and she rode on out of the barn with the fairies. As she went, she called sadly after her that his second wife had hidden one piece of straw in the corner and now the chance of saving her was lost forever. She was never seen again.

Different versions of this tale offer slight variations. One significant difference has Ellen disappear after their first child was born. Upon appearing to her husband, part of her instruction was not to tell anyone. Then, when she rode through the barn, on the thirteenth horse, she shouted out that no Leece would ever inherit the farm. Years later, when the son reached maturity, he died suddenly and mysteriously. Another version has the man find blood on the threshold of the barn in the morning suggesting that the wife was murdered by the fairies for her attempted escape.

AWM-FIOM 45–46 | GB-LWC 155–157 | HIJ-JG 60 | N-MH-02051900 | SM-MFT 79–81 | WC-WCF 19

The grey man of Ballaleece Bridge

Public | Pavement beside main road | SC 2734 8203 | 54.204810, -4.648766 | Ballaleece Bridge is on the main Peel to Douglas road, where the road turns sharply over the river Neb, immediately to the west of St John's.

In the late nineteenth century a mysterious little old grey man on a donkey used to be seen here at Ballaleece Bridge. Sightings were recorded from trustworthy people of standing in the community, but nothing further is known of this strange figure.

YLM 4.159

Tynwald Hill

Open access | Steps and gravel | SC 2776 8189 | 54.203737, -4.642337 | Tynwald Hill is beside the main Douglas to Peel road in St John's.

Walking around Tynwald Hill

It will bring you good luck if you walk clockwise three times around the base of Tynwald Hill. However, if you are carrying out a more complicated piece of witchcraft, you might need nine perambulations.

WWG-MS1 232–233

The Shiaght Mynney Mollaght

A powerful form of curse is the Shiaght Mynney Mollaght. A part of making this curse is the anti-clockwise turning of a Swearing Stone seven times inside the hollow of a larger stone. This terrible curse was sometimes done for greater effect secretly at night on the summit of Tynwald Hill and, at other times, on its north side.

DC-MI 23

Choosing the King of all Birds

A long time ago, all the birds gathered at Tynwald Hill to determine who should be their king. After long arguing about how best to judge, it was decided that, since they were birds, the one who could fly the highest would be king. So they set off from Tynwald Hill up into the sky. They went higher and higher until the eagle could fly no further. Upon seeing no other birds with him he called out, 'Ta mish Ree ny Ein, Ree ny Ein!' ('I am King of the Birds, King of the Birds!'). But just then the clever little wren flew out from hiding under the eagle's wing and flew just a little higher above him. The wren triumphantly called out, 'Cha nel, cha nel, ta mish er-y-skyn!' ('No, no, I am above him!'). So it was that the wren became King of all Birds, a thing remembered in the Hunt the Wren song on 26 December each year:

> The wren, the wren, the king of all birds
> Was caught St Stephen's day in the furze,
> Although he is little, his family is great,
> We pray you, good dame, to give us a treat.

SM-MFT 131–135

Giant's Grave

Public | Public road, close to a narrow bend | SC 2775 8194 | 54.204149, -4.642382 | The Giant's Grave is a large stone in the western wall of Glen Mooar Road behind Tynwald Hill.

The common name of this ancient burial site is the Giant's Grave, but an alternative local name for it is 'King Orry's Grave.' This perhaps identifies the giant buried here as King Orry, the revered figure of Manx-Norse history.

AJAF-ASG 73

The cursed cross slab of Tynwald Chapel

Open during daylight hours | Steps and gravel| SC 2788 8186 | 54.203522, -4.640356 | St John's Chapel is on the north side of the main Douglas to Peel road on the Tynwald Fairfield at St John's.

As well as Asruth's cross slab, which normally stands here, part of another cross also used to stand in the porch of St John's Chapel. However, when the cattle in the fields around here began to fall sick after the cross had been placed here, it was recognised to be the cause. It was secretly removed and buried, and the location of the site was never revealed, so that the cross would not be uncovered and do more damage.

WWG-MS1 217

Manannan's hill

Private land – view only | Visible from pavement | SC 2861 8171 | 54.202438, -4.629222 | Cronk y Vannin is the slightly raised ground at the south-east corner of the Ballacraine crossroads. Lying on the main road between Douglas and Peel and controlled by traffic lights, the crossroads is a short distance east of St John's.

Cronk y Vannin (Hill of Manannan) is where Manannan held his courts, presumably in a form similar to what we see at Tynwald Day. He also created his mists from here, by which he hid the Island from enemies. He is also said to be buried here within the mound.

N-IOME-21081953 | PIOMNHAS 2.3.203 | PIOMNHAS 4.2.135 | PIOMNHAS 5.5.530 | WWG-MS1 231

The cabbyl ushtey of Kerroo ny Glough

Private land – view only | Visible from road | SC 3008 8120 | 54.198310, -4.606417 | The Awin Dhoo can be seen beside Mill Road. Just over 100 metres from the main Douglas to Peel road, up Mill Road, two large slate slabs are to be seen over the hedge at the roadside, the remnants of an old footbridge over Greeba River. About five metres further upstream can be seen the Awin Dhoo flowing into the main river. The farmhouse of Kerroo ny Glough stands above this, visible through the trees.

The woman of Kerroo ny Glough lost a calf here by the stream but she could find only a tuft of its hair where it was last seen by the bank. The next day the farmer went to the same spot with the cows and was horrified to see a monstrous creature emerge from the water to tear another calf to pieces and eat it. They determined to never take the cattle close to the river again. However, one night the daughter did not return after going out for a small task on the farm and it was believed that the cabbal ushtey had taken her as well. It did not return for more cattle after that and was never seen again.

WWG-MS1 226

The phynnodderee's round meadow

Private land – view only | Visible from a quiet road | SC 2983 8075 | 54.194146, -4.609853 | Lheeaney Rhunt is a part of the Greeba Playing Fields, just over 300 metres down Ballachurry Road, a narrow road heading south from the main Peel to Douglas road at Greeba. The playing pields have a sign on the gate, to the west of the track. The large field today is formed from small older fields, of which that in the north-east corner has been identified as the Lheeaney Rhunt.

One of the phynnodderee's acts of kindness was to cut the meadow grass of this field. However, having grown complacent of the phynnodderee's help, the farmer here grumbled about the length to which he cut it. Furious, the phynnodderee let the farmer cut it himself the following year, and when he did so, the phynnodderee came after him with a scythe to stub up the roots so close on the farmer's heels that the man hardly escaped with his legs. No one was brave enough to cut the grass of Lheeaney Rhunt for several years after that, until a clever soldier from one of the garrisons took up the challenge. He cut from the centre of the field outwards in a circular fashion, always keeping an eye out for the phynnodderee, until he had completed the job without trouble.

HIJ-JG 50–51 | HIJ-JG 54 | HIJ-JG 64 | WWG-MS1 371–373

The fairies flee from the mill

Private land – view only | Visible from road | SC 2840 8236 | 54.208209, -4.632713 | St John's Mill conference centre on the western edge of the Tynwald Mills complex. It is a short walk from the car park on the other side of the river, on the Poortown Road, close to Ballig Bridge.

When this fulling mill was set up at the end of the eighteenth century, a man living close by heard a low murmuring, wailing noise very early one spring morning. On going to the door to see what it was, he saw 'multitudes of the good people' passing over the stepping stones in the River Neb here. They were heading up the side of the hill in a long line, until they were eventually lost in the mist that obscured the top of Beary Mountain. They were dressed mostly in clothes made of loaghtan wool, with little pointed red caps, and they were carrying kettles, pots, pans, spinning wheels and their other household possessions. They were moving on to somewhere quieter as they had been disturbed by the noise of the mill.

AWM-FIOM 41 | WH-DIM 104 #46 | PIOMNHAS 5.5.528 | WWG-MS1 228

Beary Mountain

Public | Rough and uneven track beyond the end of the public road | SC 2999 8335 | 54.217545, -4.608803 | Beary Mountain is south-east of Glen Helen. The summit is a walk from the top of Mill Road, which leaves the main Peel to Douglas road at Greeba Bridge.

A shepherd and his two dogs once came across an old woman at her spinning wheel just below the summit here. The dogs went close to her at first but she put something on them that made them back off in fear. The man felt that she was not quite right and they left her, but they then soon became lost and could not find their way home from the hill for two days and nights. When at home again, the man and his dogs all took sick and one of the dogs came to die.

In addition, it was here at the summit of Beary Mountain that the fairies disappeared into the mist when they fled from Ballig after the construction of the fulling mill (see previous item).

WWG-MS1 227–228

Ballalough

Private land – view only | Visible from public road, with limited pavement | SC 2630 8339 | 54.216737, -4.665493 | Ballalough is on the Poortown Road, about half a mile from Peel. It lies opposite Cronk Lheannag, the distinctive small hill to the south.

The cursed stones of Ballalough

A stone cross with carved rabbits and birds along its edges used to stand on the land of Ballalough. However, a farmer removed the stone from the keeill site and used it as a lintel, after which the cattle began to fall ill. Realising the connection, the farmer immediately panicked and buried the stone somewhere with sandy soil close to here. Since then, its location has been forgotten and the stone has remained undisturbed ever since.

PMCK-MAS 2.19 | N-IOME-24091898 | WWG-MS1 237

The tarroo ushtey of Ballalough

A tarroo ushtey used to be frequently heard bellowing at night in the curragh beside Cronk Lheannag. In around the 1870s, two young men had been out stealing apples by the Patrick Road and had taken a shortcut straight across the fields towards home. By Cronk Lheannag they saw a great beast with eyes the size of cups and lit up as if by candles come out of the curragh roaring tremendously. The men dropped their apples and ran for their lives as the tarroo ushtey came after them. It was only when they reached the road and got to the gates of Ballalough that the tarroo ushtey gave one last awful bellow behind them and plunged back into the curragh.

SM-MFT 222–223 | WWG-MS1 238 | YLM 4.155

The giant's hill

A giant wanted to make a footpath between the Isle of Man and Scotland and so set about shifting land from Glenaspet to the north of the Island. However, as he came close to Ballalough, the bottom of his creel fell out, dropping all the earth here to form Cronk Lheannag.

WC-WCF 20

Liaght ny Foawr

Private land – view only | Visible from rough and uneven footpath | SC 2748 8342 | 54.217343, -4.647371 | Liaght ny Foawr is a collection of stones partially visible on private land off of a footpath which leaves the Switchback Road westwards at the crossroads with Bayr ny Staarvey, just under half a mile north of the Poortown Road. After about 240 metres along the track, the site is partially visible looking westwards over a gate on the north side of the track.

The Manx name of this site translates as 'Giant's Grave.' This reflects the belief once common in the Island that giants were laid to rest in these sorts of burial sites.

AJAF-ASG 76–77 | HIJ-JG 72

The crossroads fire on Bayr ny Staarvey

Public | Public road | SC 2805 8357 | 54.218939, -4.638801 | A crossroads on Bayr ny Staarvey, perhaps most likely to be that towards the southern end, over Laurel Bank.

In 1847 a farmer near Poortown had been losing cattle and so he suspected that someone had put the evil eye on his stock. So he built a bonfire of coal, turf and gorse in the middle of a crossroads on Bayr ny Staarvey and he set one of the dead cows upon the top. He had skinned the animal and sold its hide to the tanner but he was advised by an older person that the fire would not work in overturning the evil eye without the complete carcass. So the skin was retrieved and also put on the bonfire before the thing was lit. The expectation was that the witch would then be drawn to the fire and so the crowd looked out expectantly. However, it was only a man, a little worse for wear after a mhelliah, who happened to wander by. Upon hearing the shouts of the crowds by the fire, he realised the situation and ran away fast, thankfully avoiding the mob's vengeful intentions.

DC-MI 27–28 | N-MS-02101847

Manannan's Chair

Private land – view only | Visible from public road | SC 2927 8568 | 54.238283, -4.621225 | Manannan's Chair is a raised area of land in a field just off Bayr ny Staarvey. The mound is visible from the first gateway on the landward side north of the public footpath that leads down to Cronk-y-Voddy.

The ancient pre-Christian ruler of the Isle of Man, Manannan, is believed to have decreed his laws and judgements here on the Chair that used to be a part of the north-western corner of the earthen mound. Some also say that it was beneath this mound that Manannan was laid to rest after his death.

On Midsummer's Eve the Manx give offerings of rushes to Manannan. This is recorded as happening in two places; at South Barrule and at a place called 'Keamool.' Although most believe this to be a lost placename, one authority in the mid-twentieth century held that there was 'no doubt' that Keamool should be identified as Manannan's Chair, and that this was the site where offerings were made to Manannan.

AWM-MN 156 | DC-MI 171–172 | WWG-MS1 235–236

A keeill made from the devil's timber

Private land – view only | Visible from public road | SC 2978 8686 | 54.248994, -4.614206 | The site of Keeill Pherick a Dromma is a distinctive raised area of land marked by a metal sign in a private field on the landward side of Bayr ny Staarvey. It is about 600 metres north of the crossroads between Cronk-y-Voddy and the coast road.

The old name of Bayr ny Staarvey is Bayr ny Mannaghyn (Manannan's Road) and it was here at the keeill site that St Patrick fought the Celtic God, Manannan. Keeill Pherick a Dromma was built here in commemoration of the saint's resulting victory for Christianity.

The keeill itself was built at the direction of St Patrick, who ordered the devil to ride the timber here over the sea from Ireland. However, once the keeill was built, the devil tore it down again. This happened a number of times until eventually a tailor agreed to sew a pair of breeches in the keeill one night to try and break the curse. However, the devil appeared as he worked and he threatened the tailor with his big head, his big clawed finger and his big cloven foot. But before the devil was able to get too close, the tailor finished his breeches and ran out the door. Furious, the devil pulled down the roof, tore off his own head and threw it after the tailor. The tailor survived, but the keeill never stood again after that.

KR-MNQ 103 | PIOMNHAS 2.3.203 | PIOMNHAS 2.3.210 | WC-IH 16 | YLM 3.4.140

Fairy women at Glen Cam

Private – view only | Visible from public road and car park | SC 29107 87615 | 54.255587, -4.624884 | Glen Cam is crossed by the road at the Devil's Elbow, where the road between Peel and Kirk Michael twists sharply over the glen. A small picnic area at the turn in the road offers convenient parking.

In the first half of the nineteenth century a man named Thomas Crellin was travelling along this road with a friend one night when they both saw two fairy women on the banks of the stream here. They were in 'bright yellow bedgowns, frisking in the moonlight.'

FP-P1   82 | N-PCG-02021901 | N-IOME-02031901

Buggane Mooar

Private land – view only | Visible from public road and footpath | SC 2787 8631 | 54.243453, -4.643126 | Buggane Mooar is the remains of a promontory earthwork on the coast 1½ miles above Peel towards Kirk Michael. It is visible from the coast road about 300 metres south of Glion Broigh, which the road crosses between Knocksharry and Lyngague.

The earthwork here has the name, Cashtal y Vuggane Mooar (Big Buggane's Castle), or simply Buggane Mooar (Big Buggane). Sadly, no stories have been passed down to us of this large buggane and their castle here.

JJK-PN 385

Meir ny Foawr

Private land – view only | Visible from public roads and footpaths | A collection of large white boulders on the hill above the Switchback Road. The stones are on private land but can be seen from the Coast Road.

The Manx name for these stones, Meir ny Foawr, translates as 'Giant's Fingers.' They were thrown here by the three-legged giant that lived on St Patrick's Isle during the time of St Patrick. The giant threw an enormous rock from St Patrick's Isle merely to amuse himself, and it broke into smaller pieces when it landed here. The mark of the giant's fingers can still be seen on some of the rocks.

Another version of the story has the giant throwing the rocks at his wife, who had fled here after an argument had flared up between them.

HIJ-JG 171–172 | JJK-PN 402 | JT-HSA 2.173–174 | PIOMNHAS 3.4.279 | WC-WCF 20 | WWG-MS3 371 | YLM 3.8.319

Crosh Vooar

Private | On private land just off the Bayr yn Ooillyn, roughly halfway between the coast road and Bayr ny Staarvey.

A large tumulus used to stand here but it was deliberately destroyed, apparently to clear out the evil which was lurking here.

LQ-GIOM 96

The Devil's Altar

Private | Altar y Jouyl is a large quartz boulder on the private land of Lhergydhoo, north of Peel.

No detailed stories have been passed down to us today of how this boulder got its name of Altar y Jouyl (Devil's Altar). However, it is said that a sacrificial offering of some sort was made near here as late as c.1870, and that a number of 'superstitious beliefs' used to be attached to the stone.

FLS C/204 | JJK-PN 375 | LQ-GIOM 78

Jurby

Although Jurby does not boast a great deal of folklore, the sites it does have are fascinating. Many will know of King Orry's landing place on the edge of the parish, but few will be aware of the curses received from disturbing ancient chapels or burial sites within Jurby or the range of stories connected to the parish church.

- The curse of a destroyed keeill [private land]
1. Jurby church
2. The landing place of King Orry
3. Cronk Carlane and the noises in the night
4. Ballacaine
- Ballamooar [private land]

The curse of a destroyed keeill

Private | On the private land of Ballaconley Farm.

In the eighteenth century the seven sons of the Conoly family here at Ballaconley destroyed the remains of Keeill Coonlagh which then stood on their land. One after another, these seven brothers then began to die, until within the year only their sister was left, Mary Conoly, who alone did not take part in the destruction. In 1751 she married a man named John Callister, and it was their heirs who held the farm through into the twentieth century.

Uncanny noises have also been heard in Ballaconley house and apparitions have been seen in the trees nearby. These have been attributed to stones from the keeill having been used in the building of the house and to the disturbance of an ancient burial place through roadworks nearby.

DC-MI 233–234 | PIOMNHAS 1.9.613 | PIOMNHAS 5.1.32 | PMCK-MAS 3.14–15 | WWG-MS2 139–140

Jurby church

Open during daylight hours | Level access | SC 3497 9848 | 54.355020, -4.540997 | The parish church overlooks the sea at West Jurby. Visible from far away against the coastline, the church is seaward from the crossroads of the Coast Road and Ballavarran Road.

Innis Patrick

Christianity was first brought to the Isle of Man by St Patrick and the place where he first landed was where the church stands today. At the time of the saint's arrival this was an island surrounded by water on all sides. Known as Innis Patrick, this is the true St Patrick's Isle.

AWM-MN 135 | PIOMNHAS 5.1.28

The psalm of destruction

One of the most remarkably outrageous vicars to have served at Jurby was a man named William Crowe. In November 1661 he was punished for several offences, including slandering both parishioners and the Lord of Mann. Another of the charges against him was that he had sung a 'psalm of destruction' against John Teare of Ballateare. The detail of this is not expanded upon, but it is likely that it was a form of curse intending to wipe out Teare and his estate. It can perhaps be assumed that this 'psalm' was given in the church, which at that time was located at a site in what is now the churchyard. It was also here, at the chancel steps, that Crowe was forced to publicly ask for forgiveness from his parishioners as a part of his punishment.

DC-MI 239–240

The candle, the skull and the midnight prayers

Sometime in the nineteenth century a light began to be seen in the church late at night. A man named Lace from Ballacreggan went with a friend to investigate but it was only Lace who was brave enough to actually enter the church at that late hour. He was surprised to find a man at the clerk's desk reading the bible by the light of a candle secured in a skull on a stick. The man explained that he had been advised to read a certain chapter of the bible at midnight in just that manner, to cure his daughter of the fits from which she suffered. After this it was observed that the daughter gradually got better.

YLM 3.10.484

The replacement priest

The vicar that used to be in charge of the church was so forgetful that he set off to fish in the river one morning, forgetting entirely that it was Sunday. When his housekeeper ran to tell him what day it was, he leapt up and rushed towards the church, but in his haste, he fell down the bank and broke his leg. In agony and unable to move, he put up a prayer to St Patrick to ask that his parishioners should not miss out on their service that Sunday. When the congregation were returning from church later, they were surprised to find the priest in pain, there down the bank, as they had received a service from someone in his likeness. At this they reflected that the clothes of their vicar that morning had appeared to shine as if they were made of precious stones.

MD-EVAF 17

The landing place of King Orry

Public | Sand, tidal | NX 3778 0153 | 54.383311, -4.499491 | At the Lhen, on the coast at the border of Jurby and Andreas. This is reached via the seaward road close to the small bridge over the Lhen Trench.

It was here that King Orry first landed on the Isle of Man. The local Manx were amazed by his arrival and asked where he had come from. He pointed up to a galaxy in the sky and said that marked the way to his country. Since then, the Milky Way has been known in Manx as 'Raad Mooar Ree Gorree' ('The Great Road of King Orry').

In some versions of this story King Orry or his followers were giants, as the Lhen is known to have seen the arrival of giants looking to make the Isle of man their new home. One of these giants that arrived with King Orry went on to make his home at Andreas rectory.

AWM-FIOM 64–65 | BN-MS3 3–11 | HIJ-JG xxxiii | JT-HSA 1.63–64 | TK-FJ 12 | WL-DPG 73 | WWG-MS1 150–152 | WWG-MS1 330 | WWG-MS3 226

Cronk Carlane and the noises in the night

Private land – view only | Visible from road | SC 3437 9705 | 54.342053, -4.549383 | Ballateare is a farm about three quarters of a mile north of the crossroads at the Cronk. The farm stands distinctively alone towards the coast, at the top of a rise on the Coast Road.

A Scottish tenant at Ballateare in the nineteenth century began to cart away the ancient mound, Cronk Carlane, uncovering burial urns. However, his family then began to be disturbed in the night by 'blood-freezing' noises and so the work on the mound was stopped and the urns were covered back over.

DC-MI 232–233 | PAS5 5.1.31

Ballacaine

Private land – view only | Visible from road | SC 3580 9709 | 54.342867, -4.527486 | Ballacaine is a private farm on the Jurby Road about midway between The Cronk and Sandygate. It is just under half a mile west of Ballavarran Road. This is believed to be the Ballacaine relevant to the folklore described here.

Nipped by the fairies

One morning a six-year-old girl went out to milk the cows at Ballacaine. As she approached the dairy, she could hear the cows calling and calling but she began to be nipped by the fairies so painfully that she almost dropped the can. When she got back to the house, the woman of the house applied a salve known as a cure for the fairies on the girl and the intensity of the pain subsided. However, the feeling of their nips remained with her for the rest of her life.

YLM 1.10.328

The old man dancing for the fairies

An old man at Ballacaine used to be plagued by the fairies. They would torment him at night in the barn where he slept with the 'cronk, cronk' of them tuning their fiddles. One damp night, when it was even worse than usual, the man had the idea of humouring the fairies instead of raging against them. So he got out of bed and began to dance, calling out, 'Play away, my little fellows; I am dancing.' The fairies then began to play for him, and they went on until he was worn out completely. The fairies then gave a polite bow, a bright light filled the barn, and the man was left alone for his first restful sleep in a long time. The fairies did not return to plague him again after that.

YLM 1.10.326

The fairies thrown into the sea

Ballacaine was once so plagued by fairies that the farm workers here feared that they might be turned into one of them if they were caught out at night. These fairies dressed in green hats and 'gaudy red fancy dresses' and they would 'scamper about in the rosy light.' They would come into the farmhouse at night and eat up the food that was left out for them, but if the food was ever missing then they would break the crockery and upset the whole room. The master had had enough of their tyranny and so he had a great meal laid out for them, and while they were eating, he sent his strongest servant to fetch a barrel and roll it into the room. Then he burst into the room and grabbed every one of the fairies to ram them into the barrel. He then nailed on the lid and rolled it into the sea, after which the fairies were never seen again at Ballacaine.

YLM 1.10.327

The Good People from the sunset land

In the 1880s an old woman recalled her youth here at Ballacaine and a particular evening when she observed 'the Good People from the sunset land' from her window. They were tiny beings in green jackets and red caps adorned with hens' feathers. These fairies had wings and were playing in the sunbeams. The girl watched as they hung from the trees and kicked their legs, rode on twigs and got up to all manner of 'capers.' However, someone called to her from elsewhere in the house and the sound caused the fairies to immediately open their wings and fly up into the sky.

YLM 1.10.327–328

Ballamooar

Private | Ballamooar is a private house on the Jurby Road east of the Cronk.

Gef, the Dalby Spook, visited Ballamooar in 1936 on a rare trip to the north of the Island when he hitched a ride on the underside of a cart. The talking mongoose reported this visit with detailed descriptions of the property, including the carpet patterns, the decoration on the fireplace, the names of the five horses and the names of the previous owners. The family connected to Gef did not know the place or the family and so they only found the opportunity to verify Gef's claims when a paranormal investigator visited from London. Upon coming to this grand house, they found that the majority of Gef's claims were accurate, others mostly accurate, but three of the 30 distinct observations were curiously false. This, like most of the stories of Gef, has never been satisfactorily accounted for.

CJ-GTM 215–220

Lezayre

There is a remarkable variety of folklore in Lezayre. Although areas such as Churchtown, Cronk Sumark or the Mooragh are key locations, few places in the Island have as rich a store of folklore as Glen Auldyn. From a moddey doo, a tarroo ushtey and a glashtin at the foot of the glen, up to the King of the Fairies at the Black Dub at the top, the glen offers a landscape teeming with bugganes, corpse lights, ghosts and more.

1. The corpse light of Regaby Gate
2. The moddey doo of the Dhoor
3. The Mooragh
4. The buggane by the Crossags road
5. Milntown Corner
6. Magher y Troddan
7. Milntown Wood
8. A place to see the doomed
9. The gigantic hare
10. The frying pan ghost
11. Daniel Dixon, the Fairy King
12. Ballakillingan
13. Gat ny Muck
14. The ghost of Kirk Christ Lezayre
15. The horned beast at the window
16. Glion ny Killey
- Billey Ghorrym [private land]
17. Cronk Sumark
18. The nine o'clock witches
19. Curing the evil eye
20. The fairies of Gob y Volley
- Chibbyr Lansh [private land]
21. The grave of the three-headed giant
22. Ballaskella
23. The Devil's Glen
24. Farrane Fing
25. Snaefell

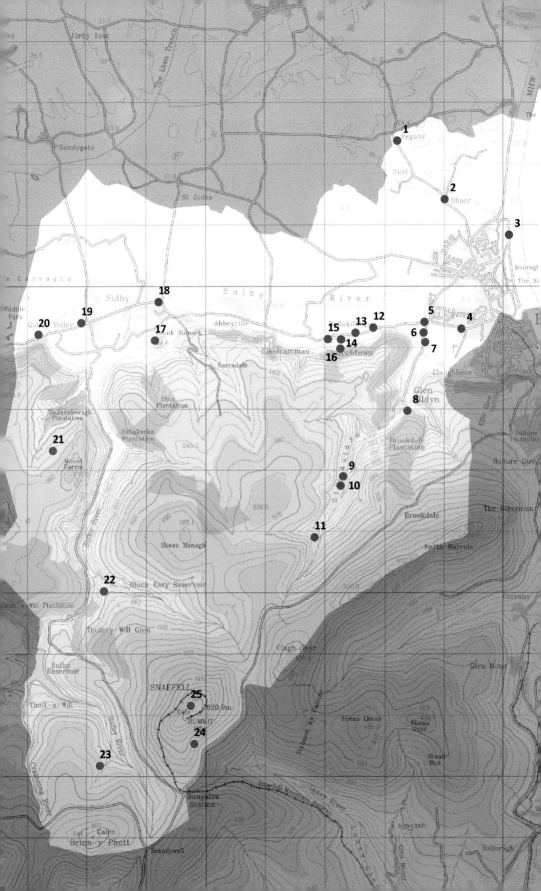

The corpse light of Regaby Gate

Public | Pavement beside road | SC 4317 9739 | 54.347889, -4.414406 | Regaby Gate used to stand just over 100 metres south of the Regaby Crossroads, on the Andreas Road by the house and the garage here today.

One evening a man was returning to Andreas from Ramsey and was close to Regaby Gate when he saw a bright light, like a ball of fire, travelling along the road in front of him. He watched as it moved towards the hedge on the right, rested on the top for a little while and then went on into the field. He followed it as it continued in the field a short while before curving back to the road, where the light finally disappeared.

Two days after this one of the man's neighbours died. At the funeral, the man was following the coffin to the church along this same road when he was amazed that, owing to the poor state of the road, they turned off exactly at the spot the light had shown, resting the coffin a moment on the top of the hedge before going over and proceeding through the field a while before returning to the road again. The route of the coffin was exactly where he had seen the light travel, and the coffin returned to the road where the light had disappeared.

YLM3 3.10.486

The moddey doo of the Dhoor

Public | Pavement beside road | SC 4400 9643 | 54.339451, -4.401167 | The Dhoor is a collection of houses on the Andreas Road, half a mile north of the turning for the Bride Road.

A moddey doo used to be well known at the Dhoor. On one occasion a man came across it here and so turned to go another way, but it followed him. He tried this way and that, but the dog was always following. It is not recorded how the man made it home safely that night.

FLS C/117

The Mooragh

Public | Pavement beside road | SC 4510 9583 | 54.33441, -4.38387 | The Mooragh Promenade at the northern end of Ramsey, by the gully beyond the first house north of the playing fields.

The moddey doo of the Mooragh

This area of the Mooragh used to be haunted by a moddey doo, and many still feel uneasy passing here at night. Perhaps a clue as to why this and 'possibly something even worse' might attach to this area of the Mooragh might be found in the land the gully leads up to being 'Cronk y Croghee' ('Hill of the Hanging').

WWG-MS3 378–379

The Mooragh tarroo ushtey

Before the park and promenade were built in 1887, the Mooragh was a damp wasteland plagued by a tarroo ushtey. The sound of its roaring and splashing at night was well known, particularly to the residents of the cottage which used to stand near here, and people would avoid the area for fear of the beast. The belief in this tarroo ushtey was so firmly held that when the foghorn was first sounded from the Bahama Bank Lightship off the shore here, the workers at the large timber yard on the north side of the harbour rushed out ready to battle the beast, armed with whatever they could find.

WWG-MS3 380 | LM 1.9.290–291

The buggane by the Crossags road

Public | Pavement beside main road | SC 4439 9432 | 54.320658, -4.394083 | The Crossags Road is between the two buildings of Ramsey Grammar School, leading off south from Lezayre Road.

In the first half of the nineteenth century a 17-year-old woman named Margaret Esther Christian was walking home to Sulby after midnight when she came across what looked to be a cat here by the Crossags Road. It walked beside her for a while but as it did so, it gradually grew larger and larger until it resembled a large horse. The woman took fright and ran as fast as she could, but after a little time the thing vanished.

YLM 3.10.486

Milntown Corner

Public | Pavement beside main road | SC 4366 9440 | 54.32117, -4.40525 | Milntown Corner is the junction of Lezayre Road and Glen Auldyn Road, at Milntown on the western edge of Ramsey.

The kindly old fairy

One night in the winter of 1912 a woman was walking out of Ramsey when her lantern went out as she approached Milntown Corner. However, just before the darkest part of the road, a little person appeared in front of her with his own lamp. He was about two feet high and wearing a red cap and a long blue coat with shining buttons on the front. He had white hair, a bushy white beard and his face was covered with hundreds of wrinkles, but his eyes were bright blue and the kindest she had ever seen. They stood silently looking at one another for a few moments and then he vanished.

WWG-MS2 248

The Milntown moddey doo

Although Milntown Corner is reputedly visited by a threatening ghost and a wide variety of beasts, including a cabbyl ushtey, tarroo ushtey and a cabbyl oie, the creature best known here is a moddey doo. This has been seen a number of times, even as late as the 1920s and 30s. It is a big black dog, nearly the size of a calf, with a long black shaggy coat and 'eyes like coals of fire.' It has been seen quietly seated or standing late at night in the dark of Milntown Corner, and when disturbed it has leapt over the road and disappeared up Glen Auldyn. The beast's unnatural threat is felt by those who meet it and it has acted as a harbinger of doom when a flood laid waste to much of Glen Auldyn after one of its appearances. It has also been seen before a death several times, such as in 1927, when a woman saw it here shortly before her father's death. Another time a doctor saw it here at two o'clock in the morning on his way to help at a birth, and it was still there when he returned, after which he learned of the baby's death.

ML2.3.15–19 | WWG-MS1 250 | WWG-MS2 255 | WWG-MS3 377

The Milntown glashtin

A farmer was returning from Ramsey with an iron coulter of a plough when he met what he thought was his own horse near Milntown. He mounted it and began to ride home, but at Milntown Corner, when he wanted to turn up Glen Auldyn, it bolted for the Sulby curragh. The farmer thrashed it with the coulter until eventually the beast submitted and turned back to go up Glen Auldyn. When it was safely in the stable, the man went into the house and sent one of his sons out to feed the beast, but it was found to have gone. This was taken as proof that it had been a glashtin and that it had returned to its home in the curragh.

A similar experience was had by another man who came across a beautiful horse with a fine saddle standing alone here one night. When he climbed up onto it, it raced off but threw him when it made a great leap. When the man got up, he found that the horse had vanished completely.

EK-CC 353–354 | N-IOME-03091898 | YLM 1.10.326

Magher y Troddan

Private land – view only | Visible from pavement beside main road | SC 4361 9440 | 54.321114, -4.406006 | Magher y Troddan is the large field just outside Ramsey, at the corner of Lezayre Road and Glen Auldyn road, below Skyhill and to the west of Milntown Corner and the Auldyn River.

The Manx name for this field, 'Magher y Troddan,' means 'Field of the Contest.' This has led some to believe that it is the site of the Battle of Skyhill. Perhaps related to this is that the field is a favourite place of the fairies.

A tarroo ushtey is also connected to this field, emerging from the river at night to endanger nearby cattle.

WWG-MS1 250

Milntown Wood

Private, but accessible as a part of the Milntown Estate, admission charge applies | Rough and uneven ground | SC 4369 9409 | 54.318354, -4.404691 | Milntown Wood can be enjoyed from within Milntown Estate, on Lezayre Road at the western edge of Ramsey. Alternatively, the Glen Auldyn Road turns off Lezayre Road and runs up the west side of the estate, beside the wood.

This wood used to be renowned for its uncanniness. People would be afraid to go past it in the dark, and some people have had to flee from strange creatures or spirits lurking here near to the mill.

DC-MI 95 | PIOMNHAS 5.2.65

A place to see the doomed

Public | Steep, overgrown, rough and uneven ground | SC 4346 9295 | 54.308109, -4.407561 | The remains of the Cabbal are in Brookdale plantation in Glen Auldyn. From the footbridge over the river into the plantation, go up the hill and take the path right. The remains of the keeill can be discerned below the footpath as it turns to the left uphill. The south-west corner of the keeill remains as a few stones jutting out from the hedge bordering the field beyond, a few metres from the path.

People used to visit the Cabbal on St John's Eve at midnight. Here they watched for lights passing along the road or by the side of the river, which would show the number of deaths that were to come within the community during the following twelve months. One year, twenty-one lights were seen dancing up the glen, foretelling of the 'great epidemic' which struck the community that year.

A possible connection between this and a practice of taking candles to the Cabbal on St John's Eve has been noted. However, little is known of this other than the Church having stamped it out as 'superstitious' in the 1630s.

One alternative account has the relevant date as Hop tu Naa rather than St John's Eve.

JJK-PN 509 | PIOMNHAS 1.9.626–627 | PIOMNHAS 2.1.27–28 | PIOMNHAS 3.1.72–72 | PMCK-MAS 4.7 | VAMD 'Hollantide' | WWG-MS1 254

The gigantic hare

PROW | Rough and uneven footpath | SC 4238 9186 | 54.297959, -4.423559 | Glen Auldyn is a glen just outside the western edge of Ramsey. Take the Glen Auldyn Road and within a mile turn off at the former chapel to cross the river over a small bridge. The glen proper begins half a mile beyond this, where the road stops and access is only by foot, along the footpath.

Two youths were poaching in Glen Auldyn one night with an acetylene bicycle-lamp, dazzling hares with the light and then knocking them over or netting them silently. However, they were startled to meet what they described as 'a gigantic hare.' They ran off down the hill in fright and did not return to poach again for some time.

WWG-MS2 272–273

The frying pan ghost

Private land – view only | Visible from steep, rough and uneven footpath | SC 4234 9174 | 54.296911, -4.424178 | At the side of the main track up Glen Auldyn, by the tholtan at Tantaloo, on a private track through the ford.

An unusual ghost has been seen coming down the steep track here by the ford. The female figure was dressed in a grey cloak and a headdress similar to a sunbonnet, and she carried a frying pan with which she threatened those she met. Her appearances were thought to be an evil omen.

WWG-MS1 256–257

Daniel Dixon, the Fairy King

PROW | Steep, rough and uneven footpath, steps, a substantial walk | SC 4191 9089 | 54.289150, -4.430223 | By the Black Dub, the remnants of a former quarry in the Glen Auldyn river, at the top of the glen, over a mile up the footpath beyond the end of the road.

A sober and upright 19-year-old man and his cousin were once in the hills gathering peat. After loading up their horses, the young man let his cousin go on ahead and he lay down near the quarry here for a rest. However, as soon as he closed his eyes he felt a weight on his chest and he looked to see a little old man sitting there. He was 'wrinkled in the most extraordinary manner; his complexion was swarthy; his teeth projected outwards; and his fingers were very slender; but both they and his legs and arms were unusually long in proportion to his body.' The young man asked who the old man was, and he replied: 'I am the Fairy King, my name is Daniel Dixon, and I live at Quay's quarry.' The young man tried to take hold of the fairy so his cousin could see him also, but he was thrown head over heels the moment he took his eyes off the little man. When he looked back, the Fairy King had disappeared and in his place were 'a number of tiny beings arrayed in brown petticoats.' These too vanished before his cousin returned.

N-IOME-03091898

Ballakillingan

Private land – view only | Visible from pavement beside main road | SC 4288 9433 | 54.320250, -4.417260 | Ballakillingan is on the north side of Lezayre Road opposite the war memorial in Churchtown. The site of the Ballakillingan chapel is at the western end of the group of trees in the middle of the field, to the east of the house. The old front gate to the estate stands on the main road at the eastern end of this field.

The buggane of Ballakillingan

A thing described as 'a sort of buggane' used to be seen walking here by the old front gate of Ballakillinghan. Those who saw it reported as being 'like a big, grey bulldog, and an awful howl on it.'

MJ 7.417

Curphey's Ghost

The chapel here at Ballakillingan fell into ruin after it was superseded sometime before 1634. By 1890, the owner of Ballakillingan, Curphey, was so indifferent to its former use that he used the old chapel as a kennel for his hounds, as he found the old box pews made perfect pens for the dogs. When the Bishop heard of this, he warned Curphey of the consequences, but he ignored him. Later, after his death, Curphey's ghost would be seen on moonlit nights walking under the beech trees and looking back to the site of the old church, shrugging his shoulders as if still indifferent to the Bishop's warning.

GQ-LOF 77

Gat ny Muck

Public | Visible from pavement beside main road | SC 4259 9424| 54.319349, -4.421659 | The road by Paddy's Field, which is the field to the east side of the Lezayre War Memorial in Churchtown. Gat ny Muck entered the field from the main road and so it is believed to be the gate there today.

Gat ny Muck means 'Pig Gate' in Manx. It got its name from the fact that it, and the road in front of it, was 'haunted by the ghost of a pig.'

GQ-LOF 15

The ghost of Kirk Christ Lezayre

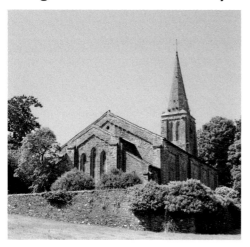

Private land – view only | Visible from road | SC 4235 9411 | 54.318151, -4.425259 | The parish church of Lezayre is on the south side of the main Ramsey road at Churchtown. The church is no longer open to the public.

Close to the start of the twentieth century, the choir were practising in the church gallery one night when one of the choristers let out a scream. Amazed, the others asked what the matter was, and the girl reported that she had seen something white at the communion rail at the front of the church. After this, the rehearsals were moved out of the church and instead took place in the schoolhouse nearby.

MJ 7.416–417

The horned beast at the window

Private land – view only | Visible from road | SC 4214 9413 | 54.318287, -4.428526 | The former schoolhouse is today a private house just beyond the western edge of the graveyard on the south side of the loop-road at Churchtown, over the road from the vicarage.

When this building was still in use as a schoolroom, an entertainment taking place here one evening was interrupted by the terrifying sight of a strange beast with horns appearing at the window. It was held by those who saw it that this was no natural animal and no explanation for its presence could be found then or after.

WWG-MS1 414

Glion ny Killey

Public | Steep, rough and uneven ground | SC 4234 9398 | 54.316996, -4.425361 | Glion ny Killey is the small steep valley over Churchtown, now a part of Ballakillingan Plantation. It is accessed by the track uphill from the Churchtown loop road, up from the Lezayre War Memorial and close to Kirk Christ Lezayre.

The Grey Lady

The upper part of Glion ny Killey is haunted by a Grey Lady. This ghostly apparition can be seen here in a robe of swishing grey silk.

WWG-MS1 259

A daughter lost to the fairies

A Lezayre girl lost interest in things and began to grow thin and listless. Her mother suspected her of having dealings with the fairies at night, so she began to watch for her in the churchyard and in the woods of Glion ny Killey. Eventually, she saw her daughter dancing with the fairies among the trees on the hillside. The woman did not dare go near to them at the time but in the morning she confronted her daughter and gave her a beating. But this was to no effect as the girl wasted away further and died not long afterwards. It was supposed that the daughter had joined the fairies for good.

WWG-MS2 228–229

Fairy music

Billie Quirk would often see and hear the fairies around his home near here but one night he heard them within Glion ny Killey as he was coming home with his brother. The sound the fairies were making was 'the most-loveliest singing in the world.' The brothers hurried to their home at the Glebe, where the music could still be heard. But when Billie tapped on the window to wake their sleeping mother to hear it, she only gave a grunt and turned over, at which the singing immediately stopped.

GQ-LOF 17

Billey Ghorrym

Private | Billey Ghorrym is an area of the private Glentramman on the side of Skyhill.

The area of the Billey Ghorrym has a dark reputation such that people would not be induced to go near it after dark and would warn their children to keep away from it at all costs. Many strange things have been seen and experienced here.

Footprints thought to be left by the fairies were found here one winter in the second half of the twentieth century. After a snowfall, a man found footprints about four inches long left in a gully in the glen here. The man scooped the snow up and carefully carried it home to measure against his own child, confirming that they were the same size as his two- or three-year-old child. He could offer no other explanation for these footprints but for their being from the fairies.

This glen is also associated with the phynnodderee, in a story perhaps better known of a site in Glen Auldyn.

GQ-LOF 13–14

Cronk Sumark

Access only | Steep, rough and uneven ground, steps | SC 3922 9412 | 54.3172447, -4.4733175 | A distinctive hill standing over Sulby. Take the Yn Claddagh road behind the Ginger Hall pub. About 300 metres along this road there is a footpath south from the road, which heads off steeply up Cronk Sumark.

Driving away evil before a wedding

It used to be the Manx custom that on the morning of a wedding young men would climb Cronk Sumark and blow cow-horns for as long as their breath held out. Although a part of this was as a celebration of the occasion, the horns were also to ward off the fairies on that important day.

WWG-MS2 130

The Grey Man of Cronk Sumark

In misty weather the apparition of the Grey Man can sometimes be seen on the top of Cronk Sumark. This mysterious figure wears a grey cloak but there are no stories recorded of who the figure might be.

WWG-MS1 264–265

The Old Maid's Hill

Unmarried women used to dance and sing in procession around the base of Cronk Sumark at night on Good Friday in the hope of gaining themselves a husband. This led to Cronk Sumark also becoming known to some as 'Old Maid's Hill.' Other accounts report this dancing around the hill as a step along the path towards becoming a witch.

WWG-MS1 264–265 | WWG-MS2 165–166

Manannan at Cronk Sumark

Cronk Sumark is one of Manannan's former homes. When enemies or other unwanted visitors approached the hill, he would make Cronk Sumark appear to be an island surrounded by sea, causing the attackers to flee in fear of being overwhelmed by the water. Manannan and his White Host of 'fairy warriors' would then charge down the hill on their horses, in pursuit of the attackers, passing through only the Claddagh's shallow ford.

Manannan can still sometimes be seen here, standing on the summit of the hill with his White Host half-veiled in mist. He can be seen wearing a crown which shining bright through the mist. It is said that if anyone were able to reach him here through the mist then they would go with him to Flaunys, his magical island out over the Western Sea, though their mortal body would be left behind to die.

MD-EVAF 12 | MD-EVAF 18–19 | MD-WCEV 20–21

The nine o'clock witches

Public | Pavement beside main road | SC 3928 9473 | 54.322734, -4.472767 | Sulby Bridge marks the eastern edge of Sulby village, at the bend in the road with the junction with Bayr Yude Noo.

Running water is said to form an obstacle for witches and other supernatural beings. It is probably as an offshoot of this that witches were sometimes to be seen at bridges at nine o'clock at night, a time when they were evidently able to cross over.

The belief in this was shown most obviously when a local parson was riding towards Sulby bridge near this time and was growing increasingly nervous as his companion deliberately went slow in order to be at the bridge at nine o'clock. Eventually, the parson lost his nerve and spurred his horse to race over at a gallop, so he was clear of the bridge just before the time when witches were supposed to appear.

WWG-MS1 263–264

Curing the evil eye

Public | Pavement beside main road | SC 3799 9440 | 54.319432, -4.492387 | The Sulby Glen Hotel is at the crossroads on the main road in Sulby, at the meeting of Clenagh Road, the Sulby Glen road and the main road through the village.

More than 100 years ago the owner of Sulby Glen Hotel was well known for his skill with cures and remedies. An example of this was when a woman fell down as if dead after watching a string of carts passing by her front door near Sulby Bridge. When her husband found her there in the doorway, he rushed here to the hotel, where the owner got a small bottle of liquid and rushed to the woman. The man put a few drops of the liquid on her lips and the woman immediately opened her eyes. Within half an hour she was speaking again and she was on her feet soon after. The man later explained that the woman's falling ill was from someone on the passing carts putting the evil eye on her. He asserted that she would have perished for certain if he had not come when he did.

MJ 5.294–295

The fairies of Gob y Volley

Private land – view only | Visible from pavement beside main road | SC 3727 9419 | 54.317296, -4.503375 | Gob y Volley quarry is on the south side of the main Ramsey to Ballaugh road, roughly 500 metres east of the Wildlife Park and half a mile west of the Sulby Glen crossroads.

One December night in the 1880s a man named Thomas Radcliffe and a friend were walking home to Ballaugh from Sulby at about twenty-five minutes before midnight. When they got close to Gob y Volley, they saw around twelve or fourteen little people running across the road in front of them and into the quarry. The two men went into the quarry to look for them, but they could find no sign of them anywhere. This left the men in no doubt that they had seen the fairies.

YLM 3.10.485

Chibbyr Lansh

Private | Chibbyr Lansh is on the hillside over the Wildlife Park and Gob y Volley.

Chibbyr Lansh has the power to cure many ailments, though it was held to be most useful for eye problems. The water should be taken at sunrise on a Sunday, when you should first walk three times around each of the well's three pools saying 'Ayns ennym yn Ayr as y Vac as y Spyrrid Noo' ('In the name of the Father and the Son and the Holy Ghost'), before daubing your eyes or other affected part of the body in a rag soaked in the water. This rag should then be left on the bushes nearby and a coin left in the well. In the past, the bushes by the well here were white with the rags, or even paper, left by those visiting the well.

The water was said to be particularly effective if it was taken at Laa Luanys (the first Sunday of harvest) 'when the books were open' (during the church service).

Two men from Sulby were once tempted to take the accumulated coins in the well for themselves. The result was that they soon fell blind and were without sight for the rest of their lives.

AWM-FIOM 120 | AWM-MN 176 | GQ-LOF 79–80 | JR-MFS 2.307 | JT-HSA 2.60 | WWG-MS1 45 | YLM 1.4.95 | YLM 1.4.102

The grave of the three-headed giant

Private land – view only | Visible from rough and uneven footpath | SC 3751 9232 | 54.300598, -4.498580 | Oaie ny Foawr is the mound beside the track below Mount Karrin, between Sulby Glen Road and the Druidale road. The public footpath takes a dogleg around the cairn, which is obvious by the boulders around it.

Oair ny Foawr means 'Giant's Grave.' One account suggests that the giant buried here is a three-headed giant named Jiarg who arrived with the Norse to the Isle of Man. After living to the end of his life in Andreas, he was buried by his wish here at Mount Karrin. It was this giant who also gave his name to Bayr Jiarg Karrin, the track which runs from here down to the Sulby Glen road.

An alternative account has this as the grave of the giant who lived at the top of Mount Karrin. He would talk to the neighbouring giant on Snaefell and the laughter between them would ring out like thunder. However, one day there was a disagreement and the giant on Snaefell threw a huge quartz boulder at his friend. Luckily for the giant here at Mount Karrin, the boulder fell short and landed near to Ballaskella.

Centuries later, a man heard about the giant buried here and so began to dig up the cairn to take a look at him. But before he had dug very far, he was seized with a great pain in his back which forced him to stop immediately. He struggled to get home and in three days he was dead.

AJAF-ASG 98–99 | AWM-FIOM 64–65 | N-IOME-03091898 | WWG-MS3 226

Ballaskella

Public ram | Steep, rough and uneven footpath, a substantial walk | SC 3838 9002 | 54.280169, -4.484052 | Ballaskella is a tholtan on the hill on the east side of the Sulby Valley close to Tholt y Will. Heading from Sulby, as the road rises into the plantation around Tholt y Will, walk down the path on the left to a stone bridge over the river. Turn right up the hillside and through the first gate. The path zigzags up to Ballaskella at the brow of the hill.

The moddey doo

A young man was walking home from Sulby on a dark and foggy night. It was around two o'clock in the morning as he started up the steep zigzag track towards Ballaskella, when an enormous dog began to follow him. The beast was nearly as big as a calf, it had glittering eyes and it growled terribly as it followed him. The man tried to hit the beast a number of times with his stick but missed each time, at which point the man realised that it was something other than natural. In the morning, when the man talked about the dog, his employer said that he too had seen the dog, and that it was best to leave it alone. The young man never again walked that path alone late at night, preferring to stay in Sulby and return in the morning if he was ever out late.

WWG-MS1 266–267

The phynnodderee and the little loaghtan

It was within memory at the start of the twentieth century that the people of Ballaskella would put out a bit of food for the phynnodderee in thanks for his help with the threshing and other such tasks around the farm. On one occasion the phynnodderee successfully collected in the sheep for the farmer here even though the phynnodderee reported that he had had particular trouble with one of the little loaghtans, having had to chase it round Snaefell three times before it was finally caught. But when the farmer went out later to see to the sheep, he found that the foolish phynnodderee had been confused, as it had been a hare that he had caught and put amongst the sheep.

FLS Q/32A

The Devil's Glen

Public ram | Steep, rough and uneven footpath, a substantial walk | SC 3831 8717 | 54.254547, -4.483589 | The Devil's Glen runs beside the Millennium Way before it reaches the Beinn-y-Phott Road.

This glen east of Glen Crammag is known either as the Thief's Glen or the Devil's Glen. Regrettably, no story of the devil is known to have been collected of this glen.

WWG-MS1 277

Farrane Fing

Public ram | Steep, rough and uneven ground | SC 39879 87525 | 54.258264, -4.459650 | Farrane Fing is a spring on the side of Snaefell. The spring forms a pool just below a large white quartz boulder towards the top of Awin Ving, the stream which runs under the Mountain Road by the Les Graham Memorial.

The water of Farrane Fing was once renowned as holy. It would be requested by those on their death beds, in the faith that it would act as a holy sacrament preparing them for death and offering a peaceful passing into the next life.

The spring was also featured in the Laa Launys practices of those down the Laxey Valley. At the start of August these people would always make a stop here at Farrane Fing as part of their annual pilgrimage to the top of Snaefell.

WC-IH 24 | WWG-MS3 179

Snaefell

Public ram | Rough and uneven ground, steps. Alternatively accessible via the seasonal Snaefell Electric Railway | SC 3982 8814 | 54.263774, -4.460846 | The peak of Snaefell is easiest reached by foot from the Bungalow, where the tram tracks cross the Mountain Road. Alternatively, a tram can be taken to the peak during summer, from the Bungalow or from Laxey.

King Snaefell

The cairn at the top of Snaefell was first built in memory of King Snaefell, who lies buried beneath it, and the mountain took its name from this great Manx king. Rather than building a memorial as we would expect it today, the mourners placed a great pile of stones over the tomb, to which visitors ever since have contributed when visiting the site.

It is believed that King Snaefell here was the most ancient, beloved and great of three different kings, the other two being buried in a similar fashion at South Barrule and at Carraghan.

GW-DIM 58 | WWG-MS1 232

The giant of Snaefell

A giant used to live on the top of Snaefell who would talk happily with the neighbouring giant on the top of Mount Karrin. The laughter between them from these conversations would normally ring out like thunder, but one day there was a disagreement and the Snaefell giant threw a huge quartz boulder at his friend. However, the boulder missed the giant on Mount Karrin and fell short to land near to Ballaskella.

N-IOME-03091898

Laa Luanys on Snaefell

At Laa Luanys, at the start of August, people used to climb to the top of Snaefell. The best record we have of what they did at the top is given in the Lonan church records of 1732:

> 'There is a superstitious and wicked custom, which is yearly continued and practised in this and the neighbouring parishes by many young people (and some of riper years) going to the top of Snaefell Mountain upon the first Sunday in August, where [...] they behave themselves very rudely and indecently for the greater part of the day.'

It is believed that this was a remnant of some now-forgotten pre-Christian practice that used to take place on the hilltops of the Island at this point of the year.

Because of this, the Church viewed the practice as problematic and tried to stamp it out. A preacher known as Paric Beg achieved this here at Snaefell by joining the crowds on the mountain at Laa Launys and preaching at them. At the conclusion of his service, he went around for the collection, which was apparently an effective way of clearing the crowds.

AWM-FIOM 121 | JR-MFS 2.305–307

Ben Ven Carraghan

Although best-known at Carraghan in Braddan, Ben Veg Carraghan has also been seen on Snaefell. In the mid-nineteenth century, a man cutting turf alone here saw this ghostly woman with her spinning wheel. Perhaps uniquely in all accounts of her, Ben Veg Carraghan spoke to the man here on Snaefell, though he never revealed to anyone what she said.

WWG-MS1 217–218

The Snaefell Café and the end of the world

The Isle of Man's greatest wizard was Caillagh ny Faashagh. He could take whatever form he liked and his favourite was to appear as a goat with big fiery eyes. He was met like this one day by a woman who asked him when the end of the world would come. Caillagh ny Faashagh gave of a number of signs of the coming of the end of the world, but the first was:

> 'The Mountains of Mann will be cut over with roads, and iron horses will gallop over them, and there will be an inn on the top of Snaefell.'

SM-MFT 190–191

Lonan

Lonan boasts many of the Island's most important folklore characters, including the phynnodderee, tarroo ushtey, giants, King Orry and, of course, the fairies. However, most distinctive to the parish are the dooinney oie and the Nikessen. While the former has a number of stories edging towards the playful or comic, the latter is remarkably dark and disturbing, making the parish's well-formed ghost stories almost pleasant in comparison.

1. The foreshadowing of a death
2. The ghost rider on Tent Road
3. The haunted house of Glen Road
4. The ghost rider of Abbey Cottage
5. King Orry's Grave
6. The cursed stones of Gretch
- Ewan y Darragh [private land]
7. The start of John y Chiarn's night with the fairies
8. Ewan Christian battles the devil
9. Chinnacan
10. Ballaragh chapel and John-y-Chiarn's night with the fairies
11. The ghost of Bayr Calloo
- A well connected to storms [private land]
12. Glen Drink
13. Agneash
14. Ballayolgane
15. Haunted Glen Foss
16. Lhergy Veg

- The tarroo ushtey of the Grianane [private land]
- Raby [private land]
17. Slieau Lhost
- The phynnodderee at Ballamilgyn [private land]
18. The man who abused the dooinney oie
19. The fairies' wine well
20. The phynnodderee of Ballalheaney
21. The two ghosts of the cottage by Glen Roy ford
- Chibbyr Pherick [private land]
- Nikkesen's Pool [private land]
- The phynnodderee's favourite place on the Glen Roy river [private land]
- A resting place for the dead [private land]
22. Kirk Lonan graveyard
23. The fairies as souls of the dead
24. The Cloven Stones
25. The Suicide Graves

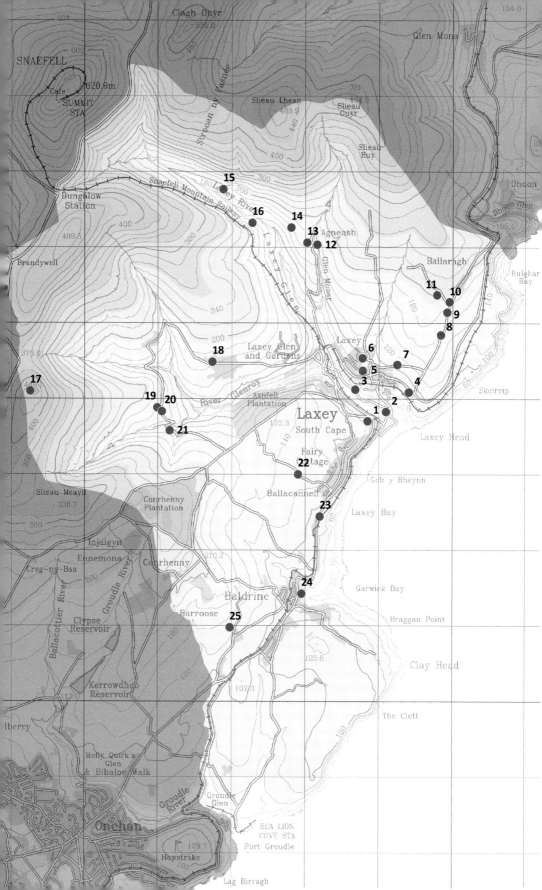

Laxey & The North

The foreshadowing of a death

Public | Pavement beside road | SC 4392 8370 | 54.225162, -4.395622 | South Cape is a stretch of the upper main road through Laxey. It is the area that bends around between Old School Hill and Lhergy Grawe.

A man was coming from Laxey village on a still clear moonless night when he heard a groan in the road ahead of him. On the clear dry road, he saw a dark patch in the middle of the highway. It looked like the shadow of an object in the moonlight, but there was no object or anything else to explain it. The man investigated, but could not understand it and so he moved on nervously. Later that night a man coming from Douglas was thrown from his horse and trap here and died on the spot.

MNHL MD522 | YLM 3.8.380

The ghost rider on Tent Road

Public | Pavement beside road | SC 4417 8382 | 54.226295, -4.391938 | The corner of Tent Road and Old Laxey Hill, by the Shore Hotel.

A ghostly white woman on a horse rides down from Abbey Cottage to the harbour in Laxey whenever a boat sounds its horn upon entering the harbour at midnight. One sighting was by a young woman in the first half of the twentieth century. She was close to the Shore Hotel at midnight when a boat entering the harbour sounded its horn, at which point a gust of wind blew out her light. The woman then saw the ghostly rider come over the bridge before her and turn down Tent Road towards the harbour. In a terrible fright, the woman rushed to her home on Glen Road, where she found her mother awaiting her, already expecting that she would have seen the ghost.

CV-OH-EC

The haunted house of Glen Road

Public | A flat parking area | SC 4369 8405 | 54.228271, -4.399364 | Edenvale was a house which stood in the open space of the recycling area on the river side of Glen Road, close to the entrance to Laxey Football Club car park.

The house that used to stand here, Edenvale, was well known to be haunted. Numerous uncanny stories are recalled by those who knew the place, including sounds of animals running around the house, machines running outside, or a person entering and walking in, all of whom were not to be seen and left no trace. Inexplicable candles and lights were frequently seen and strange noises heard from inside the house. One story was of a window that would always be unaccountably opened in the night-time, so the tenants nailed it shut, only to find the glass broken in the morning. Exorcisms were attempted but without success, as the strange occurrences and unpleasant feeling in the house persisted. Tenants did not last long in the place, until eventually it fell into neglect and was knocked down. No definite story explaining the building's haunted state is known but vague tales of an untimely death in the house used to be told.

CV-OH-EC | CV-OH-SWQ

The ghost rider of Abbey Cottage

Private land – view only | Visible from the public footpath, or from the pavement beside a main road | SC 4448 8408 | 54.228748, -4.387315 | Abbey Cottage is the last house on the landward side of the main road on the way out of Laxey heading towards Ramsey, by Abbey Lane. A public footpath goes past the house.

A long time ago, a sea captain and his young wife used to live here in Abbey Cottage. When he returned to Laxey at night, he would set off the boat's horn as it passed between the lighthouses into the harbour. At this signal the woman set off from Abbey Cottage on her white horse and rode down to Laxey to meet him off the boat. However, one day he was lost at sea and the woman died of a broken heart. Ever since then the ghostly vision of her riding to meet him can be seen whenever a boat sounds its horn upon entering the harbour at midnight.

CV-OH-EC

King Orry's Grave

Open access | Rough and uneven ground | SC 4386 8437 | 54.231134, -4.396953 | One part of King Orry's Grave is at the roadside a short distance up the Ballaragh Road from the main Ramsey road heading out of Laxey. The part of the site said to be King Orry's actual grave is down the small path on the other side of the road.

It was believed that King Orry's Grave was not just the Norse king's burial site – marked by the large standing stone known as King Orry's Stone – but also the location of his murder. Giants were also said to be buried here.

The area has a very dark reputation and in the mid-nineteenth century people could not be persuaded to travel past it after midnight.

The part of the site at the roadside has two of its central stones touching, leaving an oval opening between them. It is thought by some that people in the past might have passed through this opening in some form of ritual to cure their ailments.

AJAF-ASG 109–112 | JGC-HPECL 233 | KR-MNQ 148 | PIOMNHAS 4.3.328 | YLM 1.2.44

The cursed stones of Gretch

Private land – view only | Visible from the public footpath, uneven ground | SC 4385 8453 | 54.232564, -4.397225 | Gretch Vooar is a short distance up the Gretch Vooar Road. Starting from the Ballaragh Road at the corner immediately above King Orry's Grave, the footpath runs along the road as it goes over the ford and curves upwards until Gretch Vooar stands ahead of you.

A carved stone used to stand on the land of Gretch, covered all over with moons and stars. However, the stone was disturbed or moved by the farmer here and things started to go wrong on the farm. Realising the connection, the farmer immediately buried the stone. Since then, the location of the buried stone has been forgotten and so it remains in the ground awaiting rediscovery still.

The part of the site at the roadside has two of its central stones touching, leaving an oval opening between them. It is thought by some that people in the past might have passed through this opening in some form of ritual to cure their ailments.

WWG-MS1 237

Ewan y Darragh

Private | The former home of Ewan y Darragh is on private land on the broogh north of Laxey.

When the man who became known as Ewan y Darragh lived near here, he was courting a woman named Kirry at the Granaine. However, one night he discovered her with another man and a fight broke out in which Ewan killed the other man. Disgusted at the world and shunned for causing the death, Ewan gave up human contact and came here to live alone on the broogh. He survived here for some time living off what he could find nearby but illness and a bad winter left him destitute. However, just when at the point of death, he was amazed to find food left at his door and a copse of trees planted nearby for fuel. This was the work of the phynnodderee, whose kindness alone kept Ewan alive.

Ewan y Darragh was also renowned for his fiddling, especially as he had made his instrument from the whitened bones he found in the hills. The music he played on this fiddle was like the wild music of the winds and the streams. He played for the entertainment of the phynnodderee and the fairies who he was on good terms with. The Laxey people would sometimes also secretly come here too to listen to his playing, but if he ever saw or heard them, the music would stop immediately.

One day an unknown ship put into the bay and sent a boat in for Ewan alone. After he had boarded with his fiddle, the boat sailed away and was never seen again.

Another tale reports that Ewan joined the fairies completely and went away to their land without death. But still he returns here to play his music sometimes.

A story confirming that the spirit of Ewan y Darragh is indeed still to be found about this place tells of a Lonan man captaining a boat lost in thick fog close to the Isle of Man, when he was surprised to hear voices close to him through the fog. He called out to ask where he was and the men who were working in a field were about to shout back when they were interrupted by a voice calling out in Manx, 'Struan ny Granghie! Struan ny Granghie! Gow magh!' ('Granghie Stream! Granghie Stream! Go back!')

The captain knew the place and understood that he was in danger of hitting the rocks. He immediately swung the boat around to safety and headed towards the harbour. The men in the field did not see who had spoken but they heard the man playing the fiddle as they walked away, leading the men to believe that this was the spirit of Ewan y Darragh.

MD-EVAF 72–75 | MJ 6.360–363 | WWG-MS1 313–314

The start of John y Chiarn's night with the fairies

Public | Visible from a public road without a pavement | SC 4433 8444 | 54.231895, -4.389856 | Ballaquark is a private farm on the Ballaragh Road. It is the first farm on the landward side of the road above Gretch Vooar Road.

John y Chiarn was walking along the road outside Ballaquark one night when he met a band of fairies. He tried to get over the hedge to be out of their way, but their leader touched him with a stick and he was changed into something for carrying their luggage. They then set off, gathering in other groups of fairies, heading towards a great feast and dance at Ballure Glen outside Ramsey.

SM-MFT 146–150

Ewan Christian battles the devil

Public | On the side of a public road without a pavement | SC 4483 8483 | 54.235614, -4.382408 | The gates to Ballachrink Farm Cottages are on the landward side of the Ballaragh Road. They are about 500 metres from the sharp turn in the road before it straightens towards Ballaragh.

The devil appeared out of a shadow by the gates here one early evening when Ewan Christian was driving by after a trip south to lead a religious revival there. The devil accused the famous preacher of cheating him out of human souls through all his successful preaching, but Christian fearlessly defended himself until the argument came to a fight. Christian was overpowered and passed out, and he only got to his home in Lewaigue, Maughold, when his pony walked his cart home on its own. A week or two later Christian was dead.

Perhaps related to this, a moddey doo was well known to haunt the road here at the start of the twentieth century. A number of people were known to have encountered it near here around that time.

MD-EVAF 27 | WWG-MS2 82–83

Chinnacan

Public | A public road without a pavement | SC 4493 8515 | 54.238523, -4.380896 | The stretch of the Ballaragh Road down the hill from the final southern houses of the village, past Ballachrink to the bend in the road towards Laxey.

This stretch of the Ballaragh Road used to be well known as a place where the fairies might be met. People walking here at night would hear them whispering and chattering around them. This possibly links to the name, 'Chinnacan,' which this stretch of the road used to be known as. In the 1920s, a 90-year-old pronounced the name as 'chengaghyn' ('tongues'), which possibly refers to the sound of the fairies' whispering here.

WWG-MS3 187

Ballaragh chapel and John-y-Chiarn's night with the fairies

Public | A public road without a pavement | SC 4497 8526 | 54.239522, -4.380407| The former Ballaragh chapel is a private residence a short distance south of the heart of the village, on the corner of the Clarum Road.

The Ballaragh chapel was the first place John y Chiarn passed along the road on his night with the fairies. He had met them at Ballaquark and was transformed into something for carrying their luggage, but as the party passed by the chapel here, one of the village's barking dogs ran away with his tail between his legs as soon as he smelled the fairy travellers. From here they headed on towards Ballure for a great feast and dance.

SM-MFT 146–150

The ghost of Bayr Calloo

Public | A steep, rocky and uneven public footpath | SC 4486 8535 | 54.240285, -4.382083 | The Bayr Calloo is today also known as the Clarum Road. It leads up into the hills from the former Ballaragh chapel, a short distance south of Ballaragh village.

The ghost of a young woman often used to be seen on this road. Many people attested to having seen her, including the postman.

WWG-MS3 185

A well connected to storms

Private | Chibbyr Gorran is a well on private land near Croit ny Claghbane.

Great gales and thunderstorms will occur if this well ever runs dry, and the rain that falls in those storms will be sufficient to fill the well again. Storms and natural disasters will also occur if the well is ever destroyed or drained. It has also been suggested that the weather can be influenced here by the correct use of the well's water in a charm.

WWG-MS1 42

Glen Mooar and the Hills

Glen Drink

Private land – view only | Visible from the public footpath, steep, rough and uneven footpath, steps | SC 4324 8603 | 54.245841, -4.407273 | The glen east of Agneash. From the car parking area close to the chapel in Agneash, take the small path to the north-east down between the houses. It crosses a small bridge, climbs up past a house and emerges to drop down to a bridge over Glen Drink itself.

The fairies driven off by a Methodist

The root of 'Glen Drink' has been claimed by some to be 'rink' rather than 'drink,' an obsolete Manx word for dancing. It is not known whose dancing is responsible for the naming, but it might be the fairies, as they were well known here.

However, around the 1820s a Methodist minister began holding services in a house in the glen every other Sunday. This came to drive the fairies away and by the 1870s they were no longer to be seen in the neighbourhood.

HIJ-JG 105–106 | JJK-PN 259 | MK-FIOM 30

Taken by the fairies for the night

A man was walking home late one night at Glen Drink when it suddenly began raining very heavily. He climbed over the hedge to shelter under some trees but it was just as wet there as on the path. He went to climb back over the hedge but, although he walked and walked, he could not find the hedge again. He had been going a long time when he commented aloud on his surprise at the size of the orchard he found himself in and which he had never seen on that bare hillside before. At this point his legs went weak and he felt himself taken up in a great company of people who rushed him off. He did not know where he was until morning when it grew light and he found himself on the bare mountainside close to Glen Drink.

N-RWT-03121898

The stolen child

At a house in Glen Drink a baby was left unattended for a short while and when the parents returned, they found the cradle empty. The parents set off looking for the child and eventually found the baby unharmed about half a mile away. This strange occurrence was explained as an attempted abduction by the fairies.

N-IOMT-10061939

Agneash

Public | On a public road with some parking space | SC 4311 8605 | 54.245998, -4.409313 | Agneash is a small village up the Mines Road, nearly a mile above the Laxey Wheel.

Fairies as common as rabbits

The fairies used to be regularly seen around Agneash. Indeed, towards the end of the nineteenth century someone here would see three, four or even six fairies every day when going about their work on their farm. The fairies were so numerous that they took no notice of them and seeing one was no more remarkable than seeing a rabbit.

WWG-MS1 307

The Agneash Changeling

A mother in Agneash once left her baby in the cradle when she went to the well. But by the time she returned, the fairies had exchanged the baby for a fairy child. Wisely, the woman kept away from the cradle and let the child cry until eventually the fairies realised that the fairy child was being neglected. They then returned and swapped the woman's own child back again.

There was at least one other instance of a changeling here in the village, but no details are known to have been recorded.

N-IOMT-10061939 | PIOMNHAS 4.3.368

Ballayolgane

Private land – view only | Visible from a public road without a pavement | SC 4288 8625 | 54.247730, -4.412982 | Ballayolgane is the last inhabited building on the right-hand side of the track from Agneash village towards the Snaefell Mines.

The phynnodderee of Ballayolgane

The phynnodderee used to help on the farm here at Ballayolgane. If his work here was like elsewhere, it would have been of great swiftness and strength but without payment. It is likely that the phynnodderee moved on from here after he took offence at the farmer's gift of clothes.

MNHL MD522 | WWG-MS1 283 | YLM 3.8.380

Fairies in red trousers and blue coats

The old couple who lived here at Ballayolgane in the 1870s regularly saw the fairies on their land around here. The woman reported that they were 'like little boys, dressed in red trousers and blue coats.'

HIJ-JG 106

Haunted Glen Foss

Public | Rough and uneven footpath | SC 4196 8676 | 54.252033, -4.42731 | The mines track where it crosses Glen Foss on the way from Agneash up towards the Snaefell Mines. The track drops down to a bridge over the glen, about two thirds of a mile beyond Ballayolgane Farm.

In the 1930s, Glen Foss was considered 'the most haunted ground in the whole area.' An old woman in a red cloak was just one figure who haunted the area here. She has been seen in a number of places in the Island, but no one has ever been able to discover anything about her. In addition to this, this area is also haunted by the spirits of dead weavers in white cloaks, who can be seen between midnight and two in the morning around here. They are associated with the flax mill which used to stand close by.

N-IOMT-10061939 | WWG-MS1 303–304

Lhergy Veg

Private land – view only | Visible from a rough and uneven footpath, or partially visible from the Snaefell Mountain Railway | Lhergy Veg is today a tholtan below the electric railway line in the Laxey Valley. It is visible from the mines track on the opposite side of the valley, or from the railway.

A man named James Callow lived here in the mid-nineteenth century but he was better known as the 'Fairy Doctor' or 'Fairy Tailor' because of his closeness to the fairies. He sometimes received help with his tailoring from the fairies. More than this, they would transport him wherever he needed when he requested it. Rather than take a horse to Ramsey for the materials of his trade, he would go out onto the hill behind his house and call out:

'Sleih ny voynrey, sleih ny shee,
Tar dys shoh as hroggal mee.'

(This means, 'Fairies, come here and lift me.)

He would then be lifted through the air to his destination for his errand and then back again. Because of this, he was able to make the long journey to Ramsey to buy material and back in only twenty minutes. Another version has it as only taking five minutes. Having heard of this ability, some Americans invited the Fairy Tailor to the opening of a new railway. There he took bets that he could beat the train to its destination, and so made an enormous sum when he did so. However, the Fairy Tailor met his end soon after this when he was shot by an embittered enemy who was jealous of his ability.

The large rocks lying outside Lhergy Veg cover passageways into the earth where the fairies live. When people still lived in the house, they would hear the fairies frequently emerge to sing and play amongst these stones.

Also underground here are two giants who once came up from under the flagstones. The weavers of the house were at home when the giants pushed up through the floor, but at the first sight of them the men fled. However, the men regained enough bravery to return to look in through the window. They saw a male and a female giant sitting by the chiollagh with 'things like horses' blinkers and bridles' on their heads and 'something else rising above their heads like a sort of helmet.' The weavers ran off for help but by the time they returned the giants were gone.

FLS STW/C | MD-EVAF 27–28 | PIOMNHAS 4.3.330 | WWG-MS1 296–299

The tarroo ushtey of the Grianane

Private | The ruin of the Grianane is on private land hidden in trees at the top of a gully above the tram tracks in Laxey Valley.

This farm came to be deserted because of a tarroo ushtey. The fearsome water bull would emerge from the stream at night and roar around the house trying to find a way in. The inhabitants eventually had to bar the doors with furniture and stay up through the night in order to ensure their own safety. After this went on too long, they were driven away completely, and the Grianane fell into ruin as no one was brave enough to take up living there after them.

This tarroo ushtey is perhaps linked to Berree Dhone, the caillagh of the Corony Valley, as it was occasionally referred to as Yn Dhow Vargad (Margaret's Ox), suggesting a possible association with Margad y Stomachey from the Berree Dhone song.

Separately to this, strange sounds can sometimes be heard near the Grianane, like voices or music. Some link this to a hallowed well close to the nearby stream but nothing further is recorded to offer an explanation. Dogs and horses do not like the place and will avoid it however they can.

WWG-MS1 296 | WWG-MS3 386

Raby

Private | On the private land of Baljean Farm, up the Laxey Valley.

The spiders' shawl

The woman of Raby was deserted by her maid just when there was a great deal of important spinning to be done. In despair, she went to the river to ask for help, of either the river or the spiders directly. They took pity on her and the spiders gathered together and completed the spinning with ease. But, more than this, they also spun for her from their own thread a shawl of miraculous beauty and delicacy. This shawl was kept in the family for generations but it has now sadly been lost.

A variation of this tale has the woman as a flax weaver who was regularly helped in her work by the fairies, to whom she called by the river.

PIOMNHAS 4.3.331 | WWG-MS1 291–294

Kewley of the Horns

When Nicholas Kelly lived here, a woman known as Darrady Dorrady Kewley swore away his life. When Kelly brought her to court, she denied the claim and proclaimed that if she was telling a lie then may horns grow on her head. When horns did indeed begin to grow on her head, she was forced to wear a covering over her brows to hide them and her family then became known as Kewley ny Kerka (Kewley of the Horns).

MNHL MD522

Glen Roy & The South

Slieau Lhost

Public ram | Steep, rough and uneven ground | SC 3932 8409 | 54.227271, -4.466361 | Slieau Lhost is a hill standing over the Mountain Road on the Douglas side of Windy Corner.

At Oie Voaldyn (30 April), Midsummer and Hop tu Naa, people used to light a fire on the summit of Slieau Lhost and dance around it, summoning in the change of seasons and warding off the evil which is most potent at those times of the year.

Also at Oie Voaldyn, a man might see a vision of his future wife here. He must take a newly sharpened sickle and cut certain herbs with it in silence as he goes up, as well as gathering some gorse-bons and rushes. At the top of the hill a large sod should be cut and the man should stand in the bare earth that is revealed. He should then repeat a charm whilst building a fire with the gorse and rushes under his own feet. As soon as it is alight, he should step out and throw the herbs in the flames, after which he will see his future wife appear in the smoke and flames. When the fire dies out, the sod should be replaced.

Spectral fires have also sometimes been seen at the summit here by people below. No remains or marks of burning could be found when the ground was later examined by daylight.

At sunrise on the morning of Laa Boaldyn on 1 May (in some accounts it is Easter morning) the figure of a tall youth can be seen moving across the summit of the hill from east to west by those standing at the foot of the hill.

It used to be a Manx custom that on the morning of a wedding, young men would climb the hill and blow cow-horns as long as their breath held out. Although a part of this was to celebrate the occasion, the horns were also blown to ward off fairies on that important day.

If you are in a dispute with someone, it is said that you can get the better of them if you run around the cairn at the top of the hill three times.

A particular moss also grows here which is useful in love charms.

WWG-MS2 110–112 | WWG-MS2 130

The phynnodderee at Ballamilgyn

Private | Ballamilgyn is a private farm north from the Baldhoon Road, not far from Laxey.

The phynnodderee used to help on the farm here at Ballamilgyn. If his work here was like elsewhere, it would have been of great swiftness and strength but without payment. It is likely that the phynnodderee moved on from here after he took offence at the farmer's gift of clothes.

MNHL MD522 | WWG-MS1 283 | YLM 3.8.380

The man who abused the dooinney oie

Public | Public road without a pavement | SC 4181 8447 | 54.231444, -4.428388 | Baldhoon is a community of houses along the Baldhoon Road about half a mile beyond the edge of Laxey. The Baldhoon Road leaves the main road through Laxey heading steeply uphill at the crossroads with Church Hill Road by the petrol station.

A man from Baldhoon was drunk and foolish enough one night to shout at the dooinney oie when he heard him warning of oncoming bad weather by blowing his horn on the top of Lhergy Grawe. The man began by shouting, 'Save thy wind and go thy ways home!' but the dooinney oie did not react until the man went on and the dooinney oie leapt up and chased after him. The man ran for his life, crossing the stream at the stepping stones, while the dooinney oie leapt over the river in one bound. The man rushed to the home of a religious man he knew not far away and reached the house just in time to slam the door shut before the dooinney oie. The furious shouts of the dooinney oie then shook the thatch of the house as if there was a storm of hail stones but the Baldhoon man remained safe inside. The man was only able to return home safely after morning had arrived, and he was never so foolish as to shout at the dooinney oie again.

SM-MFT 197–202

The fairies' wine well

Public | Rough and uneven ground close to the road | SC 4108 8386 | 54.225717, -4.439359 | Chibbyr Feeyney is the remarkable stone-built roadside well close to Glen Roy, on the south-west side of Glen Roy Road, between the driveway to Glen Roy Farm and Brundal House.

As with other wells of the same name, Chibbyr Feeyney (Wine Well) is said to be where the fairies collect their water. This water then becomes wine and is served at their fairy feasts. Although the water is fine for human consumption, if a person drinks the wine, it will put them in the power of the fairies forever.

A recess in the wall on the way down the steps to the water was perhaps used for offerings of some sort.

WWG-MS1 32 | WWG-MS1 34 | WWG-MS3 199

The phynnodderee of Ballalheaney

Private land – view only | Visible from the public road without a pavement | SC 4110 8383 | 54.225436, -4.438971 | Ballalheaney is an abandoned farm close to Glen Roy at the side of Glen Roy Road. It is at a sharp corner of the road between Brundal House and the driveway to Glen Roy Farm.

The phynnodderee used to help on the farm here at Ballalheaney. If his work here was like elsewhere, it would have been of great swiftness and strength but without payment. It is likely that the phynnodderee moved on from here after he took offence at the farmer's gift of clothes.

MNHL MD522 | YLM 3.8.380

The two ghosts of the cottage by Glen Roy ford

Public | Public road without a pavement | SC 4116 8360 | 54.223449, -4.437871 | Cronk y Thona is the hill of Glen Roy Road from the bridge over the river of Glen Roy itself, up to Ballacollister Road on the south-east side.

A man and his son were away sailing on a coal schooner between Whitehaven and Liverpool when the man's father passed the lane to their cottage here by the river late one night. He heard the click of the gate opening and closing and saw two men following him up Cronk y Thona. The man grew nervous and hurried up the hill, but still the two figures swiftly overtook him. As they passed him, quickly and silently, the older man saw that their faces were as black as coal. It was later discovered that it had been on that night that the two sailing men had died at sea.

YLM 3.10.482–483

Chibbyr Pherick

Private | Chibbyr Pherick is a well in an overgrown glen below the Ballacollister Road, about half a mile from the Axnfell Plantation.

This holy well was formed when St Patrick visited the Isle of Man and his horse stumbled here and dislodged a turf with its hoof. Water sprung from the ground and so St Patrick took the first drink from the newly formed well. It has been known as Chibbyr Pherick (Patrick's Well) ever since.

If you drink here, you must leave an offering of some kind or else you will become lost as you go on with your journey. Another version of this has it that you will go astray or experience some bad luck if you pass the well without saying, 'Perick, bannee mee!' ('Patrick, bless me!').

In the 1880s Chibbyr Pherick was held as one of only five wells from all over the Isle of Man to be identified as a particularly important curative well by 'the older generation of Manx people, especially for eye problems. However, it fell into neglect and obscurity when the fair ceased to be held here on old Laa Boaldyn (12 May).

AWM-MN 144 | EK-CC 93 | JT-HSA 2.60 | JT-HSA 2.121 | MD-EVAF 14 | MQ 1.9.766–767 | N-IOME-11061910 | PIOMNHAS 2.4.529 | PMCK-MAS 4.40 | WH-MM1 146 | WWG-MS1 52

Nikkesen's Pool

Private | Nikkesen's Pool is in the Awin Ruy, near to its junction with the Glen Roy River, on private land below Ballalheaney.

Nikkesen's Pool was well known for being a dangerous place, even before the beautiful girl from Ballaquine was lost there. She was out looking for the calves, calling out, 'Kebeg! Kebeg! Kebeg!' to them when a great mist came down and enveloped the valley. A sweet voice then called out to her, 'Kebeg's here! Kebeg's here!' The girl replied, 'I'm comin'! I'm comin'!' and went towards the sound, but she was never seen or heard of again.

She was not the only victim of Nikkesen (sometimes alternatively given as Nyker, Nikki, or Nykrsán), the legendary water-goblin who lives within this dark pool. Sometimes he would lure girls to the pool by taking the form of a handsome young man, after which they were never seen again. Other versions report his sometimes taking the form of a horse or pony for the same end.

On moonlit nights Nikkesen leads his victims onto the meadow by the pool here, trooping them around and then dancing in a circle. There are reports that people would sometimes come to watch this macabre spectacle from the sloping land around.

Evidence of the pool's uncanniness can also be seen in that it remains at the same level even when the river is in flood.

AWM-MN 208 | JJK-PN 266 | PIOMNHAS 4.3.328 | SM-MFT 87–88 | WWG-MS1 284–288 | YLM 3.9.445

The phynnodderee's favourite place on the Glen Roy River

Private | In the Glen Roy River below the abandoned Ballalheaney Farmhouse. Although the location of the site is not known for sure, the name 'Spreigh Vedn' suggests a waterfall, which is to be found here below a field of the same name.

A place known as Spreigh Vedn on the Glen Roy river used to be a favourite place of the phynnodderee. No specific stories are known of him here, but perhaps it was to here that people came when seeking his help for their farms.

Today this pool is known locally as the Drowning Pool, owing to a suicide which took place here in the first half of the twentieth century.

WWG-MS1 283

A resting place for the dead

Private | The Crosh is a piece of masonry on private land near to Poolvilla.

It used to be the custom that funeral processions would only ever go along certain traditional paths towards the parish church. Along these routes would be particularly reverential spots where the body could be set down and the bearers could take a rest. These large stones were one of these sites for the resting of corpses on the way to Lonan Old Church. The name, the Crosh, suggests that perhaps a cross used to stand here.

FLS KM/C | FLS STW/D | WWG-MS1 282

Kirk Lonan graveyard

Open during daylight hours | Uneven ground, close to a public road | SC 4297 8299 | 54.218490, -4.409840 | Kirk Lonan is on Church Road, which turns up the hill from the main Laxey to Douglas road close to the southern edge of Laxey.

The corpse lights of two miners

One night the parson of Kirk Lonan saw candlelight hovering in the churchyard, then another light began to hover in another part of the churchyard, and then they both went out. Shortly after this two miners were killed in an accident and they were buried in graves exactly where those lights had been.

N-IOME-01101898

Soil from the newest graves

In the 1890s the vicar here noted that soil was being taken from the newest graves in the graveyard. It was being used in a charm of some sort, but the vicar was not able to discover how or for what it was used.

MNHL MD522 | YLM 3.8.379

The fairies as souls of the dead

Private land – view only | Visible beside the main road, at a dangerous bend in the road without a pavement | SC 4318 8243 | 54.213557, -4.406304 | The former Lonan Schoolhouse is the final seaward house before the main Laxey to Baldrine road crosses the tram tracks.

In the 1880s this schoolhouse was plagued by fairies in the night-time. No matter how securely the master, Tommy the Clerk, locked or bolted the doors, the fairies would always get in. However, when the tram line was built in 1894, it passed directly behind the schoolhouse and unearthed a number of stone coffins. After these were removed by the authorities, the schoolhouse was never again visited by the fairies.

MQ 1.7.617 | WWG-MS3 367–368 | YLM 2.115

The Cloven Stones

Private land – view only | Visible from the quiet road without a pavement | SC 4292 8142 | 54.204343, -4.409823 | The Cloven Stones are a group of large standing stones occupying the front garden of a private house on Lower Packhorse Lane, about twenty metres down from the main road through Baldrine.

The Cloven Stones mark the grave of a Welsh Prince who was invading the Island but was slain on his first engagement with the Manx. He was buried here where he fell.

Before the 1800s the owner of the land here employed some workers to take down the stones. But upon arriving at the site the man turned around and saw his home on fire. He rushed back to the house but found everything as normal. However, upon looking back to the stones, it now appeared that they were on fire. He saw this as a warning to him and so he called away the workers from their task. This is why the stones remain with us today. One commentator saw this illusion as originating with the fairies, who were seeking to protect a site important to them.

It has been said that the stones clap when it is thundering or when the church bells ring.

At the start of the nineteenth century, it was reported that 'several supernatural tales' were connected to the Cloven Stones. However, unfortunately no other such tales are known to have been recorded.

GW-AIOM 175 | HIJ-JG 100 | HAB-HIOM 237 | JGC-HPECL 235–236 | JT-HSA 1.267 | KR-MNQ 212 | PIOMNHAS 4.3.326 | SH-HSDV 93 | WWG-MS1 296

The Suicide Graves

Public | Beside the quiet road without a pavement | SC 4203 8086 | 54.1990588, -4.4231642 | The tops of two stones protruding out of the ground on the eastern side of the Baroose Road just before Pack Horse Lane turns off to Harrison Farm.

These two stones are all that remain visible of the graves of two suicides. These people lived in a house which used to stand in the field to the north, but after their suicide they were not welcome in the parish churchyard and so were buried here instead. Nothing further is known of the deaths or why it was specifically here that they were laid to rest.

WWG-MS1 280

Malew

Malew is one of the Island's richest parishes for folklore. Particular focal points are South Barrule and Castle Rushen, both of which have a surprisingly varied wealth of tales, including ghosts, giants, King Orry, Manannan, pre-Christian rites, miraculous wells, a buggane and the fairies. Other remarkable locations include Ballahick, one of the Island's best-known sites for the lhiannan-shee; St Michael's Isle, with its chilling tale of Father Kelly's ghost; the Folly, which has a history of very strange occurrences; and Kirk Malew, where a mistake in funeral customs led to a dead woman having to be secretly exhumed one night in 1863.

1. Castle Rushen
2. Castletown Square
3. The charmer and the fairy pig
4. The dog and the woman with the enormous teeth
5. The Green Lady of Scarlett
6. The spirit guardian's light
7. Hango Hill
8. Father Kelly and the ghost of St Michael's Chapel
9. A sense of the dead
10. The Folly
11. Ballahick
12. The Broogh
13. The small man of Cashtal Rhunt
14. The haunted ship burial
15. Kirk Malew
16. The miraculous cross of the Cross Four Ways
17. Fairy Bridge
18. Grenaby
19. The Green Lady of Cronkbreck
- The Fairy Hill, the rum and a dead man [private land]
- Godred Crovan's Stone [private land]
20. The Death Coach of Solomon's Corner
21. Men being stoned as they plough up a keeill
- The moddey doo of Ballagilbert [private land]
- The shiny ghost [private land]
22. The Round Table
23. The giant's rock on South Barrule
24. South Barrule

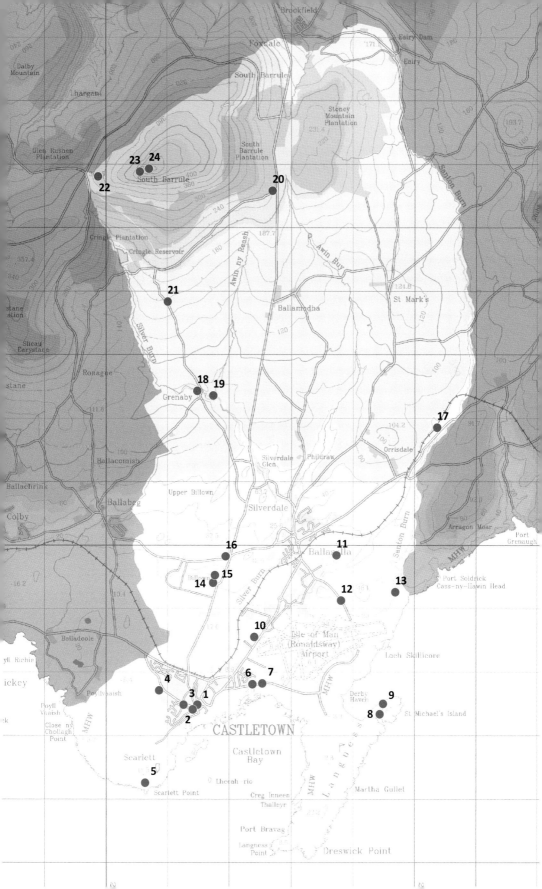

South of the Cross Four Roads

Castle Rushen

Open Easter to October. There is an admission charge to enter the site | Some of the castle has level access, but the inside includes steep narrow steps | SC 2652 6746 | 54.073763, -4.652945 | Castle Rushen is in the centre of Castletown. The main gate opens towards the Cain pedestrian bridge over the harbour. Chibbyr Hidey is in the middle of the inner courtyard.

Ghosts

A ghostly woman is well known in Castle Rushen. She has been seen all over the castle, including in rooms where there were no means of entering. Her presence has been known since at least the 1710s, when she was held to be the spirit of a woman executed for murdering her child.

One remarkable account from this time was of a man who saw her in the wind and rain late one night by the gate outside the castle. He approached to check on her welfare, but she moved through the closed gates and disappeared.

The Countess of Derby was also said to haunt the castle. Her spirit used to walk along the castle walls at night, as was seen by a considerable number of people over many years. This is likely to be related to the white apparition which used to be seen on the ramparts during the time when soldiers were still stationed in the castle.

An alternative ghostly figure wore 'medieval' clothes, and is to be seen in the corridors of the castle but comes out to the walls at the stroke of midnight, where she was seen nightly by the inmates of the prison here.

AWM-FIOM 71 | BN-MS3 23 | EK-CC 364 | GW-DIM 36–37 | HAB-HIOM 364 | FLS S/14-A | MT 32 | JT-HSA 1.285 | JT-HSA 1.304–305

The giant's brass shoes

When digging an extension to the Earl of Derby's wine vaults, about fifteen metres underground, the workers discovered a massive pair of brass shoes. These shoes were enormous and could only have belonged to a giant.

GW-DIM 71–73

The sleeping giant

Although now closed up, the caverns under the castle used to be renowned for their magnificence. People would go down to admire them, but they did not return. In around 1670 an unusually brave man descended into the caverns, leaving a thread behind him so that he could find his way back. He went down for over a mile into the dark depths until he came upon a grand house illuminated by many candles. He knocked on the door and a servant answered, who asked what he wanted. The explorer replied that he wished to go as far as he could, so the servant showed him through the house and out the back door, where the way led on.

The man walked a great distance further and came upon another house, grander and better lit than the last. He was about to knock at the door but he thought to first look through the window. He saw an enormous giant, at least 14 feet high and ten or eleven feet around the body. He was asleep in a room of black marble, lying on a table with his head on a book and with a great sword by his side. The explorer grew frightened at the sight and returned to the first house, where the servant let him through again.

As the servant was showing him back through the house, he told the explorer that he would not have returned if he had awoken the giant, though he could not reveal who the giant was or what that other place was. After that the man retraced his steps up to the surface of the earth, the entrance was closed and no one has dared to go back ever since.

AWM-FIOM 63–64 | HAB-HIOM 363–364 | GW-DIM 5-6 | JT-HSA 1.303–304

The blind giant

A group of young men armed with staves and torches decided to go down to investigate the tunnels under the castle. After a short while they came across a very large old blind man sat on a rock 'as if fixed there.' Upon hearing the men approach, the giant spoke to them, asking about the state of the Island. After a while in conversation the giant put out his hand to shake one of the men's hands. Thinking quickly, a man offered the plough-share which he had with him. The giant squeezed the iron together and was pleased with the man's apparent strength. 'There are yet men in the Isle of Man,' he observed.

HIJ-JG 136 | MD-DT 197–198 | WH-MM1 172

The fairies overthrown from Castle Rushen

Castle Rushen was first the stronghold of the fairies. They ruled over the whole Island and held off attack from outsiders by a magic fire which caused the Island to be forever hidden in mist. However, in about 100BC the fire went out one day and the Island was revealed to human beings, who soon attacked and gained victory over the fairies to win Castle Rushen from them. However, these people then lost the castle to giants, but they were later able to defeat them and gain the castle permanently at last.

AWM-FIOM 37-38 | GW-DIM 7 | WWG-MS1 329–330

The wishing well

The well inside the inner courtyard is called Chibbyr Hidey. It has the power to grant wishes if you walk around it seven times, wish hard as you go, and then drop a coin in.

WWG-MS3 235–236

Castletown Square

Public | Level pedestrianised public space close to parking | SC 2649 6741 | 54.073336, -4.653376 | Castletown's main square is in the centre of the town, outside the walls of Castle Rushen.

The Battle of Summer and Winter

On Laa Boaldyn (1 May), the first day of the summer half of the year, people from all over the Isle of Man used to come here to watch a battle between two groups of people dressed as Summer and as Winter. The Winter group was eventually driven out of the town as far as Scarlett, at which point the fight was over. There was then a great feast in the square, with much food, drink and dancing. As many fiddles as possible were employed for the music and people enjoyed 'games of every kind' that were on offer here.

JC-MR 52–55

The end of the witch of Slieau Whallian

A witch caught trying to kill someone with a charm was rolled in a spiked barrel down Slieau Whallian but survived, and so was brought here to Castletown. Every parish on the Island then sent three horse-loads of heather for the fire onto which she was put. When the flames came to consume her, her heart burst so violently that it caused a report so loud that it was as if it came from a cannon.

N-IOME-03091898

The charmer and the fairy pig

Public | Level pedestrianised public space close to parking | SC 2635 6748 | 54.073883, -4.655544 | Arbory Street runs from the main square in Castletown north-west to the first road, The Crofts, beyond which it becomes Arbory Road and goes on towards Castle Rushen High School and the Buchan School.

A boy named Ned Quayle lived near the Sloc and late one day he went out looking for his mother when she had not returned home from the hills. On the hill he came across a little white pig and he began to chase it, thinking that it must belong to a neighbour. The boy then noticed that the pig's tail was feathery and spread out like a fan, its ears were long and its eyes burned like fire. The boy was almost led over the brogh but stopped just in time, turned and ran home frightened, with the pig chasing him all the way.

When the boy had made it home safe, his grandmother identified the animal as a fairy pig. Ned developed a fever and went to bed but when his mother came into his room, he was shocked to see that she had the same eyes as the pig. At the sight of this a sharp pain went through his right leg which was so intense the leg could not be touched. This incredible pain persisted for days and even stopped him eating, so Ned's father took him in a cart to a charmer who lived in Arbory Street.

The charmer sent everyone but the boy out of the room, laid Ned on the floor and locked the door. The man got down a large book, opened it up and pointed with his left hand to a picture of a plant. With his right hand he made the sign of the cross over Ned's leg and said:

'Ta mee skeaylley yn guin shoh ayns ennym yn Ayr, as y Vac, as y Spyrryd Noo, Ned Quayle. My she guin, ayns ennym y Chiarn, ta mee skealley eh ass yn eill, ass ny fehyn, as ass ny craueyn.'
('I dispel this fairy shot in the name of the Father, and of the Son, and of the Holy Ghost, Ned Quayle. If it is a fairy shot, in the name of the Lord, I dispel it out of the flesh, out of the sinews, and out of the bones').

The pain immediately left the boy and never returned, but a mark remained on his leg where he had felt the stab for the rest of his life.

SM-MFT 104–107

The dog and the woman with the enormous teeth

Public | Public road with pavement | SC 2596 6771 | 54.075773, -4.661698 | Arbory Road by the old windmill. Sometimes referred to as 'the Witches' Mill,' the former mill is today a distinctive privately owned tower towards the eastern edge of Castletown, next to Castle Rushen High School.

When a man set off for Castletown one moonlit Saturday night, he found a very large dog waiting for him at his front door. The dog walked with him all the way until he reached the old windmill, where it disappeared. When the man returned later, there was a very tall woman stood here by the windmill at the same spot as where the dog had disappeared. She joined him in the road and began to walk beside him. The man was too afraid to look at her or say a word but when they reached Balladoole Lodge she left his side and the man took courage and turned to look at her. She turned and grinned at him, showing the largest teeth he had ever seen on a person or animal.

KR-MNQ 189

The Green Lady of Scarlett

Public | Rough and uneven ground, tidal | SC 2572 6625 | 54.062640, -4.664515 | An obvious heart-shaped pool on the rocks at Scarlett. The pool is roughly ten metres long and is clearly visible from the Raad ny Foillan outside of high tide. It is 200 metres along the path from the Scarlett Nature Discovery Centre, close to the remarkable building in the field above.

A ghostly Green Lady used to be seen by this heart-shaped pool at Scarlett. Reports from children who sometimes saw her here before World War II describe her as not sinister and without a sense of foreboding; she was felt to be a protective presence for the children playing here.

CV-OH-BS

The spirit guardian's light

Public | Public road with footpath | SC 2746 6781 | 54.077186, -4.638768 | The Promenade is to the north-east of Castletown, bordering the shore towards Hango Hill and Langness.

In the 1920s a woman enjoyed the protection of some form of spirit. As well as warning her away from danger on at least one occasion, the spirit would sometimes light her way when walking at night. This was witnessed by her nephew and another boy as she walked along the Promenade one evening in 1928. In the morning the nephew asked her why she had had been carrying an electric light but he was surprised to hear that she had been carrying nothing at all. The woman believed that this protective spirit caring for her was the spirit of her deceased mother.

WWG-MS2 90–91

Hango Hill

Open access | Rough and uneven, beside road with pavement | SC 2760 6780 | 54.077215, -4.636596 | Hango Hill is the distinctive grassy rise with ruins on the top. It is by the shore above Castletown, on the road towards Derbyhaven, by King William's College.

Illiam Dhone's blood

It used to be considered unlucky to let blood fall on the ground, especially when it was from an important person. So when Illiam Dhone was executed here in 1663, blankets were laid on the ground so that not a drop of his blood would touch the earth. In fact, some accounts hold that no blood came from his wounds, even as the bullet hit his heart.

AWM-FIOM 145 | HIJ-JG 142

The ghostly women

A man was once walking from Castletown to Derbyhaven a little after one o'clock in the morning. When he got as far as King William's College he saw a woman coming towards him in an old-fashioned cloak with the hood pulled up over her head. He crossed the road to let her pass, but she crossed to his side. He crossed back but she followed him again. Now close, he held his hand up to keep her away and cried out, 'In the name of the Almighty, what is it?' At this the woman slipped past him and disappeared. It is believed that this was the spirit of a person who was murdered here.

KR-MNQ 141

The Mollagh Vooar

Hango Hill and sometimes the shore below is haunted by a moddey doo known as the Mollagh Vooar. It is an enormous black dog the size of a calf but it does not have a head. It is not often seen by humans, but dogs see or sense it more frequently. They take extreme fright at this moddey doo, often without their owners experiencing anything to account for their dog's terror.

This ghostly presence has been linked to the historical appearance of a black dog in Castletown sometime before the 1850s. One day a black dog began screaming and howling around Castletown and so a group of men began to chase it out of town. But they did not go beyond Hango Hill as it was here they took fright that the dog was other than natural and the gang of people ran back to town as fast as they could.

MT 31 | WWG-MS1 323–324 | YLM 1.9.290

Father Kelly and the ghost of St Michael's Chapel

Open access | Rough and uneven ground | SC 2952 6734 | 54.073689, -4.607144 | St Michael's Chapel is the ruined church on St Michael's Isle (also known as Fort Island). The island is connected by a causeway to the northern end of Langness.

A priest named Father Kelly had a dream in which St Michael appeared and showed him to a church on the island off Langness. Father Kelly looked in through the window and saw himself kneeling in prayer amidst rich and beautiful decorations. The priest took the dream as a vision of the future and so set about building the chapel here. However, when the building was complete, he found that he did not have the wealth to buy the riches in his dream.

One evening he was in the chapel praying to St Michael for an answer to his problem when he heard voices outside. Father Kelly listened closely and heard them digging and then heaving something heavy into the ground before covering it over and going away. A storm arose soon after and a ship was wrecked. Only one man survived long enough to reach shore and with his dying words he confessed to Father Kelly that he and the others had buried stolen treasure outside the chapel. After the man died, Father Kelly dug up the chest and was delighted to be able to deck the church with its sumptuous treasures. However, he was uneasy with how he had come by these treasures and so he would often stand out on the rocks near here looking out to sea pondering whether it was right to have claimed these treasures.

One day the sister ship to the one which had been wrecked sailed in and the crew recognised the treasure in the church. Father Kelly then went missing and when the people of Derbyhaven came to look for him here, they found him hanging from the rafters over the altar and all the treasure gone. The chapel was not used after that and it soon fell into ruin. It is said that Father Kelly can still sometimes be seen on calm moonlit nights standing on the rocks looking out to sea.

Another version of the story has Father Kelly strangled at the altar, and his ghost is not to be seen, but it can be heard moaning inside the chapel with 'a noise like the jingling of money.' This can be heard at night if you strike the wall of the chapel. Another version of the tale tells us that this moaning is to be heard at midnight in the chapel.

Presumably it was Father Kelly's ghost that was seen in the 1860s after a large ship struck St Michael's Isle, causing the death of forty of its crew. A group of Manxmen were then employed to hack up the wreck to remove it and the task took them into the night. At midnight the workers saw a white thing like a person stood moaning in the door of the chapel. The men immediately refused to do any more work there that night.

A variation of this story tells of some pirates coming to hear of the treasure hidden at the chapel. In the process of taking it, the pirates heartlessly murdered the priest, but not before he had cursed them. This curse came into almost immediate effect as a hurricane arose as the pirates were setting sail and their ship was driven back onto the rocks, causing all lives to be lost. Ever since then a jingling of money and some dying moans can be heard in the chapel at midnight.

Perhaps also connected to this is the ghost of a sailor who can be seen walking up from the shore and over the land at about sunset.

EF-MSR 160–162 | MT 32-33 | WH-MM 239–247 | WWG-MS1 321–322 | YLM 3.4.159

A sense of the dead

Open access | Rough and uneven ground | SC 2957 6749 | 54.075062, -4.606453 | The shore of St Michael's Isle facing Derbyhaven and Ronaldsway Airport, connected by a causeway to the northern end of Langness.

In the times of the Norse Kings of Man and the Isles, the invading army of John Dugaldson were killed and drowned by the forces of the defending Manx here in 1250. This is thought to be the reason why there is a persisting 'murky atmosphere' felt here to this day.

WWG-MS1 321–322

The Folly

Public | Pavement beside main road | SC 2749 6854 | 54.083776, -4.638815 | The main road close to Ronaldsway Airport, outside the Manx Aviation and Military Museum. The Folly itself was a tower that used to stand within the site of the car park here.

The headless black calf

This area has a long-standing reputation of being haunted. One of the many strange things that have been seen and experienced here was a headless black calf with a chain rattling behind it which a girl was terrified to see by the Folly.

WWG-MS2 215

The midday presence

If you walk down the main road here at midday, you will have the uncanny sensation that someone is walking beside you. This sometimes inspires panic in those who experience it.

MT 30 | WWG-MS1 365

The White Lady of the Folly

A ghostly White Lady can be seen moving silken footed at twilight or in the early evening by where the Folly used to stand.

WWG-MS2 245

The man taken at the Folly

Sometime around the 1870s a preacher named Sainsbury and a friend were walking home by here when they heard music from the barn that stood nearby. As well as the music being beautiful, it was also accompanied by 'a burst of aethereal song, surpassing all human power.' The preacher recognised this as of the fairies and that nothing good would come of investigating it, but his headstrong friend went off into the barn to listen. The preacher walked on, but when his friend did not emerge, he went back and shouted for him. However, the man was not to be found anywhere and so the preacher then hurried on to Ballasalla to gather more people for a search. When they returned to the barn, there was no music at all, and the man was never seen again.

MT 30–31 | WWG-MS1 365

The tall man

Two people were walking from Ballasalla to Castletown one winter's evening when one of them noticed an incredibly tall man walking close beside them. This man was so tall that his head was higher than the trees which stood here at that time. Neither of the pair said anything of their new companion but when they reached the wall that was 15 to 20 feet high, which stood around the orchard here at that time, the tall man slipped over the wall without difficulty and disappeared. The man who had observed this was then shocked to hear from his companion that she had not seen the tall man at all.

YLM 3.4.157

Ballahick

Private land – view only | Visible from rough and uneven public footpath through a working farm | SC 2882 6983 | 54.095820, -4.619192 | Ballahick is a private farm on the public footpath which runs between the main road leaving Ballasalla north-east towards Douglas, and the small road running along the north-east side of Ronaldsway airport, accessed through Balthane Industrial Estate.

The White Lady of Ballahick

A man was walking home from Derbyhaven when he heard singing and dancing inside a barn here at Ballahick. He went to investigate and when he found a group of women dancing inside, he joined in. He danced with them a while until the sweat was coming off him, so he took a woman's apron and wiped his brow. From this moment on, the White Lady he was dancing with never left him alone. It even got to the point that she would be under the table as he ate. She was with him like this until the day he died.

An alternative account has the man escape after the woman repeatedly tried to have him wipe his sweat with her apron, to which he cried out, 'Lord, have mercy upon me!' At this, the people and the food and drink all disappeared in an instant, leaving him entirely alone but safe.

GB-LWC 154 | MJ 6.363

The lhiannan-shee of Ballahick

A young man was coming home late at night and saw a light on at Ballahick. He had thought that the farm was unoccupied and so he went to see for himself. At the gate he met two women who invited him in and he found two or three pairs of people dancing inside. He started to dance with one of the women and by the end of the evening he had kissed her. But when the dancing stopped and all the others departed, she followed him home, and everywhere else afterwards, haunting him till the end of his days. It was believed that it was the kiss which gave this lhiannan-shee the power to follow him, even over the sea.

An alternative version of this tale has the man named Mickleby, who met the two women by a stream before going to the dance, where he was doomed by wiping his sweat on a part of one of the women's dress. Forever after that the woman would appear standing at his bedside when he lay down to sleep at night. The only way he could be rid of her was to throw over her and himself a linen sheet which had never been bleached.

EW-FFCC 124–125 | KR-MNQ 135

The Broogh

Private land – view only | Visible from a public road | SC 2883 6910 | 54.089296, -4.618617 | The Broogh is the small hill to the north-west of Ronaldsway Airport. It can be approached through the Balthane Industrial Estate. Upon emerging into fields, the Broogh can be seen to your left, with a large radar dish on the top.

Among the flat land of Ronaldsway this conspicuous mound has a reputation for being uncanny. This is especially felt to be the case at night. This has suggested to some that the hill is the location of an ancient burial site.

WWG-MS1 321

The small man of Cashtal Rhunt

PROW | Rough and uneven ground, at cliff-edge | SC 2977 6925 | 54.090880, -4.604373 | Cashtal Rhunt is a coastal earthwork standing over Cass ny Hawin at the foot of the Santon Burn, north-west of Ronaldsway Airport.

The remains of this Iron Age promontory fort, sometimes known as Cashtal Rhunt (Round Castle), is haunted by 'the diminutive figure of a man.' Nothing further of this figure is known.

WWG-MS1 526

The haunted ship burial

Private land – view only | Visible from a public parking space with a pavement | SC 2682 6939 | 54.091151, -4.649528 | Skibrick Hill has a standing white boulder at the top, obvious to the west beyond Kirk Malew churchyard.

An early recorded form of this hill's name is 'Skiprig,' which means 'Ship Hill.' This perhaps links the site to a ship burial, and so the site is taken to be the burial site of a person of importance, with the white boulder standing as their grave marker. It is believed that assemblies or sacrifices would once have been periodically held here, and that the place has been haunted.

WWG-MS1 363–364

Kirk Malew

Open during daylight hours | Some uneven ground | SC 2683 6944 | 54.091687, -4.649329 | Kirk Malew is the parish church, one mile north of Castletown along the Crossag Road towards the Cross Four Ways and Ballamodha.

The Fairy Cup of Kirk Malew

A man was out at night when he heard music so beautiful that he could not resist following. He was led for miles until he came to an open common where a large group of fairies were sat at a feast. A silver cup was passed round for him to drink from but before he did so one of the fairies, whose features seemed familiar to him, quietly warned him not to drink it if he wanted ever to return to his family. So the man found a way to pour the drink out onto the ground without being seen and so avoided having to drink it. Soon after, the music stopped and with it all the fairies disappeared. The man was then left alone in a field far from home, but still clutching the silver cup. This he brought here to Kirk Malew so that he could be safe from the fairy item. It was used here for the communion wine for many years afterwards.

AWM-FIOM 41–42 | GW-DIM 28 | HIJ-JG 161–162

Swearing on a person's grave

Compurgation was a church practice officially outlawed in 1609, though it continued for decades afterwards. In order to prove your word in a case relating to a dead person, you had to go to the person's grave and lay down on your back upon it. An open bible was then put on your chest and around you knelt a number of 'compurgators' (witnesses) who watched as you swore the truth of your claim. One of the cases known to have taken place after the practice was outlawed was in 1616 at the grave of a man named Christopher Younge here in Malew. Remarkably, it was the Deemster, Thomas Samsburie, and his wife, Jaine Samsburie, who carried out the compurgation to prove that Younge's will was incorrect in claiming that Samsburie was in debt to him.

N-IOME-08101898

Digging up the dead to untie knots

In 1863 a woman named Morrison died and was buried here in the churchyard. However, when she was laid in her coffin, knots were mistakenly left in the cap and shroud which she was wearing. It was because of this that her spirit could not rest and so came back to haunt her home. Members of the family appealed to the vicar to allow them to dig her up to fix the knots, but he dismissed them as foolish and superstitious. So, in desperation, at six o'clock on Easter morning, 5 April 1863, two of the woman's brothers-in-law went to the graveyard, dug her up and untied the knots in the clothes themselves. The men were caught and brought to trial, but they were let off with only costs and a severe censure.

N-MH-20051863

Forced to renounce the devil

The wife of an MHK, Jane Caesar, of Ballahick, was accused of keeping her ailing husband alive for years through diabolic practices, stealing the productivity of neighbouring lands to boost her own, and taking clippings from a bullock's hooves before selling it, apparently for 'a sinister purpose.' In 1659 she was brought to trial for witchcraft and although she was found not guilty, she was ordered by the Governor to publicly denounce the devil in front of the congregation here at Kirk Malew. After initially refusing, Jane Caesar eventually proclaimed, 'I defy the divil and all his works,' but then went on to issue a curse on her accusers, 'May those who brought me to this scandal never see their eldest children in the estate my youngest are in!'

DC-MI 16–17 | PIOMNHAS 5.2.71–72

Burying the wren

The custom of Hunt the Wren on St Stephen's Day (26 December) was to take the dead bird around the local community before burying it in a churchyard. Although the historical record for this is not known, a particular curious historic version of this at Kirk Malew was described in the 1970s. The wren was paraded around Castletown before daybreak and then brought along Malew Street and here to the church. In 'a secluded corner' of the graveyard everyone gathered in solemn silence as a small grave was dug, after which they sang 'O colb ec shee' ('O body at rest') as the bird was interred in the grave. A living wren in a small cage was then hung inside the wren bush, and the Hunt the Wren dance was performed around it. At the conclusion of the dance, the living bird was set free and the wren pole was broken up and burnt on the dead wren's grave.

ML 2.3.35–36

The miraculous cross of the Cross Four Ways

Public | Public road with a limited pavement, close to some parking | SC 2702 6981 | 54.095008, -4.646652 | The Cross Four Ways is the meeting of the roads between Colby and Ballasalla, and Ballamodha and Castletown.

A cross used to stand here at the Cross Four Ways, to which people would bring their sick children. In the writings of Bishop Foster in 1634 we learn that the children would be laid at the cross, presumably in the faith that a miraculous cure would follow.

JJK-PN 614 | WWG-MS2 187–188

North of the Cross Four Roads

The Fairy Bridge

Public | Public road without a pavement | SC 3046 7185 | 54.114484, -4.595261 | The Fairy Bridge is a small bridge marked with white walls on the main road between Douglas and Ballasalla. It is half a mile north-east of the steep stretch of road where the Old Castletown Road is met and under which the railway line passes.

Although this bridge probably only became known as the Fairy Bridge in the mid-twentieth century, usurping the name from Ballalona Bridge nearby, today the bridge here enjoys wide renown as a place favoured by the fairies. In recent decades it has become normal for notes and offerings to be left here for the fairies, frequently appealing to them for their favour in some form. Longer established is the saying of a greeting to the fairies for luck as you pass over the bridge, often in Manx as 'Moghrey mie, Vooinjer Veggey' ('Good morning, fairies'). This has been widely practiced since around the 1950s.

Manx motorbike racers from the south of the Island in the 1960s used to come here to the bridge to have a word on the fairies in order to gain good luck for their upcoming races. They judged the success of this by the fact that the five racers who did this went on to become the only Manx people at that time to gain World Championship points in their racing.

CV-YT-BK1 | Add

Grenaby

Public | Quiet public road | SC 2657 7242 | 54.118335, -4.655111 | Grenaby is the area about Grenaby Bridge over the Silver Burn on Kerrowkeill Road. The bridge is less than 100 metres down the hill from Ballamaddrell Road (coming from Ballabeg).

The haunted road at Grenaby

Many strange and mysterious things have been seen at or experienced here along this road. These include fairies, a witch only one foot high, an enormous cat with great flaming eyes nearly as big as saucers, a cow-like water monster, a tall man without a head, and 'something dark like a big chest or box' that used to move about the road here.

One particular story is from a man who was coming from Castletown at daybreak when he saw a man walking down the hill carrying a coffin. At the bridge here, this man and his burden disappeared.

FLS Q/10-C | KG-TMC 67 | WWG-MS1 355–357

Jimmy Squarefoot

The most famous strange inhabitant of Grenaby was Jimmy Squarefoot, a man with a pig's head, complete with two great boar's tusks. He was originally in service to a giant who lived on Cronk ny Arrey Laa, who would ride him all over the Isle of Man and even over the sea. When this giant eventually went away, Jimmy Squarefoot moved to Grenaby, where he became well known. Sadly, few specific stories of his activities are known, but travellers coming through here would receive a terrible fright when he would rush out at them with his 'gleaming tusks and gnashing fangs.'

WWG-MS1 355-357

The Green Lady of Cronkbreck

Public | Steep, rough and uneven ground, steps | SC 2683 7236 | 54.117819, -4.651074 | Chibbyr Feeayr is an impressive stone-built well on the public footpath south-west of Grenaby. From Grenaby Bridge, go beside the stream, across the field, over the ford, and Chibbyr Feeayr is beside the path on your left.

A ghostly Green Lady was sometimes seen by this well in the 1920s. Nothing is known of this spectre or why it haunts this area.

WWG-MS1 32

The Fairy Hill, the rum and a dead man

Private | The Fairy Hill is a mound on the private land of Orrisdale Farm.

The Fairy Hill has its name as the fairies are known to live here. However, in around the mid-nineteenth century, a farmer wanted the hill levelled for ease of ploughing but he could only induce two people willing to carry out the work when he added to the generous fee the promise of as much rum as they could drink. Foolishly, the keg of rum was delivered as the work was only just beginning and one of the men immediately set to drinking. Soon he had drunk so much that he had to be carried home, but he died either on the way or as he arrived home. The other man took such fright at this that he refused to do any more work on the site. The mound has remained untouched ever since that time.

WWG-MS1 359 | WWG-MS2 221

Godred Crovan's Stone

Private | The site of where the stone once stood is visible from the public footpath roughly 500 metres to the west of the Old Parsonage in St Mark's. From within the final field before the footpath meets Bayr Ruy, the site where the boulder stood is visible over the hedge to the south.

One day in around 1060, Godred Crovan was in his castle on the top of South Barrule when he and his wife argued until she left the castle to be away from him. When she got as far as here near St Mark's, she thought she was out of range of his vengeance and so turned around to shout at him again. However, Godred picked up an enormous boulder and threw it at her from where he stood on the top of Barrule. It hit her here and killed her instantly. Weighing 20 to 30 tons, the boulder lay untouched for centuries. However, in the 1820s it was broken up and part of it was used in the building of the old St Mark's parsonage, where it is supposed to keep residents of the building free of arguments and disagreements.

AWM-FIOM 27 | AWM-MN 223 | HIJ-JG 96 | JGC-HPECL 171–172 | YLM 3.11.503

The Death Coach of Solomon's Corner

Public | Public road without a pavement | SC 2777 7558 | 54.147042, -4.638477| Solomon's Corner is at the meeting of the Ballamodha Road and Corlea Road.

The area around Solomon's Corner has a dark or uncanny reputation. A number of strange sights or experiences have been had here but one of the most remarkable is the Death Coach that can be seen on dark nights running by here, along the Corlea Road or, more commonly, westwards into Windy Common. The coach is all black, with black horses and piloted by a headless driver.

WWG-MS1 343–344

Men being stoned as they plough up a keeill

Private – view only | Visible from public road | SC 25996 73809 | 54.130595, -4.664596 | Kerrowkeeill Chapel is set back on the north-east side of the Kerrowkeill Road, a little over half a mile down from the Corlea Road.

The large slab at the end of the wall outside Kerrowkeeill Chapel is from the keeill which used to stand behind the chapel. In about 1873 a man named Mylchreest became the new owner of the land and he instructed his men to plough up the remains of the keeill. One of the men, Tommy Kelly, was very disturbed by having to do this work and so he was horrified when 'sharp stones seemed to pierce his flesh' as he set about the work. He appealed with Mylchreest and he told them to hold off the job, but by that time the destruction had already been done.

FLS Q/10-C | JRB-AS6 6

The moddey doo of Ballagilbert

Private | A private lane leading from a tholtan westwards to the Silverburn.

A moddey doo lurks on this lane. The beast, unlike most of its kind, is missing a head, though perhaps this only adds to its fearfulness.

WWG-MS1 347

The shiny ghost

Private | On private land by the Silverburn below the Corlea Road.

A man was once walking beside the river here and at a bend in the path he saw a man ahead who was wearing something like 'an oilskin coat, all shiny.' The man tried to catch this other person's attention by shouting, but without success. A little further on, the figure suddenly vanished.

A similar story has the figure in a homespun woollen coat with bright buttons as large as saucers. A separate time he was also seen in a low-crowned, broad-brimmed, rabbit-skin hat. This account identifies the figure as a buggane.

Other people have had similar experiences in the same place resulting in such 'unsurmountable fear' that they would never return to the glen.

EK-CC 369–370 | WWG-MS1 354–355

The Round Table

Public ram | Rough and uneven ground | SC 2472 7574 | 54.147471, -4.685236 | At the western foot of South Barrule close to the Round Table crossroads. A small mound close to the road towards Colby.

The fairy feasts

The Round Table is used by the fairies as a table for feasting and drinking. It was from such a feast here that the legendary Fairy Cup of Kirk Malew was obtained. A man was out at night when he heard music so beautiful that he could not resist following. He was led for miles until he came here to the Round Table, where he found a large group of fairies sat at a feast. A silver cup was passed round for him to drink from but before he did so, one of the fairies, whose features seemed familiar to him, quietly warned him not to if he wanted ever to return to his family. So the man found a way to pour out the liquid on the ground without being seen and so avoided drinking it. Soon after this the music stopped and with it all the fairies disappeared. The man was then left alone in a field far from home, but still clutching the silver cup. This he took to Kirk Malew so that he could be rid of the fairy item. It was used there for communion for many years afterwards.

Another tale of this site as a dining table was that it was square, but the soldiers from up on South Barrule fell out over who was to sit at its head. To ensure peace between them, the corners of the table were cut off to make it round. This story has also been suggested as possibly once having been associated with Finn MacCooill and his residence at the top of South Barrule.

AWM-FIOM 41–42 | GW-DIM 28 | WWG-MS1 337–339

The silent man-spirit

A man named Clague was on his way to Douglas one fine starry night and as he was coming to the bog close to the Round Table, a man appeared and walked silently beside him. This man was wearing a long swallow tailcoat and a very high drum hat, and he gave no reply when the traveller tried to speak to him. Clague was not frightened of this strange man but was more puzzled as they walked in silence until here at the Round Table, where the strange man went off in a different direction and left Clague to go on alone. Later it was discovered that someone had been attacked and almost killed by something like a bull in those bogs, which led Clague to believe that the silent stranger was a 'man-spirit' who had come to put him past the danger.

YLM 3.4.158–159

The giant's rock on South Barrule

Open access | Steep, rough and uneven ground | SC 2563 7587 | 54.148950, -4.671364 | Creg yn Arran is a prominent rock visible against the skyline from the base of South Barrule. Creg yn Arran is just off the footpath, about 50 metres below the remains of the stone wall about the summit of South Barrule.

The giant that used to live on Cronk ny Arrey Laa once quarrelled with his wife and in anger threw rocks at her as she ran away from him. One of these rocks landed here on South Barrule, forming what came to be known as Creg yn Arran.

The name is popularly explained as 'Rock of the Bread,' so named because bread used to be left here for the soldiers stationed at the top of South Barrule. However, it has been suggested that the story of leaving food like this might have originated in an older story of leaving offerings to the fairies here.

WWG-MS1 328–329 | WWG-MS1 339 | WWG-MS1 356

South Barrule

Open access | Steep, rough and uneven ground | SC 2577 7592 | 54.149450, -4.669302 | South Barrule is the highest hill in the south of the Isle of Man, located seven miles directly west of Douglas.

Manannan's home

Mannanan is the great pre-Christian deity who ruled over the Isle of Man with kindness and in peace. His palace was here on the top of South Barrule and it was from here that he worked his magic to cover the Island with mist to hide it from potential invaders. The Manx would bring a bundle of rushes here as their annual rent for living on his Island. This was done on Midsummer's Eve, or St John's Eve (the evening before Tynwald Day). It is a custom which is continued today.

AIOMS 26–29 | AWM-MN-28 146 | EW-FFCC-06 120 | KR-MNQ-72 221 | MD-WCEV 20 | SM-MFT 203–208

The resting place of King Barrule

South Barrule takes its name from a great king buried here at its peak. Rather than building a memorial as we would expect it today, the mourners of King Barrule placed a great pile of stones over the tomb, to which people when visiting the site have contributed to ever since. Kings are also buried at the top of Snaefell and Carraghan.

GW-DIM-12 58 | WWG-MS1-74 232

Laa Luanys

People used to bring an offering to the ancient pre-Christian god, Lug, at the top of South Barrule on Laa Luanys at the start of August. In the nineteenth century 'crowds' of people would come to the top of the hill, to which some in the Church took offence. So, a preacher named William Gick took it upon himself to denounce the people carrying out the practice as 'pagans.' By the twentieth century the custom of ascending the hill had become hidden under the tradition of gathering bilberries on this day.

Another Laa Luanys tradition at the end of the nineteenth century was for people to come to the cairn at the top of the hill at the start of August. They would take rocks from the pile and scratch their initials on them, before then returning the stones carefully to where they first got them. It has been suggested that drinking from the spring at the top of the hill was also a part of this tradition.

JC-MR 80–81 | JR-MFS 2.305–307 | WWG-MS3 271–272

Other residents

Other accounts have different characters living at the top of South Barrule. When Finn McCooil was living on the Island, it was a buggane or a giant who lived here. Stones were thrown from here in a competition of strength by three giants, landing at The Four Roads, Ballacreggan Corner and Cronk Skibbylt in Rushen. Another giant threw a stone from here to kill another giant where he stood in Santon. At the start of the Norse era, it was Godred Crovan who lived here, and threw a stone from the hill at his wife in St Mark's. Later, the terrible Baron Kitter lived in a castle here, but it was set alight through the workings of the witch, Ada, so Kitter's cook called loudly and successfully from here to warn Baron Kitter on the Calf of Man.

AWM-FIOM 27 | EF-MSR 168–171 | HIJ-JG 175 | HIJ-JG 96 | JGC-HPECL 171–172 |
JT-HSA 2.177–178 | KR-MNQ 230 | PIOMNHAS 4.3.269 | SM-MFT 45–49 | YLM 3.4.160

The disappearing well of South Barrule

On the level ground north-west of the peak of South Barrule is Chibbyr yn Rhullic, a well which gives exceptionally good water and which can cure your ailments. However, if you ever happen across it and drink, you will not be able to find it again that day, even if you have only taken a few steps away.

JR-MFS 2.307 | KR-MNQ 221 | WWG-MS3 237–238 | YLM 3.4.166

All the treasure of the Isle of Man

The ancient Caillagh ny Ghueshag (Woman of the Spell) left the prophecy that:

> 'Tre trieghyn jeh trieghyn Finn,
> Birchys Vannin cooyl Rhullic-y-Doon.'
> ('Three feet of Finn's feet from the wall of Rhullick y Dhoon lies all the treasure of the Isle of Man.')

Some believe that this refers to the flat area on the top of South Barrule. Finn is the giant, Finn MacCooil, which suggests that the three feet would be a considerable distance. It used to be believed that this prophecy referred to the Foxdale mines, but perhaps the true treasure is yet to be found.

EK-CC 321 | WWG-MS1 327–328

Captive of the armies of fairies

The southern slopes of South Barrule used to be thought of as 'probably the most fairy-haunted part of the isle.'

A woman was once walking over South Barrule when she came across two armies of fairies about to do battle. The battle was to commence when a bell was rung, and so she rang it herself. However, when she did so, both fairy armies attacked her instead and kept her captive for three years before she escaped.

EW-FFCC 120 | YLM 1.9.290

The ghostly couple

Some people were on South Barrule cutting turf in the middle of the day when a fog fell across the hillside. When it cleared, they saw a finely dressed old gentleman and a lady walking on the side of the hill. They thought the couple could be the minister and his wife but then they suddenly disappeared. One of those who saw them thought it was a lhiannan-shee.

YLM 3.4.162

Marown

With the buggane of St Trinian's, Marown has one of the best known of all Manx folklore tales. However, the parish has a lot more than this, including two distinctive tales of the phynnodderee, a holy well renowned for its cures, and a wonderfully detailed account of the problems that resulted from clearing away a keeill. However, at the head of all of these are Marown's fascinating and varied connections to St Patrick.

1. The men who tried to take stones from the Braaid
2. St Patrick's Chair
- The Fairy Orchard [private land]
3. The phynnodderee and the sieve
4. St Trinian's Chapel
5. The surprise witch trial
- Lhiabbee Pherick and St Patrick's curse [private land]
6. The White Lady of Ballafreer
7. The farm of the trolls
8. Chibbyr Roney
9. The curse of the Rheyn keeill

The men who tried to take stones from the Braaid

Open access | Steep, rough and uneven ground | SC 3252 7656 | 54.157482, -4.566422 | The Braaid Circle is in a field to the west of the main road, about 750 metres north-east of the Braaid roundabout.

In around the 1860s two men were employed to remove stones from the Braaid Circle for use in the building of a wall. However, as soon as the men had started, one of them was seized with a terrible pain in one of his legs, and the other got a similar pain in his arm. They at once stopped their work and went home, leaving the stones as they were and as they have remained ever since. The leg and arm of the men never improved and they remained useless for the rest of the men's lives.

AWM-FIOM 154

St Patrick's Chair

Open access | Steep, rough and uneven ground | SC 3165 7795 | 54.169618, -4.580420 | A collection of cross slabs in a field south of Crosby. About half a mile south of Old St Runius' Church, take the footpath heading west up from the road. The collection of stones that make up Patrick's Chair are in the centre of the third field on the south-west side of the path.

Christianity was first brought to the Isle of Man by St Patrick, and these stones mark the site where the saint first preached the gospel on the Island. Some hold that the saint himself sat on the stones, and that anyone who does so now will never be weary. In the late nineteenth century the owner of the land reported seeing lights coming 'up and down' here and that sometimes, on a dark night, St Patrick's Chair would be seen to suddenly light up.

AWM-MN 122 | HIJ-JG 66 | MD-EVAF 15 | PIOMNHAS 2.1.18 | PIOMNHAS 3.3.222 | RP-MA 35 | WC-IH 14–15 | WWG-MS1 368–369 | YLM 2.2

The Fairy Orchard

Private | The Fairy Orchard is a small group of trees around Ballaquinnea keeill on private land south of Glen Vine.

The group of trees around this keeill site is known as the 'Fairy Orchard.' Sadly, no story has come down to us to explain the name, but it is likely that this wood was once a favourite of the fairies.

JMM 3.49.153

The phynnodderee and the sieve

Private land – view only | Visible from a road without a pavement | SC 3299 7836 | 54.173787, -4.560244 | The former Glen Darragh Mill is a private house south of Glen Vine. About 500 metres along the Glen Darragh Road, south from the lights in Glen Vine, the building is obvious with the old waterwheel at its side at the junction with Ellerslie Road.

Although the phynnodderee was kind and helpful, he could also be frightening due to his vast size, hairy body and his fiery eyes. So when he saw a light at the mill here and put his big head in at the door, Quaye Mooar's wife, who was inside sifting corn, took fright. However, she thought quickly and gave him a sieve. 'If thou go to the river and bring water in it, I'll make a cake for thee,' she said, 'and the more water thou carry back, that's the bigger thy cake will be.' The phynnodderee went to the river with the sieve but all the water he tried to get fell right through. In anger he threw away the sieve and called out:

'Dollan, dollan dash!
Ny smoo ta mee cur ayn,
Ny smoo ta goll ass.'
('Sieve, sieve, dash! The more I put in, the more there is going out')

By the time the phynnodderee got back to the mill, the woman had made her escape.

SM-MFT 52–53

St Trinian's Chapel

Private land – view only | Visible from a main road with a pavement | SC 3175 8018 | 54.189667, -4.580174 | The remains of St Trinian's Chapel can be seen in a field on the north side of the main Douglas to Peel road. It is at the bottom of the hill west of Crosby, in the field opposite the small layby.

The buggane

Accounts vary as to the origin of St Trinian's Chapel, but the most common is that it was first built by someone in thanks for surviving a shipwreck. Some accounts attribute the wreck itself to the demon which was later to also destroy the church.

After the walls were erected, whenever they tried to put a roof on St Trinian's Chapel, a buggane came in the night and pulled it down. A brave tailor called Timothy took a wager that he would remain inside the church and sew a pair of breeches the next time the roof was on. So, when the roof was next put on, he went there and was sewing the breeches by candlelight when the terrifying buggane rose up out of the ground. Covered in black hair, with tusks and fiery eyes like torches, the buggane called out dreadfully to the tailor to look at his big head, but Timothy only replied, 'I see, I see!' and went on sewing faster. Next the buggane heaved his arms and body out, calling to the tailor to look at them, but he received only the same response from the tailor. Next, the buggane showed his terrible claws and his cloven foot, but the tailor replied with only, 'I see, I see!' and sewed yet faster. Before the buggane could finish his next sentence, Timothy finished the last stitches and leapt out of the window. The buggane was furious and pulled down the roof before chasing after the tailor. Timothy ran for his life, with the buggane following on behind at great speed. The buggane was gaining on the tailor and was very close just as Timothy leapt to safety over a wall into sanctified land. The buggane could not follow the tailor and in fury he ripped off its own head and threw it at Timothy, but it narrowly missed and exploded nearby. Timothy survived, but St Trinian's has never had a roof on it after that night.

AWM-FIOM 60–61 | FG-AIOM 169 | GW-AIOM 177 | HAB-HIOM 238 | JT-HSA 2.61 | KR-MNQ 103 | MD-DT 202–203 | N-MH-02061847 | N-MH-08041875 | SM-MFT 163–170 | TK-FJ 19 | WL-DPG 102 | WWG-MS1 366–368 | YLM 2.30

Removed stones

There are several stories connected to people suffering after removing stones from St Trinian's Chapel. This was so remarkable a feature of the site in the mid-nineteenth century that it was said that 'no one will touch a stone of it.'

A particular story from the nineteenth century was of a young stonemason who took a stone from the chapel for use in a wall of an outbuilding nearby. After this the young man suddenly became very ill, with his body becoming covered in sores. He was in this way for many months before someone realised the cause of the illness and returned the stone to the church. After this he made a quick recovery to full health.

Another time a man named Kelly went to take a large stone from the chapel as a cornerstone for a new building at Rock Farm. As he lifted the stone, he felt a sharp pain go through his knee, which only grew worse as he continued to pull it to the site of the new building. After that, he was forced to lie in bed, where he remained incapacitated for many years until a friend suggested that the stone might be the cause. The stone was then removed back to the chapel, after which Kelly soon recovered.

Separately, a boy who lived in a mansion at the foot of Greeba fell ill and was wasting away dangerously. No one could discover the cause until someone recalled that the boy had taken a small stone from St Trinian's Chapel when he had been here with friends. The stone was found and returned, and the boy made a recovery soon after.

Stones from St Trinian's were also used in the tower of the new Braddan Church. It was these stones that caused the spire to fall down twice in storms not long after its consecration in 1876. After that, the spire was taken down completely.

In the late nineteenth century a man named E.B. Wood took stones from the ruins of the chapel to build a pigsty at his farm in Crosby. It was only when all the pigs that he put in the sty had died that he realised the error he had made. He pulled the sty down and returned the stones to the church, after which no more of his pigs fell ill.

At the start of the twentieth century the Vicar of Marown, Rev A.E. Clarke, obtained permission from the landowner to have the site cleaned up. The rubbish was removed, revealing a good deal of surplus loose earth and a number of large granite stones lying around. The stones were used to help build a small tower and the earth was spread about the field in which the church sits. However, soon after this the owner of the land, a Mr Corlett of Rock Farm, fell ill. Corlett was adamant that this was a result of the work on the site and so he demanded that the earth was raked up and returned to the church. This was done and very soon afterwards Corlett made a full recovery.

The power of the chapel also extends to the field in which it sits, as it should never to be put to grain, despite being the best farming land in all the parish. In the late nineteenth century this taboo was ignored and wheat was grown here. It was recognised as the finest wheat in the parish that season, but people would still not so much as touch even one ear of it. When the crop was cut and stacked, the farmer suddenly died. When the heir took over the farm and sowed crop in the field that following year, he too died, leaving the farm to pass out of the family.

FLS B1/A | HIJ-JG 53–54 | N-IOME-24091898

The surprise witch trial

Private land – view only | Visible from a main road with a pavement | SC 3203 7996 | 54.187850, -4.575749 | A private house on the south side of the main Douglas to Peel road at the brow of the hill over Crosby. On the west side of the house is written 'Halfway House.'

In 1843 a Marown farmer named Quine lost two cows and a horse in quick succession. He attributed the cause to witchcraft and so he successfully had a warrant for trespassing made and called a jury for a trial to take place here at the Halfway House inn. However, once the trial was underway the questions gave little attention to trespassing but instead centred on whether the witnesses knew of any witchcraft done to the animals. Eventually the farmer's sister-in-law was felt to be the cause and so was found guilty of trespassing on the farm 'in any shape or form' and was sentenced to pay an enormous fine, utterly out of proportion to the apparent crime of trespassing. However, the conclusion of the trial was interrupted when some boys set a hare loose in the room. The animal was taken for the witch and so was immediately caught and killed. 'You shall not trouble Quine again!' they called out in triumph, thinking they had arrived at the perfect punishment for the witch. However, since Quine's sister-in-law remained present, they recognised their error. When the whole story reported in the papers, the farmer and the others involved were mocked for their credulity and foolishness.

AWM-FIOM 84 | N-MH-10011844 | JT-HSA 2.168–170

Lhiabbee Pherick and St Patrick's curse

Private | Lhiabbee Pherick is a large flat rock on the private land of Ballafreer, to the north of the main road between Union Mills and Glen Vine.

It was St Patrick who brought Christianity to the Isle of Man and he continued to visit the Island afterwards. It was on one of these visits in around 444 that he visited Ballafreer seeking a location for a chapel and, when he was in the field he had decided on, he pricked his foot on a thorn. In anger, the saint cursed the ground and so it has never grown crops to this day. However, St Patrick immediately regretted his anger and did penance for it by spending the night sleeping on a large flat rock with his head on the quartz boulder which has now rolled a short distance away. The large flat rock has ever since been known as Lhiabbee Pherick (Patrick's Bed). The rock today bears a carved inscription of unknown antiquity reading, 'Leabba Pheric.'

Variants of this tale include St German as a companion for St Patrick here, and that the curse on the land was specifically against crops that could be used to make alcohol.

JJK-PN 166 | JMM 3.49.159 | MD-EVAF 15 | PIOMNHAS 3.1.69 | PIOMNHAS 3.1.82 | WC-IH 12 | WWG-MS1 369–370

The White Lady of Ballafreer

Public | Rough and uneven ground | SC 3443 7859 | 54.176327, -4.538347 | The White Lady is at the gatepost in front of Ballafreer, a farm to the north of the main road between Union Mills and Glen Vine. The farm track is private but the site is accessible on foot by the public footpath that runs between the main road close to Glenlough to Trollaby Lane at Trollaby Farm.

This remarkable quartz pillar has had special importance for centuries and it has acted as 'an object of reverence, of wonderment, of admonition and of fear for many.' It used to be a custom for women about to be married or looking to become pregnant to come here to perform a rite before sunrise for luck in their endeavours. They would take a mouthful of water from Chibbyr Pherick (which enters the stream below the track a short distance to the west) and then walk three times around the White Lady jesh-wise (clockwise). They would then swallow the water and say: 'Ayns yn Ennym Yee, as y Vac, as y Spyrryd Noo' ('In the Name of the Father, the Son, and the Holy Ghost').

N-IOME-21081953 | WC-IH 13–14

The farm of the trolls

Public | Public road without a pavement | SC 3470 7887 | 54.178866, -4.534244 | Trollaby Lane leaves the main road at the western edge of Union Mills. The glen runs up the right-hand side of the road, leading up to Trollaby Farm.

One possible root of this farm's name is in the Old Norse for 'farm of the trolls.' It has been suggested that the trolls (or goblins) used to be known to live in the glen close to the farm.

AMW-MN 207 | JJK-PN 170

Chibbyr Roney

Private land – view only | Visible from steep, rough and uneven ground | SC 3491 8060 | 54.194531, -4.531983 | Chibbyr Roney was a well to the west of West Baldwin. It was on the south side of the track which leaves the Ballalough Road just past the Rhyne. Although it was washed away by a flood in around 1930, it was in an embankment roughly ten metres from where the track crosses the River Rheyn.

This holy well was once considered so important that the parish boundary of Marown juts out from the river here to include it. The well's water was renowned for its cures, especially if taken when 'the books were open' (i.e. during a church service). One known method of taking the cure here was to spit on a round white stone and place it into the water, thus transferring your ailments to the care of the well. This was especially effective for problems of the eyes and reports exist of old people who had relied on glasses for years who were able to thread a fine sewing needle with the naked eye after taking the water.

The well was also known to cure warts if you washed them in the water and then left a bit of silver or a white stone behind in the well.

If the water was drawn in this correct way, its curative quality could even last being bottled and taken away for someone unable to visit the well in person.

Rather more ominously, this well is known as a haunt of the lhiannan-shee, who waited here for a lone man she could attach herself to.

AWM-MN 145 | FLS Q/1-A | PIOMNHAS 10.1.84–85 | MJ 4.253 | WC-IH 23–24 | WWG-MS1 66 | WWG-MS2 239

The curse of the Rheyn keeill

Private land – view only | Visible from a public road without a pavement | SC 3502 8075 | 54.195927, -4.53044 | The site of the keeill was in a field to the west of West Baldwin. Nothing remains of the keeill itself today, but it was west of the centre of the field opposite the Rhyne on Ballalough Road.

When the keeill was still standing, the owner of the Rhyne farm took a portion of the roof for use in the farmhouse. But such unearthly noises then began to be heard in the house that the wood was returned to the keeill within the fortnight.

Despite this, a later owner named Kewley levelled the keeill and removed gravestones for buildings around the farm, resulting in years of bad luck. Strange noises were heard from the yard, as if his horses were out and terrified, galloping about furiously, but upon going out Kewley discovered all the horses at peace in the stables. Then the son who had carried out the work died, followed by other of Kewley's children falling ill or dying, then Kewley himself died, followed by his wife losing her mind. The tenant farmer who followed fared little better, as he first lost four cows and three horses to disease, and then the threshing mill mysteriously broke and defied any attempts to fix it. At first the mill was powered by a windmill that had been built using some of the stones from the keeill, but that began of its own accord at night, or went with such tremendous fury, shaking the whole building as soon as it was started, that it had to be taken down. The mill was then worked by horses but it still refused to work, repeatedly breaking no matter how many times it was fixed. The tenant farmer was forced to leave and the owner tried desperately to hide the state of the farm from the neighbours, knowing that they would attribute it to the levelled keeill and its lingering curse on the land. Eventually, the stones from the keeill were removed and buried as best they were able to, close to the site the keeill.

AWM-FIOM 154 | HIJ-JG 36–38 | YLM 3.10.483–4

Maughold

Maughold is one of the Island's strongest folklore parishes, boasting a number of bugganes, terriu ushtey, ghosts, giants and even a fairy hill in the middle of a modern housing estate. Although there are numerous pockets of folklore, such as around Ballure, Lewaigue and North Barrule, a stand-out area for folklore is Maughold Village, in part thanks to St Maughold, whose tales are amongst the most brilliant of all Manx saints' tales.

1. The final drinking place of Charlie Chalse the charmer
2. Chibbyr y Woirrey
3. Killeaba Fairy Hill
4. Ballure Glen
5. The curse of Old Chalse Ballawhane
6. The strange place on Lewaigue Hill
7. The White Lady of Lewaigue
8. Ewan Christian and the Kione Prash
9. Port e Vullen
10. Kirk Maughold
11. The Guriat Cross
12. St Maughold's sarcophagus
13. The blood-charmer of Baldromma
14. Maughold Head
15. St Maughold's Well
16. Port Mooar
17. The Jalloo
18. The roar of the tarroo ushtey
- Hee Kerna [private land]
- Gob y Chashtal [private land]
19. The failed fire at the crossroads
20. Ballasloe
21. Dem ny Tarroo Ushtey
22. The phantom coach below Ballavelt
23. The Big Man of Ballure
24. Ballagilley
25. The buggane of Gob ny Scuit
26. The ghostly horse of Park Llewellyn
27. North Barrule
28. Clagh Hoit
29. Blood-charming at Ballasaig
30. Boayl ny Niee
31. Passing a mysterious woman by the Hibernian
32. Something in the ditch outside Ballaglass
33. Kitty the wise woman of Cardle Vooar
34. The Gob ny Scuit spirit's false warning
35. Corony Bridge
36. The red woman and the weaver
37. The Londhoo's ghost
38. Cashtal yn Ard
- Charming at Rhenab [private land]
39. A ghostly horse near the Barony gate
- Creg y Foawr [private land]
40. Port Cornaa
41. The glashtyn by Ballagorry Chapel
42. The meeting place of witches
43. The moddey doo at Glen Mona
44. The fairies blowing their hunting horns
- The Ree Mooar ny Howe [private land]
45. The ghost of a drowned girl
46. Meir ny Foawyr
47. Dreem y Jeeskaig

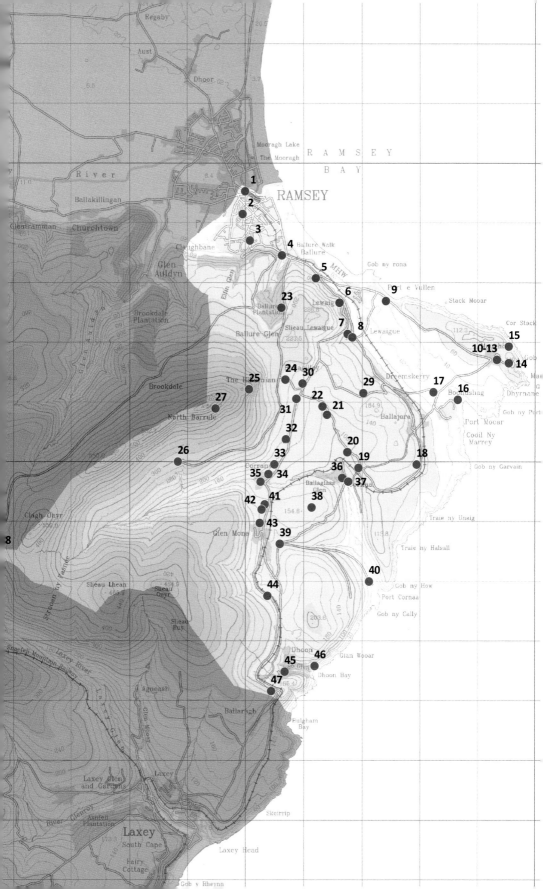

Ramsey to Maughold Head

The final drinking place of Charlie Chalse the charmer

Public | Paved level ground | SC 4507 9452 | 54.32267, -4.383667 | The Friendship Inn used to stand at the end of Collins Lane, at the harbourside close to the Swing Bridge in Ramsey.

Charlie Chalse was son of the legendary Chalse Teare of Ballawhane and he himself was a highly respected charmer in his own right. However, Charlie Chalse had troubles with alcohol and one night after a bout of heavy drinking here in the Friendship Inn, he stumbled out over the road, fell straight into the harbour and drowned.

JR-MFS 2.295–296 | WWG-MS2 181

Chibbyr y Woirrey

Public | Rough and uneven ground | SC 4503 9414 | 54.319272, -4.384134 | Chibbyr y Woirrey is a well, today filled in and covered over by a canopy within Coronation Park in Ramsey, between the main road to the Mountain Road and Prince's Road.

The well hidden underneath the false fairytale-like structure is Chibbyr y Woirrey (St Mary's Well). In addition to being well known for its excellent drinking water and for never drying up, the well's water was also used in love charms or with certain herbs to divine the future. However, the well fell into neglect until it was covered over in the 1930s with the development of Coronation Park (previously known as the Chibbyr Woirrey field).

WCR-MRP 43 | WWG-MS1 78

Killeaba Fairy Hill

Public | Steep and uneven ground, beside road with a pavement | SC 4517 9371 | 54.315410, -4.381726 | Killeaba mound is a small grassy hillock in the middle of the modern housing development at the top of the residential road named Killeaba Mount, which comes off Lheaney Road, the final road seawards on the way out of Ramsey towards the Mountain Road.

Another name for Killeaba mound is the Fairy Hill. Although no specific stories of fairies are recorded here, similar sites around the Island with this name are known to have fairies living inside and were often to be seen with fairies on the top at night.

WWG-MS1 420

Ballure Glen

Public | Pavement beside a main road | SC 4571 9344 | 54.31320, -4.37328 | Ballure Glen is on the Maughold edge of Ramsey. The main road to Laxey crosses it over Ballure Bridge at a dark turn in the road close to the tram tracks.

Ewan Christian's conversion

It was here at Ballure Bridge that Ewan Christian met a ghostly woman or 'unearthly presence.' This meeting caused him to change the course of his life, converting from his previous wild life to one of ardent Christian zealotry.

This ghostly figure has been linked to the White Lady of Lewaigue Bridge, who some have identified as the spirit of one of the women Christian wronged in his earlier wayward life.

WWG-MS2 75 | WWG-MS3 359 | WWG-MS3 414–415

The Carrasdhoo Men's store

The Carrasdhoo Men were a murderous gang who had their base on the north side of Ballure Glen not far from the shore, and a store further up the glen. They would bring the things they gained through smuggling and wrecking here to enjoy them. The historic accounts of the Carrasdhoo Men have left some commentators wondering if there was 'something other than human' about them.

WWG-MS1 385–387 | WWG-MS2 258–259

The great fairy gathering

It was in Ballure Glen that a great gathering of the fairies took place. A man named John y Chiarn was caught up in it after they had come across him by Ballaragh and turned him into something for carrying their luggage. The gang of travelling fairies gathered in groups of different fairies as they came here, where they turned off up the glen to a great feast with much drinking and dancing. There was cowree, binjean, oatbread, cheese and tramman wine. The music was played on fiddle, flute, clarinet and drum, by a number of fairies up on a big rock as the others danced around. Although the festivities were to go on for a fortnight or so, John y Chiarn was returned to his home shortly after arriving, when one of the fairies touched him with a stick.

SM-MFT 146–150

Fairies capering in Ballure Glen

The fairies were well known to be regularly seen in Ballure Glen in the 1820s and they were even seen walking around in broad daylight. They were recorded as being 'like merry little men and women,' they were dressed 'nicely' and they 'sang most sweetly, while they danced and capered beautifully.'

N-IOME-03091898

The Ballure cabbyl ushtey

A cabbyl ushtey, also here referred to as a 'glashtin,' lives in the river in Ballure Glen. It emerges from the stream at night in a form almost identical to a natural horse. It lingers at the roadside hoping that someone will try to climb onto its back, at which point the cabbyl ushtey rushes into the stream and drowns their unfortunate victim.

This cabbyl ushtey used to be so well known that a rumour of its being in a field by the glen one day in 1863 led to hundreds of people immediately rushing out from Ramsey to catch a glimpse of it. However, the crowds met with only disappointment as the beast had gone by the time they got there.

KR-MNQ 99 | HIJ-JG 152

The buggane of Gob ny Scuit at Ballure shore

The buggane of Gob ny Scuit sometimes used to visit Ballure shore. He would get here in just three strides from his home on the side of North Ballure.

WWG-MS3 372-373

The curse of Old Chalse Ballawhane

Private land – view only | Visible from a pavement beside a main road | SC 4630 9305 | 54.309882, -4.364078 | The Folieu inn is the ruined two-story building on the landward side of the main Ramsey to Laxey road, shortly after the turning for Port Lewaigue.

Old Chalse Ballawhane was legendary for his skill at charms and other cures. Although most stories of him are from Andreas, one is from his visit to the Folieu inn when the stagecoach he was travelling in stopped here on the way to Ramsey. The landlord recognised Old Chalse and called on him to sort out two drunk men who were causing him trouble. As Old Chalse went to speak to the men, the coachman lost his patience and tried to leave without him, but the horses would not budge while Old Chalse was not in the coach. After Old Chalse had finished speaking to the men, he told the landlord that they would not bother him further and then he left. The two drunk men then headed home but did not make it as one woke up in the morning to find himself in the Cornaa glen, and the other passed out in the road with swollen and damaged fists after mistaking a tree for his companion and trying to beat it for not speaking to him.

N-RWT-03121898

The strange place on Lewaigue Hill

Public | Public road with limited pavement | SC 4669 9267 | 54.306531, -4.357858 | The junction of the main Ramsey to Laxey road and the Dreemskerry Road which leads down to the Venture Centre.

A man was once here at the top of Dreemskerry Road when he saw the greyish form of a woman and her small dog walking down the main road towards him. Before they reached him, the dog ran across the road and disappeared, and the woman appeared to melt into the hedge on the opposite side of the road. He went to look at the spot in the hedge but there was no way for someone to pass through and no explanation of where she had gone.

Other tales of strange occurrences or dark feelings are reported on this stretch of the road. In a separate incident, two men were walking near here one night when they were passed by a spectral funeral complete with a coach and a procession of mourners. In the crowd following the hearse the men both recognised a man they knew. Within a week that man had died.

A similar appearance of a dark horse-drawn coach, though without an accompanying procession, has been seen in recent years late at night further down the Dreemskerry Road towards Lewaigue.

WWG-MS2 246–247 | WWG-MS3 395 | Add

The White Lady of Lewaigue

Public | Public road without a pavement | SC 4684 9212 | 54.301683, -4.355272 | Lewaigue Bridge is a short distance down the Dreemskerry Road from the main Ramsey to Laxey road. The bridge crosses the river at the Venture Centre, just before the road splits between the Dreemskerry Road and Jack's Lane.

A ghostly White Lady is sometimes to be seen or experienced on the bridge here or seen moving silken-footed at twilight or in the early evening in the glen just above. She was first recorded in the early twentieth century, but she remains independently known today as sightings still take place.

For at least a century, people here have avoided Lewaigue Bridge at night or at midnight. However, in the early eighteenth century, people would come from as far away as Ramsey on moonlit nights to catch a glimpse of the White Lady. One account describes her as being seen in the glen below the bridge in white clothing and her feet shining in fine shoes. The sight of her troubled those who saw her.

Some accounts say that the White Lady originated with Ewan Christian, better known as 'Christian Lewaigue,' when a woman he wronged returned as a ghost to hound him around his home here at Lewaigue and as far away as Ballure Bridge on the edge of Ramsey. According to differing accounts, the White Lady is viewed as either the good or bad angel of Christian Lewaigue's life.

The White Lady once came into the house at Lewaigue, the former home of Ewan Christian. She walked past the owner and up the stairs with her silk dress rustling and wet, causing the person to give up the house entirely. A later sighting of her was by a man named Harrison, a later owner of the house, who was out on the road between Lewaigue and the bridge one night when she walked past him with her skirt rustling. The man turned and saw her go into the farmhouse. A generation later it was at this same spot that a man saw and heard nothing, but his otherwise perfect dog refused to pass. It stood frightened at a point against the hedge, backed off slowly and then turned and bolted up the road.

Some today still avoid crossing Lewaigue Bridge at night.

GB-HLSM 1.417–418 | WWG-MS2 245 | WWG-MS3 358–359 | WWG-MS3 414–415 | Add

Ewan Christian and the Kione Prash

Private land – view only | Visible from a public road without a pavement | SC 4690 9208 | 54.301319, -4.354291 | Lewaigue is a private house a short distance up the hill from the Venture Centre, at the junction of the Dreemskerry Road and Jack's Lane.

Lewaigue used to be the home of Ewan Christian, who was a great figure of Manx folk history with many unusual stories told of him.

It was Christian who built the Kione Prash, a brass head that could not only reveal the future and the secrets of the past, but it could also to cast out the devil and his league of bugganes, moddee doo, lhiannan-shee, ghosts and others from the Island. However, the thing was made using materials Christian had gained from the devil and so he was only able to build it by using one of the devil's potions which enabled him not to have to sleep for seven years. But when the night came for the Kione Prash to be finished and to speak at last, the potion went missing, taken by Christian's jealous servant. So it was that Christian fell asleep before midnight came around and the Kione Prash came to life with much steam and noise. However, all it could say before the crank-head of the brain-gear broke was one sentence:

'Traa ba, as Traa la
As Traa ella na be Me bra.'
('Time was, Time is, and Time shall ever be')

The head then exploded, blasting the roof completely off the shed that Christian had built it in. He then had to pay off his debt of seven years' sleep, but in so doing he wasted away and died. After this his servant cast the tools and materials of the Kione Prash off Maughold Head, but the box in which the devil brought them to Lewaigue was still to be seen in the glen in the 1830s.

Christian was also well known for battling spirits during his lifetime. He battled the devil at Ballachrink, Lonan, and he banished whatever spirit it was who was pinching and hitting a girl in the night-time in Jurby. Christian sat with this girl for three nights until he finally saw the invisible spirit open the door and lift the sheets, prompting Christian to act. He could also communicate with the spirits of the dead, as he did when a deceased neighbour came to his bedside to tell him where his will was to be found, after which Christian was able to locate it in the dead man's mattress, as he had been told. Another time a dead person's spirit stopped him in the road to tell him of hidden money, which Christian passed on to the person's family.

It was also said that Christian could still be seen around Lewaigue long after he had died, as he returned in spirit to see how the place he so cared for was fairing.

Stories of another ghost associated with Lewaigue are in the proceeding item.

WK-KP 399–413 | WWG-MS2 77–81 | WWG-MS3 415

Port e Vullen

Public | Public road without a pavement | SC 4750 9267 | 54.30678, -4.34543 | Port e Vullen is a collection of houses along the road from Ramsey towards Maughold village, around the bottom of Jack's Lane. The Guriat Cross stood on the seaward side of the road, a short distance up the hill towards Maughold past the speed limit signs, almost opposite the gate on the other side of the road.

The Guriat Cross

A woman broke the sabbath by spinning on a Sunday and then setting off to take the wool to the weaver. However, as she was getting over the hedge by her home here at Port e Vullen, the wind caught the balls of wool and blew her and the wool back. She cursed the wind and in response she was immediately turned to stone with her five balls of wool. Here she remained, stood at the roadside for hundreds of years.

When the cross slab stood here at the roadside it was known as a wishing stone. People would make a wish as they touched their hats or curtsied at the cross. Funeral processions would stop here and perform an 'elaborate ceremonial' of some description before going on towards Maughold churchyard.

Today known as the Guriat Cross, it was moved in 1894 from the roadside to the cross house at the parish church, where it can still be found today.

AJAF-ASG 159 | HIJ-JG 185 | JF-TIOM 160 | JT-HSA 2.30 | WWG-MS2 455 | WWG-MS3 289–291

The gap in the funeral procession

A woman was watching the funeral procession of her sister-in-law's father. As it passed along the road here at Port e Vullen she noted a gap between two of the carts. She knew that the traditional belief was that such a gap foretold of another funeral soon to pass along that way but she thought little of it. However, within a fortnight her mother had relapsed into an illness and died. The daughter made no connection to the earlier funeral procession, as their home was at Cardle Veg, where the normal route to the church would be down from the Hibernian. However, there had been a heavy snowfall that day and so the procession was forced to go around to the Folieu and down through Port e Vullen, along the very route of the previous funeral.

FLS G18/A

Kirk Maughold

Open during daylight hours | Some uneven ground | SC 4930 9169 | 54.298554, -4.317308 | Kirk Maughold is the church in Maughold village.

The whispering bones of Kirk Maughold

In the 1860s some men were employed to replace the steps at the communion rail. During their work some bones were disinterred and they were left exposed as two of the men went for lunch. The third man was then left alone and he heard whispering or murmuring all over the church during the time that they were away. When the other men returned, they reinterred the bones and the noises ceased.

AWM-FIOM 155

The smiting of Gilcolum

In 1158 a man named Gilcolum was among the Norse who sailed into Ramsey Bay. Knowing of the riches here at the monastery of Kirk Maughold, Gilcolum got permission from his leader, Somerled, to plunder the place. News of this reached the community here, at which some fled to hide but many more stayed to cry through the night for god's mercy through St Maughold. Their prayers were answered as St Maughold returned from the dead to appear to Gilcolum in his dream. After identifying himself to the Norse plunderer, the saint raised up his pastoral staff and used it to stab Gilcolum in the heart three times. Gilcolum let out great screams at each stab and when his men ran to him, they found him in great pain. Barely able to speak, he asked for messengers to be sent here to fetch the priests of Maughold to intercede for him with the saint. However, the priests refused to help him and, only six hours into the next day, Gilcolum died in great agony and with 'a swarm of large revolting flies' flying around his face and mouth. When news of this reached Ramsey, the remaining Norsemen left at the next tide and Kirk Maughold remained safe from their plunder.

GB-CKMI f.38r–f.39r | JT-HSA 1.99–100

The Guriat Cross

Public | Some rough and uneven ground | SC 4928 9167 | 54.298344, -4.317563 | The Guriat Cross is cross no. 69 in the cross house in the churchyard of Kirk Maughold.

This large cross with five raised balls on its face used to stand at Port e Vullen. See 'The Guriat Cross' at Port e Vullen for details.

St Maughold's sarcophagus

Public | Some rough and uneven ground | SC 4939 9169 | 54.298556, -4.315842 | A large stone sarcophagus on the eastern side of the churchyard of Kirk Maughold. It lies on the grass just inside the path, a short distance down the slope from the gate towards Maughold Head.

This large stone trough is associated with the story of St Maughold's sarcophagus. St Maughold's bones are said to lie within it, but they cannot be seen. A spring of pure water used to flow from the sarcophagus, which delivered either instant health or death to those brave enough to drink it. Norse invaders tried to take the sarcophagus but without success as the deeper they dug to get it out, the deeper they found it went down into the earth.

Although this trough is known to have lain outside the graveyard before 1878, it was originally dug up from within the graveyard.

AWM-FIOM 23 | HIJ-JG 186 | YLM 1.11.386

The blood-charmer of Baldromma

Private land – view only | Visible from an area of some rough and uneven ground | SC 4919 9167 | 54.298319, -4.318873 | Baldromma is the private farm bordering the south side of Kirk Maughold churchyard.

Perhaps the most celebrated blood-charmer of the north of the Island used to be the Primitive Methodist preacher who lived here at Baldromma, Jim Crellin. He was the son of Juan Richard Crellin of German and he died not long before the 1930s. One time a poor castration six miles away at Smeale in Andreas left blood audibly pouring onto the straw and it was clear that the bull would die. A man was sent to Jim Crellin, who said his charm from his home here in Baldromma. Miraculously, the bull's bleeding stopped immediately.

WWG-MS2 191 | WWG-MS3 323–324

Maughold Head

Open access | Steep, rough and uneven ground, close to a cliff edge | SC 4962 9164 | 54.298174, -4.312271 | Maughold Head is the distinctive headland over the sea behind Kirk Maughold. It is most easily reached from the car park at the end of the single-track road which leads around the outside of the churchyard.

St Maughold predicting the weather at Laa'l Breeshey

St Maughold appears each year on Laa'l Breeshey (1 February) to stand at the top of Maughold Head. He holds his pastoral staff out vertically in his right hand and turns around slowly. The direction in which he finishes his turning shows how the weather will be for the coming year, with south being best for farmers, and north worst.

WWG-MS1 384

Samson's Stone

Samson was once here on Maughold Head and threw an enormous granite boulder across Ramsey Bay, all the way to Cronk ny Arrey Laa on the Bride Hills. The imprint of Samson's hand could be seen on the top of the standing stone, until coastal erosion cut away at the land and the rock was lost into the sea.

WWG-MS1 221

The death of the Purr Mooar

A wild boar used to terrorise the north, killing sheep and causing other nuisances for the farmers who lived close to its home near Skyhill. Eventually the people gathered together to be rid of the beast and they hunted it all the way from Skyhill to Maughold Head, where they arrived just in time to see it roll off the cliff. As it hit the waves below it turned into a great fish and swam away. Although the source is not definite at this point, it is probable that the Purr Mooar turned into a porpoise, the Manx name for which is 'muc varrey,' which literally means 'sea pig.'

WWG-MS1 274

The whistling of mermen

The whistles of mermen used to be heard from the coast around Maughold Head. These whistles were a warning of coming storms.

YLM 3.4.159

St Maughold's Well

Open access | Steep, rough and uneven ground | SC 4963 9192 | 54.300706, -4.312375 | St Maughold's Well is a stone-lined spring on the broogh behind Maughold Head. Take the rocky track to the left at the foot of Maughold Head. At the end of this track, go through the gate on the eastern seaward side of the car park and follow the steep path downhill until you reach a gate through the stone wall. The path from here leads directly to the well.

St Maughold's Well is the Isle of Man's most renowned holy well for cures and wishing. It was used by the saint himself and it is reported to offer cures to a wide range of ailments, but particularly problems of the eyes. The water was also good for curing non-physical disorders, and it acts as a charm against the fairies and evil spirits.

The best time to take the water is at sunrise on Easter Day or at Laa Luanys (recognised here on the first or second Sunday in August), especially during the church service. Another day when the well was especially visited was on 25 March by women desiring children.

To take the water you should 'teem' the water three times with your right hand before bathing your eyes or whatever else ails you in the water. Those taking the water should then leave behind in the water a coin, a bent pin, a metal button or a cross made of two pieces of straw. Alternatively, another effective way to take the water is to dip a rag in (perhaps using it to bathe your ailment) and then to leave it on a bush nearby. When the rags rotted away, the ailment would also disappear.

People from far away and even from off the Island used to visit the well in droves for cures. Many stories exist of the well's miraculous success, including restoring perfect eyesight and even undoing a man's hair loss. The water was also believed to help women fall pregnant if drunk in the correct manner. It was sometimes bottled and carried to people as far away as Douglas who were unable to visit the well in person.

At the start of the twentieth century many people within Maughold and beyond knew this well as 'St Patrick's Well.' The story was that it was St Patrick who first formed the well, when his horse leapt up the hillside from the sea, and one of its hooves struck the ground here and formed the spring.

AWM-MN 144 | EK-CC 94 | GB-HLSM 1.410 | HIJ-JG 190 | JGC-HPECL 231 | JF-TIOM 160 | JJK-PN 275 | JJK-PN 285 | JR-MFS 2.307 | JT-HSA 2.41 | JT-HSA 2.60 | JT-HSA 2.121–122 | MQ 1.9.766 | MQ 3.17.85 | N-IOME-11061910 | PIOMNHAS 10.1.84 | PMCK-MAS 4.20 | RJK-SIOM 10 | RP-MA 8–9 | SH-HSDV 102 | WCR-MRP 43 | WH-MM1 145–146 | WS-AIOM 144 #43 | WWG-MS1 61–62 | WWG-MS3 326–328

Lower Maughold

Port Mooar

Public | Rough and uneven ground, close to parking | SC 4874 9102 | 54.292347, -4.32553 | Port Mooar is a large bay south of Maughold village. It is reached via the first road seawards south of the village, about half a mile from the village green.

St Maughold's landing point

Maughold was the leader of a band of robbers in Ireland until St Patrick put him in shackles, threw the keys into the sea, and cast Maughold out to sea in a small rudderless boat large enough for only himself. After drifting on the waves, he landed here at Port Mooar, where he was taken in by the fledgling Christian community. He went on to eventually reach such faith that the keys to set him free were miraculously found in a fish.

WWG-MS1 383–384

The tarroo ushtey's landing point

A tarroo ushtey used to come ashore here at Port Mooar. It would then go off to meddle with the cattle, giving them calves which came out speckled or spotted and poor beasts compared with other calves. This went on until the tarroo ushtey was almost caught at Glen Auldyn, after which it fled and was never seen again.

GB-HLSM 1.414

The Jalloo

Public | Public road without a pavement | SC 4832 9116 | 54.293431, -4.332088 | The Jalloo is an area along the road south of Maughold village. It is between the turning to Port Mooar and the Ballajora tram stop. At the northern end of The Jalloo is the Dreemskerry Hill road heading west.

The Manx word 'Jalloo' normally means spectre, phantom or ghost when in a place name. No stories have been passed down of how the name was gained here, but perhaps it has a connection to the wayside cross which is believed to have once stood here at the road junction.

JJK-PN 298 | WCR-MRP 96

The roar of the tarroo ushtey

Private land – view only | Visible from a road without a pavement | SC 4801 8995 | 54.282542, -4.336153 | Ballafayle e Kerruish is a private farm roughly halfway along the Maughold Road between the Hibernian crossroads and Maughold village. About a quarter of a mile south of the Ballajora crossroads the view opens out across to Maughold Head, and Ballafayle is the next farm on the seaward side.

The tarroo ushtey of Dem ny Tarroo Ushtey, near to Ballavelt, roared so loudly that it could be heard here at Ballafayle. On one occasion a man here died shortly after hearing its roar, though it is not recorded whether the roar was the cause or merely an omen of his death.

WWG-MS3 381

Hee Kerna

Private | A cave on private land south of Port Mooar.

This cave is said to connect all the way to Gob ny Scuit on North Barrule and it is because of this that the buggane of Gob ny Scuit is sometimes seen or heard here on the shore.

An old man named Corkill used to live nearby at Straledn and he would come down to the shore early in the morning to look at what the tide had brought in. One day he came across the buggane stood here, at the mouth of Hee Kerna. The beast said to Corkill, 'If you don't look at me, I'll not look at you.' Corkill wisely did that and moved on quickly.

Another story of this cave's connection to North Barrule has it as the dooinney oie who moves between the two sites, as he can be heard in both places shouting out his warning of oncoming storms.

Separately, in around the 1880s a girl found a little lump of gold on a rock above the high-water mark near here. She eventually sold it for a large sum of money to a Liverpool pawnbroker but, although there was a great deal of searching, no further gold was found. This mysterious discovery of gold was understood as being the work of the fairies.

WCR-MRP 95 | WWG-MS3 211 | WWG-MS3 231 | WWG-MS3 374–375

Gob y Chashtal

Private | Gob y Chashtal is a coastal headland on private land south of Port Mooar.

An alternative name for this ancient promontory fort is 'Gob ny Garvain,' pronounced at the start of the twentieth century as 'gowan,' suggesting that it is derived from the Manx for 'Headland of the Smith.' It is associated with a story of a magic or fairy blacksmith named Culann. It was to here that Conchubar, the King of Ulster, came on the recommendation of an oracle or wise person, to have a sword and spear made by Culann. While waiting for his sword to be made, Conchubar was walking on the shore near here and came across a beautiful sleeping mermaid. He tied her up to stop her escaping, but when she awoke, she explained that she was Teeval, the Princess of the Ocean, and she promised that if he let her go, she would give a shield made by Culann extraordinary powers. Conchubar freed her and had the shield made to her specification, with her face on the front and her name written around it. This he took back to Ireland and whenever he was in battle he looked at the shield and invoked her name, and the strength of his enemies would leave them and flow into him and his men. By this he was able to gain a great kingdom.

Another story reports that the magic smith's daughter was a mermaid and would entice men to follow her into the sea, where she became a leader of the souls of the drowned. This mermaid enchantress was identified by some as Tehi Tegi, an enchantress linked to the wren hunted at Hunt the Wren.

Another story relates this site as connected to the sword Macabuin, which had the power to cut through anything, until it was outwitted by a concoction created by the witch, Ada. See Kitterland, Rushen, and Peel Castle, German, for further details.

Independently of these stories, a fisherman from Port Mooar was once sailing here at night when he saw the promontory lifted up. Revealed beneath it was a long deep cave, out of which came a strange greenish light.

AWM-FIOM 9–10 | JJK-PN 297 | MD-CTM 25 | SM-MFT 115–120 | WWG-MS1 381–382 | WWG-MS2 362–363

The failed fire at the crossroads

Public | Public road without a pavement | SC 4701 8988 | 54.281553, -4.351486 | The crossroads of Maughold Road, the Quakers' Road and the track leading down to the foot of Ballaglass Glen.

In the 1880s or 90s the farmer at Crowcreen was plagued with bad luck and the last straw was one of his cows giving birth to a dead calf. He followed the advice of the local miller and piled up a cartload of gorse here at the crossroads. After dousing the gorse with oil, the farmer put the calf on the top and set the bonfire alight. As the calf burned, it was expected that the person who had put the witchcraft on the farmer would be compelled to come here to the fire. However, although a crowd gathered to watch what happened, the farmer was disappointed that the fire did not compel any culprit to arrive, and his luck continued afterwards as it had before.

WWG-MS3 338–339

Ballasloe

Private land – view only | Visible from a public road without a pavement | SC 4682 9014 | 54.283889, -4.354489 | Ballasloe is the collection of houses north-east of Ballaglass Glen. It is on the south side of the Hibernia Maughold Road, a short distance from the turning off towards Ballaglass Glen.

Curing a crazed sow

The farmer at Ballasloe once had a remarkably fine and valuable sow. A Manx-American, who was visiting from Illinois, praised the sow highly after which the sow refused to eat, broke out through the fields and then almost drowned in the mill ditch. Recognising that it had gone mad from the visitor's jealousy, the farmer sent for Teare of Ballawhane, who sent back a bunch of herbs collected from his garden and instructions for their use. The sow was so far gone by the time the messenger had returned the eight miles back to Ballasloe that they had to suspend the beast on ropes from the ceiling to get it up on its feet. After putting a stick in its mouth to stop it biting them, they boiled the herbs into a broth and poured it down the pig's throat. The people then retired for their own meal and when they returned, they found the sow back to full fitness and eager for its next feed.

WWG-MS3 315–316

Singing at the smithy

A blacksmith's shop used to be here at Ballasloe. Some men were passing here at three o'clock one morning when they were surprised to hear a number of people singing, one of whom they recognised. They realised that the people were not actually there, and that it was an ill omen for the near future. Indeed, they were proven right, as the man whose voice they had heard was dead within the week.

A similar ill omen was also heard here when the blacksmith, a man named Matt Summers, heard a hymn being sung just outside the building when no one was physically there. Two days later, a man who lived close by died, and at the funeral the same hymn was sung as was heard here by the blacksmith.

WWG-MS3 396

Dem ny Tarroo Ushtey

Private land – view only | Visible from a public road without a pavement | SC 4647 9078 | 54.289516, -4.360248 | Dem ny Tarroo Ushtey is the damp and boggy ground leading down towards the stream opposite the gates to Ballavelt, on the Hibernia Maughold Road, down from the Hibernia Crossroads.

As the name suggests, Dem ny Tarroo Ushtey is the home of a tarroo ushtey. The beast emerges from here to roar loudly and to meddle with nearby cattle, later resulting in stillbirths or other such birth abnormalities. One particular sighting of the tarroo ushtey here reports it as black and smaller than normal cattle. A young lad of Ballavelt saw it in one of the fields of Ballavelt and reported it to his father. However, the beast was gone by the time the father got there, and so the son was punished for appearing to have deceived his father.

Another time the tarroo ushtey's roar was loud enough to be heard at Ballafayle, with terrible consequences.

WWG-MS3 195 | WWG-MS3 380–381

The phantom coach below Ballavelt

Public | Public road without a pavement | SC 46393 90906 | 54.290620, -4.361490 | The narrow and winding stretch of wooded road into Maughold that comes off downhill eastwards from the Hibernia crossroads on the main Ramsey to Laxey road, finishing not for after Ballavelt.

This stretch of road is well known for being a place where 'much of a spectral nature' has been seen or experienced. One example of this is a phantom horse-drawn coach which can be seen making its way towards Kirk Maughold between one and two in the morning. Some accounts report that its appearance foreshadowed death.

WWG-MS3 395

Ballure into the Hills

The Big Man of Ballure

Public | Steep, rough and uneven ground | SC 4570 9258 | 54.305422, -4.372940 | A stream by the track which runs along the eastern edge of the plantation in upper Ballure Glen. It is easiest reached from the Rhowin Road, which runs from the Gooseneck to the Hibernian. The stream is obvious above the track at the bend just over 300 metres down from the end of the paved road.

A peddler named Willy Carberry was coming up this road one moonlit November night when he stopped here to have a drink from the stream. As he knelt down to drink, he looked up and saw the Big Man of Ballure standing over him on the opposite bank. As tall as half a telegraph pole and with a long staff on his hand, Carberry knew it was the giant who helped the Christians of Ballure but who was rarely seen as he was so reclusive. Taking fright at the sight of the Big Man, Carberry jumped up and ran away.

WWG-MS3 370

Ballagilley

Private land – view only | Visible from a public road without a pavement | SC 4576 9136 | 54.294466, -4.371400 | Ballagilley is a private farm beside the road between the Hibernian crossroads and the Gooseneck. The farm is distinctive for its waterwheel on the building by the road.

The Ballagilley changeling

At reaping time here at Ballagilley, a woman laid her baby on the ground close to the hedge of the field and she set to work. Another worker paused a moment in their own labour and he looked up to see a little red woman come in and take the baby, leaving another child in its place. The changeling baby then let out a terrible cry, but before the unsuspecting mother could go to it, the man held her back and told her to wait. They looked on for a minute or two as the child screamed, and then the little red woman re-emerged and laid the true baby back safely on the ground. The fairy woman then picked up the screaming changeling and disappeared with them through the hedge.

WWG-MS3 356

The giant leaning on the hedge

People walking along the road on moonlit nights here by Ballagilley used to see 'a big, big man' with his arms folded leaning on the hedge on the south side of the road here. Nothing further is recorded of this figure, nor of his possible relation to similar figures known close by.

FLS R/11-E

The buggane of Gob ny Scuit

Public | Very steep, rough and uneven ground, a committed walk | SC 4515 9120 | 54.292860, -4.380709 | Gob ny Scuit is a gully on the very steep eastern face of North Barrule, damp with a spring of water running down the exposed rock face.

The buggane of Gob ny Scuit used to be one of the best-known of all bugganes in the Isle of Man. It was said to be the terrifying transformed form of a man who committed murder in the corner of a field at Ballagorry and then fled here to avoid capture. When he died, he transformed into a buggane and he has haunted this place ever since.

Accounts of the buggane's appearance vary, but he has been reported as a man covered in gore, a terrifying horned bullock, and as a man with the head of a cat with great fiery eyes. His cries or howls were legendary in the parish, striking fear into all who heard it.

An alternative version has this buggane helping farmers with threshing or warning them of oncoming bad weather with his call of 'Ha-oo, ha-oo!' enabling the Maughold farmers to get in their harvests successfully. This role of his has perhaps led to him being confused with the dooinney oie, better known in Lonan.

Gob y Scuit is said to connect via a long underground passage to Hee Kerna, a cave on the shore south of Port Mooar. The buggane sometimes travels through this and has been seen on the shore at Hee Kerna.

The famous Teares of Ballawhane visited Gob ny Scuit to try and drive the buggane away, but without success. One account has a man known as Jemmy-Jem Jem-beg Jem-mooar uncover the shouting as merely the wind on the rocks here but it does not explain the sightings.

AWM-FIOM 61 | AWM-MN 160–161 | GB-HLSM 1.407 | WK-MI 508–512 | WCR-MRP 93 | WWG-MS1 392–393 | WWG-MS3 231 | WWG-MS3 372–375

The ghostly horse of Park Llewellyn

Public | Steep, rough and uneven ground, a committed walk | SC 4391 9000 | 54.281698, -4.399123 | Park Llewellyn Road by Park Llewellyn, a tholtan on the uphill side of the track leading up the Corony Valley. It is most easily accessed from the Rhowin Road between the Hibernian crossroads and the Gooseneck.

Two shepherds were caught in heavy rain late one night between one and two in the morning, and so they were sheltering on the track close to Park Llewellyn House. They were surprised to hear the sound of 'a tremendous heavy horse, galloping like thunder' coming up the track. The men looked but saw nothing as the invisible horse leapt the gate into a field above and galloped on towards North Barrule.

WWG-MS3 384

North Barrule

Public | Steep, rough and uneven ground, steps, a committed walk | SC 4428 9093 | 54.290173, -4.393964 | North Barrule is the Isle of Man's second highest peak. It is a long and committed walk from the Black Hut on the Mountain Road, or a shorter but very steep climb from the Rhowin Road between the Hibernian crossroads and the Gooseneck.

The resting place of King Barrule

North Barrule took its name from a great King buried here at its peak. Rather than erecting a monument as we would expect today, the mourners placed a great pile of stones over King Barrule's tomb, to which people visiting the site have contributed ever since. Kings are also buried at the peaks of Snaefell and Carraghan.

GW-DIM 58 | WWG-MS1 232–233

King Orry's great strength

King Orry, the great Norse ruler of the Isle of Man, was incredibly strong and powerful. One day King Orry thought to entertain himself by throwing an enormous rock from where it lay at the top of North Barrule down into Bulgham Bay below. But the rock came back up the hill of its own accord, three times, with King Orry throwing it back down each time. On the fourth time, the rock remained where it landed in Bulgham Bay.

It is possible that this story used to be told of Manannan rather than King Orry, as the name of the rock is 'Creg Vanannan,' which translates from the Manx as 'Manannan's Rock.'

WWG-MS1 316–317

The glashan

The glashan was a figure very much like the better-known phynnodderee. He was big and hairy, was very strong and helpful to farmers, but he was disdainful of clothing. A glashan used to help around North Barrule, gathering and driving in straggling sheep.

KR-MNQ 105

The White Horse

Around the 1850s two men were out searching for sheep buried in the snow on the slope of North Barrule above Park Llewellyn, when the men looked up and were surprised to see a white horse on the crest of the hill. It was smaller than normal, similar to the traditional Manx pony believed to be long extinct. The men recognised that it could not be a normal horse out in that weather, so they knew not to go any closer to it. The horse watched them working for a quarter of an hour and then moved away northward and out of sight over the ridge.

WWG-MS3 382–383

The final sighting of Ben Ven Carraghan

The ghostly appearance of a young travelling spinner from Maughold used to be well known on Carraghan in Braddan. She was murdered there by someone seeking her money, and her spirit, known as Ben Ven Carraghan, would frequently be seen on the hill with her spinning wheel and slumped down with her head on her arm as if in worry or woe.

Sometime around the 1860s a man decided to confront this spirit and so he and some others approached her from different sides so that she could escape. The woman could not get away and so approached one man, causing his dogs to begin to tremble and even shed tears. The man fell ill immediately and was in a bad way for six months afterwards. Ben Ven Carraghan then moved towards a small gully and vanished, but it was later discovered that she was seen here on North Barrule at that precise moment, heading in the direction of Maughold Head. This was the last time was she ever seen.

HIJ-JG 128–129

Dancing around the Oie Voaldyn fire

Oie Voaldyn (the evening before 1 May) is a dangerous time, when you are most exposed to witchcraft, bad luck and the effects of evil spirits. So fires are lit to drive off danger and evil from your land. This used to be frequently done on hills, and traditionally a fire was lit here at the peak of North Barrule, around which people danced with straw torches. After the conclusion of the dancing, one person was left behind to watch over the embers of the fire, ensuring that it was not tampered with in any way and its positive effects for the year ahead would be fully enjoyed.

A fire was also lit here for similar reasons at the other end of the year, at Hop tu Naa.

WWG-MS1 392

Clagh Hoit

Public | Steep, rough and uneven ground, steps | SC 4084 8852 | 54.267449, -4.445488 | Clagh Hoit is a short distance from the Black Hut and the Mountain Road. From the parking area of the Black Hut, nestled into the north-eastern side of Snaefell, cross the road and go over the stile. Follow the stone wall for 200 metres until it meets the wall heading north. This corner is Clagh Hoit and the site of the former cairn.

A boundary-cairn used to stand here to help those travelling between Laxey and Sulby on the rough track that used to run here. One account reports it as featuring a white boulder so large it 'would have filled the breadth of Parliament Street in Ramsey and stood nearly as high as the houses.' It was at the meeting point of three parishes and a number of strange things have been seen here. Travellers would often hear music and voices here, though they could not see anything or find where the sounds came from. A particular strange occurrence here was when a man known as Robbie the Plumber came across a donkey stood alone and unattended, but as Robbie was looking at the beast it changed into a black dog and ran off along the road towards Ramsey.

WCR-MRP 44 | WWG-MS1 417–418 | WWG-MS3 385–386

From Slieau Lewaigue to the Corrany

Blood-charming at Ballasaig

Private land – view only | Visible from a public road without a pavement | SC 4710 9114 | 54.292948, -4.350722 | Ballasaig is a private farm on the north side of School House Road, the narrow road which leaves the main Ramsey to Laxey road at almost its highest point on Slieau Lewaigue.

A bull was once castrated poorly here at Ballasaig and the wound would not stop bleeding. A blood-charmer was sent for but he could not stop the flow and so instead they sent for his wife, also a blood-charmer, even though she was attending a birth close to Cornaa and was rather drunk at the time. She recited a charm to stop the blood where she was, over a mile away from the bull and a note taken at Ballasaig confirmed that the bleeding stopped at that exact moment.

WWG-MS3 323

Boayl ny Niee

Public | Rough and uneven ground | SC 4607 9129 | 54.293972, -4.366709 | Boayl ny Niee is beside the public footpath running alongside Struan ny Niee, the stream between the Hibernian and Ballaberna. At the lowest point of the Ramsey to Laxey road, just north of the Hibernian crossroad, a footpath leads off eastwards. Follow this path alongside the stream, Struan ny Niee, until you reach a slope coming down to the stream from a gate in a field opposite. Boayl ny Niee is believed to be this area of the stream.

Boayl ny Niee (Place of the Washing) gets its name from it being where the fairies wash their clothes at night. A particular report of this was of a fairy woman all in red who emerged from the river one night to wash her clothes by the light of a candle which she would put on the rocks beside her. Seeing the fairy washers here is an omen of bad weather coming.

An alternative account of how this place got its name, and the river its name of Struan ny Niee (Stream of the Washing), begins with a band of Norse invaders defeating the Sulby men at Sulby Claddagh and then heading over the hills into Maughold. Here they were routed by the Maughold men at Slieau Lewaigue. After every one of the enemy was put the death, the Manx came here to Boayl ny Niee to wash the blood off themselves, causing the river to run red as far as the Cornaa Mill.

JJK-PN 628 | WWG-MS3 183 | WWG-MS3 351–353

Passing a mysterious woman by the Hibernian

Public | Public road without a pavement | SC 4591 9108 | 54.292025, -4.369058 | About 100 metres to the Laxey side of the Hibernian crossroads, on the main Ramsey to Laxey road, roughly where the traffic signs stand today for the Ramsey-bound traffic.

A man was walking home from the Corrany one moonlit night when he met a woman walking the opposite way as him here in the road. He called goodnight to her but he received no reply. He called again and was ignored again. Enraged, he took hold of her dress and she covered her face with her arm. He called out, 'I'll find out who you are, if I have to follow you to Douglas!' To which the woman replied, 'You don't know me and you never will.' The man was unclear what happened next but he suddenly found himself standing alone on the road with his knife open in his hand with the blade facing behind him. He continued on his way but by the time he reached home he was 'feeling queer' and so went straight to bed.

A few days later he called on a woman he thought it could have been on the road that night, but he was surprised to learn that the woman had been on a boat at the time of his encounter. She had planned to get off at Ramsey but the boat unexpectedly skipped the town and went on straight to Douglas. The explanation of the man's experience was then believed to be that it was this woman's distressed spirit projected onto the road where she should have been at that time. However, the words the strange figure had spoken remained difficult to interpret, unless they had some secret meaning.

WWG-MS3 412–414

Something in the ditch outside Ballaglass

Private land – view only | Visible from public road with a pavement | SC 4576 9036 | 54.285514, -4.370895 | The farm of Ballaglass is on the main Ramsey to Laxey road. The two white pillars of the gates are on the seaward side on the road, just north of where the road drops down to the Corrany.

A man set off from Ballaglass just before daybreak but, as he came out of the gates here, his horse noticed something black in the ditch outside. The horse refused to go further, but the man persisted and forced the horse on. However, later in his journey, in Santon, his horse fell down dead and he himself lay ill for months afterwards.

WWG-MS3 386

Kitty the wise woman of Cardle Vooar

Private land – view only | Visible from a public road without a pavement | SC 4558 8995 | 54.281744, -4.373526 | Cardle Vooar is a private farm on the landward side of the main Ramsey to Laxey road, a short distance north of the Corrany.

A woman named Kitty, well known for her skill at cures and charms, lived here at Cardle Vooar more than 100 years ago. One story recorded of her is of how she successfully cured a man's swollen big toe by having him put it in the midden as she quietly said a charm over it.

WWG-MS3 330

The Gob ny Scuit spirit's false warning

Private land – view only | Visible from a public road without a pavement | SC 4548 8978 | 54.280251, -4.374997 | The former Cardle Chapel is on the upland side of the main Ramsey to Laxey road. Now a private residence, the former chapel is just north of the Corrany.

When midway through the service one Sunday morning here at Cardle Chapel the congregation heard the Buggane of Gob ny Scuit high up on North Barrule shouting, 'Cluck hoods!' ('Gather in!'). Heeding the warning, they finished the service quickly and headed straight out to gather in the corn, working through the night until it was completed. However, much to their surprise, the following day turned out fine, and in the night following they heard the Buggane again, shouting loudly in his enjoyment at how he had tricked them all.

WWG-MS3 373–374

Corony Bridge

Public | Public road with a pavement | SC 4534 8965 | 54.279056, -4.376988 | Corony Bridge is at the Corrany, on the main Ramsey to Laxey road, at the bottom of the hill north of Dhoon School and Glen Mona.

The headless monk

A headless monk used to be seen at Corony Bridge and in the fields north-east of here. Sadly, no story remains of who this spectre was or where they came from, though some have claimed that it used to be a practice in the Island to cut off the heads of monks before they were buried.

WWG-MS1 399

The fairies lined up along the walls of the bridge

Corony Bridge was one of the meeting points for the fairies on their way towards a great feast and dance in Ballure Glen. The fairies of the Corrany mustered here and arranged themselves into rows along the walls of the bridge, holding up their coloured lanterns on the ends of sticks to light the way for the fairies coming from Lonan. After this Lonan crowd had passed through, the Corrany fairies fell in behind and went on towards Ballure. Among their number was John y Chiarn who had been changed into something for carrying their things after he had met them near to Ballaragh.

SM-MFT 146–150

Ballaglass Glen and South

The red woman and the weaver

Public | Steep, rough and uneven ground | SC 4674 8969 | 54.279843, -4.355581 | The Lag Vollagh road is the rocky track which begins directly opposite the lower entrance to Ballaglass Glen, close to where the road turns to cross the bridge. The location where the weaver sat is probably on the low wall overlooking the house.

In the second half of the nineteenth century a weaver was walking from Douglas towards his home at Port Mooar when he took a rest just at dawn here on the hedge. When he opened his eyes again a little red woman was sat on his lap. He went to grab her, but she quickly slid down and got away from him. He called out in amazement, 'Ta mee rieau dy clashtyn dy row ny ferrishyn ny noon as noal ayns Ellan Vannin, as dar Yee ta mee fakin nane noght!' ('I've always heard there were fairies going to and fro in the Isle of Man, and by God I'm seeing one tonight!').

WWG-MS3 354–355

The Londhoo's ghost

Public | Steep, rough and uneven ground | SC 4684 8965 | 54.279491, -4.354055 | The wood visible from the bridge on the road below Ballaglass Glen. Looking downstream, it is on the left, up above the private gardens of the former mill. The public footpath which passes by the woods can be accessed via the Lag Vollagh track directly opposite the lower entrance to Ballaglass Glen.

The ghostly apparition of a giant deer can be seen in these woods. Its great antlers are unmistakably similar to those of the giant deer now on display in the Manx Museum. This ghostly apparition was known as the Londhoo (also, curiously, the Manx name for the blackbird).

WWG-MS1 400–401

Cashtal yn Ard

Open access | Steep, rough and uneven ground | SC 4622 8923 | 54.275473, -4.36325 | Cashtal yn Ard is at the top of the hill south of Ballaglass Glen. Access is via the single lane road which runs between the bottom of Ballaglass Glen and the Aah Lhaggagh ford off the road to Port Cornaa. Where the road twists sharply around a house, a signpost marks the footpath leading off north-west up the hill. The site is 200 metres up the hill, beyond the tholtan.

Although today universally known as Cashtal yn Ard (Castle of the Height), in Victorian times the dominant name for this site was Cashtal Ree Gorry (King Orry's Castle). This name relates to the legendary Norse ruler of the Island, frequently believed to be a giant, who was perhaps believed to have lived here in a castle or fortification, the remains of which can still be seen today.

A curious story of this area relates how the tracks of a mysterious creature were found in the snow one winter. Although they were found all across the northern Maughold farmlands, they were most clearly visible here at the Ards. The tracks were described as being of a four-legged creature with 'half a hoof on each foot, one in front of the other.' The mysterious creature was never discovered or identified.

AJAF-ASG 167 | JT-HSA 2.27 | N-MS-17031877 | OS-25-VIII.7 | RP-MA 9 | WWG-MS3 384–385

Charming at Rhenab

Private | Rhenab is a private farm at the top of the single lane road running between the bottom of Ballaglass Glen and the Aah Lhaggagh ford off the road to Port Cornaa.

A family named Joughin once lived here at Rhenab and were very skilled in charms. One of their charms was written on a piece of paper and given to a neighbour to be worn in an amulet against toothache. The charm read, ''Peter stood at the gate, and Christ came passing by. Christ said to Peter, 'Why are you so down-hearted?' 'Because my teeth ache, Lord.' 'I'll give you power over the toothache for ever.'' The charm worked for the entirety of the woman's life and was eventually passed to another family member.

More than 100 years ago, after the time of the Joughins, a man at Rhenab was suffering from a painful swelling under his big toe which hindered his walking. He called on a woman named Kitty from Cardle Vooar who was well known for her skill with charms and cures. She had him put his bare foot into the midden here at Rhenab as she repeated a charm quietly under her breath. The cure was successful and the swelling was soon gone.

WWG-MS3 330–331

A ghostly horse near the Barony gate

Public | Public road without a pavement | SC 4567 8862 | 54.269882, -4.371474 | The old Barony gate is close to the Aah Lhaggagh ford on the road to Port Cornaa. It can be recognised by the single gatepost by the house up the road from the ford. The other gatepost can still be discerned in the undergrowth on the other side of the road.

Two children from Thalloo Queen were on their way to get a doctor when they heard the sound of a galloping horse coming up behind them here. They stopped and looked but could see nothing, despite the sound of the hooves getting closer and closer. When the phantom horse was close to the girls, it stopped and nothing more was seen or heard.

WWG-MS3 384

Creg y Foawr

Private | Creg y Foawr is a rock in the riverbed of the private glen below the Aah Lhaggagh ford, below the road towards Purt Cornaa.

This rock was thrown here into the glen by the foawr (giant). The two white streaks on the rock are the marks left behind from the foawr's fingers. The rock has been named as Creg y Foawr (The Giant's Rock) ever since that time.

JJK-PN 288 | WCR-MRP 54

Port Cornaa

Public | Rough and uneven ground, close to parking | SC 4721 8799 | 54.264634, -4.347444 | Port Cornaa is the bay closest to Glen Mona, accessed via the loop road opposite the Glen Mona Hotel or close to the Dhoon. The narrow road to Port Cornaa comes off eastwards from this loop road and reaches the shore after 1½ miles.

The tarroo ushtey of Port Cornaa

A tarroo ushtey used to be sometimes seen around the boggy pools inland from the shore here. One sighting of it was when a man named Jimmy Fayle saw the beast lying out on the bank of pebbles before dark as he returned home along the glen road.

WWG-MS3 382

The giants landing at Port Cornaa

It was at Port Cornaa that a group of sea-giants first arrived on the Island. After securing the lower valley, they made their way up North Barrule, where a fight broke out. Their two leaders argued and then began hurling rocks at each other, two of which are still to be found in Bulgham Bay.

WWG-MS1 317

The home of the man who befriended a mermaid with apples

A young man named Sayle used to live with his family in a house close to the shore here. One day he was on his own out in his boat at Bulgham when he met a mermaid who asked after his old father. When the older man was told of this later he told his son to take apples with him the next time for the mermaid, as she might bring luck on the family. Sayle did this, and the mermaid was delighted. She took an apple and chanted:

> 'The luck of the sea be with you, but don't forgetful be
> Of bringing some sweet lan' eggs for the children of the sea.'

The family had great luck from then on but Sayle came to almost live at sea for all the time he spent out around Bulgham. He was accused of being idle and so he made up his mind to sail foreign, but not before he had planted an apple tree over the rocks for the mermaid where she was normally to be found. After he left, the mermaid missed him and eventually she set off after him. Neither of them was seen again. A part of Bulgham Bay retains the name 'Gob ny Ooyl' ('Headland of the Apple'), from the tree Sayle planted for the mermaid there.

SM-MFT 75–78

The glashtyn by Ballagorry Chapel

Private land – view only | Visible from pavement beside main road | SC 4541 8925 | 54.275482, -4.375734 | Ballagorry Chapel is on the northern side of Glen Mona, beyond the Dhoon School. The chapel has long been closed as a place of worship.

In around the 1880s the field here at the chapel was just boggy ground and it was from here that the old woman living close by would hear a glashtyn 'tearing' at night in the field. The creature, however, was only ever heard but never seen.

WWG-MS3 382

The meeting place of witches

Private land – view only | Visible from main road with pavement | SC 4539 8919 | 54.274940, -4.376000 | The top of Creg ny Mult, the hill overlooking Dhoon School in Glen Mona.

The hilltop of Creg ny Mult was noted in the 1840s as the most important meeting place for witches. This was particularly so at Oie Voaldyn (the evening before 1 May), when a number of women met here under the leadership of a witch who assigned them positions of responsibility and initiated new witches to their number.

WK-MI 537 | WWG-MS1 414–415

The moddey doo at Glen Mona

Public | Visible from road with a pavement | SC 4532 8896 | 54.272838, -4.376903 | The drainage ditch from the upper fields on the main road through Glen Mona. The walled-in drainage ditch is at the end of the row of terraced houses on the Ramsey side of the village.

Two men returning home from the North Laxey Mine in the Corony Valley were passing through Glen Mona in the moonlight at about two in the morning when they heard a splashing from the spooyt here. They were terrified to see a large beast coming out of the ditch that was black, half the size of a calf and with eyes 'blazing like saucers.' The beast went over to the opposite side of the road where it headed on down the road towards the farm. In telling of the sighting to friends the next day, the two men discovered that it was already known of, as 'the Moddey Doo of the Rhenab Road.'

WWG-MS3 377–378

The fairies blowing their hunting horns

Public | Visible from a road with a pavement | SC 4545 8775 | 54.261977, -4.374282 | Balellin is a private farm between Glen Mona and the Dhoon. Coming from the south, it is the first farm on the east side of the main road after the Glen Mona loop road turns off over the tram tracks and down the hill. The old entrance to the farm is today marked by the redundant gateposts to the south of the present entrance.

The leader of a group of fairies blew his ram's horn outside the Ballelin gates as they rode by here one night. Amongst their number was John y Chiarn, who had met them near Ballaragh and was changed into something for carrying their things when one of the fairies had touched him with a stick. They were heading on towards Ballure for a great feast and dance.

SM-MFT 146–150

The Ree Mooar ny Howe

Private | Barony Hill is a private hill between Port Cornaa and Dhoon Glen. A short distance to the south of the small copse of trees plainly visible from the main Ramsey to Laxey road are the remains of Keeill Vael.

Sometimes in dark and misty weather a mysterious figure known as Ree Mooar ny Howe (the Great King of the Hill) can be seen here by the old keeill site. Little is known of this figure but in the 1920s he was still to be met here and the children of Glen Mona were warned when going to the Barony Hill, 'Mind yourself, or the Ree Mooar ny Howe 'll be after you.'

This is likely to be connected to the tumuli here; said locally in the 1920s to be the burial place of 'the heroes and the champions.'

FLS R/11-E | PIOMNHAS 2.1.15 | WWG-MS1 380–381

The ghost of a drowned girl

Public | Steep, rough and uneven ground, a committed walk | SC 4575 8646 | 54.250541, -4.369081 | Inneen Mooar is the large waterfall in Dhoon Glen, close to the southern edge of Maughold Parish.

The name of this impressive waterfall, Inneen Mooar, means Big (or important) Girl. It has been said that this name comes from a girl who drowned in the pool below the waterfall and her ghost has haunted the place ever since.

An alternative story might possibly connect to the glen having been a favourite place of a sea-woman of some kind who was vaguely remembered here at the start of the twentieth century.

WWG-MS1 387

Meir ny Foawyr

Private – view only | Visible from steep, rough and uneven ground, a long distance away, a committed walk | SC 4625 8657 | 54.251609, -4.361457 | Meir ny Foawyr are two enormous slabs of rock standing on the crest of the next headland north of Dhoon shore at the bottom of Dhoon Glen. The site is not publicly accessible, but it is visible from a long distance away, from the brooghs on the upper footpath through the glen.

These two enormous stones are the Meir ny Foawyr (Giant's Fingers). One story of how they got this name is that they are a giant husband and wife who have somehow become petrified.

A more detailed story is that two giants fell into an argument here at the bottom of Dhoon Glen. The husband and wife were stood on opposite sides of the glen throwing rocks at each other, and these stones landed here along with the single one on the crest of the headland close by. Reports say that the sound of these giants arguing can still be heard here on rough winter nights.

In addition to this, this is a good place to make a wish, if you stand squeezed between the stones of the Meir ny Foawyr, facing out to sea and with your palms placed flat against each stone.

WWG-MS3 219 | WWG-MS3 291 | WWG-MS3 371

Dreem y Jeeskaig

Private land – view only | Visible from the public road without a pavement | SC 4553 8614 | 54.247551, -4.372221 | The site of Dreem y Jeeskaig is below the Ballaragh Road at the bend up from the Dhoon. The land of Dreem y Jeeskaig bordered the Ballaragh Road and ran alongside the Keeym Crossags footpath which drops back down to the Ramsey to Douglas road.

The famed preacher, Ewan Christian of Lewaigue, was called to deal with an extremely evil, violent and obstinate spirit here at Dreem y Jeeskaig. The first time he came, the spirit told him to come again alone another night. This Christian did, and although no one discovered what passed between them, the spirit was never seen again and Christian was never quite the same.

This is perhaps linked to the moddey doo that also used to be seen here lurking around the roadside at Dreem y Jeeskaig. In around the 1840s, a boy named Kewley of Booilley Mooar was driving home from Ramsey with his father when their horse saw the moddey doo here. The horse shied and threw the father and son from the cart before bolting for home. As they picked themselves up, Kewley and his father saw the moddey doo leap out over the cliff edge.

WWG-MS3 379–380

Michael

Although much folklore in Michael is on private land, what is available to be publicly visited offers a fascinating range of tales. Particularly important is the keeill on Bayr ny Staarvey, built by the devil under St Patrick's orders, but suffering the same fate as the better-known St Trinian's in Marown. Also particularly noteworthy are the range of accounts of the collecting of a tune still be heard today from the fairies in the Michael hills.

1. Cronk y Croghee
- The curse of Ballacarnane Keeill [private land]
2. Glan Beasht
3. Spooyt Vane
- Samson's Rock [private land]
- The Giant's Foot [private land]
4. Saved by a child's crying
5. Capturing the fairy tune, Slieau Curn
6. The cap of Nan y Caillagh
7. Carn Vael
8. Capturing the fairy tune, Druidale
9. Jack the Giant Killer
10. Orrisdale

Cronk y Croghee

Private land – view only | Visible from a pavement beside the road | SC 3226 9154 | 54.291875, -4.578711 | Cronk y Croghee is on the main road north of Kirk Michael. The site of the former mound is 200 metres north of the petrol station, opposite the road heading seawards towards Orrisdale.

During improvements to the main road in 1889 Cronk y Croghee was cut into and inside the small hill were found cross-slabs and burial urns, indicating that it was an ancient burial mound. It has also been suggested that this was the site of a Tynwald meeting of 1422. However, the Manx name translates as 'Hill of the Hanging,' and it is believed that this relates to its being the place of execution for the Bishop's court. This is perhaps connected to a moddey doo which haunts the area.

At the start of the twentieth century this hill began to be known as 'Fairy Hill,' but no particular stories behind this name are known.

FLS K/106 | JJK-PN 439 | JJK-PN 441 | WC-IH 107 | YLM 2.123

The curse of Ballacarnane Keeill

Private | The remains of the keeill are on the private land of Ballacarnane Beg, a farm above the main road south of Glen Mooar between Kirk Michael and Peel.

Around 400 years ago a family named Mylrea owned Ballacarnane and, despite knowing them to be gravestones, the father and the five sons decided to clear away the stones around the keeill. The mother and the daughter protested, but the men ignored them and completed the job. As a result of this, within the year all the men had died and just the women were left. When that daughter eventually married, it brought the farm to the Cannell family, who have owned it ever since.

An alternative version of this occurrence has it as seven sons in around 1700.

CV-YT-JC | PIOMNHAS 1.9.610 | PMCK-MAS 3.11 | WWH-MS2 140

Glan Beasht

Private land – view only | Visible from a pavement beside the road | SC 3052 8931 | 54.271256, -4.604168 | Glan Beasht is a place in Glen Mooar not far below the main road. The site remains only in name today and cannot be located precisely.

Although the meaning of the placename is unclear, it has been suggested that 'beasht' might refer to a buggane or some other frightening being, such as a tarroo ushtey or a cabbyl ushtey. Further down the glen is a place once known as Coan Argid (money or silver hollow), which was perhaps related, with the beast acting as a protector of the treasure there.

WWG-MS3 205–206

Spooyt Vane

Public | Steep, rough and uneven ground, steps | SC 3077 8879 | 54.266687, -4.600054 | Spooyt Vane is a waterfall in Glen Mooar, south of Kirk Michael. From the coast road north of the glen, take Bayr Balleyleigh, signposted to Bayr Garroo. After about 500 metres, turn off southwards to the car park. Walk from here further along the track and over the stream. The glen entrance is on your right. Follow the path down towards the river for the waterfall.

Contemporary archaeologists suggest that Spooyt Vane could be a site of pre-Christian religious significance. This aspect of the waterfall has been suggested as a possible reason why the nearby keeill was constructed here at the arrival of Christianity in the Island.

AJAF-ASG 188–189

Samson's Rock

Private | Samson's Rock is a large boulder on private land in the upper part of Glen Mooar.

This large rock got its name after it was thrown here by the biblical figure, Samson. He did this as a demonstration of his great strength after he had been blinded. The marks of his fingers and thumb can still be seen imprinted on the rock from where he gripped it.

It is also said that either Samson or John Wesley preached from this rock when visiting the Island.

WWG-MS1 421 | WWG-MS3 227

The Giant's Foot

Private | The Giant's Foot is an obvious foot-shaped indentation in bedrock on private land in the upper part of Glen Mooar.

This remarkable footprint was made by a giant who got here to the Isle of Man from Ireland in only one, or three, strides.

WWG-MS1 422 | YLM 1.10.308

Saved by a child's crying

Public ram | Steep, rough and uneven ground, a committed walk | SC 32703 87835 | 54.258745, -4.569870 | The old quarry buildings in Glion Kiark, above Barregarrow. The only public access is a long and steep hike down from Sartfell.

When the slate quarry here was still operating, shifts were working day and night. One night when the manager went on his midnight round of the site, he was horrified to find that a landslide had covered the place where the men had been working. He rushed down to Barregarrow to get help to dig them out, but he was surprised to find the men already there safe in their homes. The men explained that they had a habit of going to the mouth of the quarry each night at ten o'clock to see what the weather was like, but when they did so that night, they heard a child crying on the hillside above them. They grew scared at the sound and decided to go home. It was this mysterious and unexplained sound that saved their lives.

FLS Q/41 B

Capturing the fairy tune, Slieau Curn

Public ram | Steep, rough and uneven ground, a committed walk | SC 3418 9064 | 54.284384, -4.548740 | Slieau Curn is a hill standing in the distance over Kirk Michael. It is best accessed via one of the footpaths marked on the OS map.

One snowy New Year's Day morning a man went up to the hills to check on his sheep. As he was coming back towards Slieau Curn he heard the fairies playing a tune on the big fiddle. He committed the tune to memory and set off towards home. However, by the time he had got here to Slieau Curn he had forgotten the tune and so he had to go back to listen again. Eventually he learnt it properly and held it in his memory all the way home. Because he had been out all night, it was now Sunday morning and so his wife was scandalised when he got in and began to play the tune himself. 'Paddy boght, ny moghrey Jy-doonee t'ayd?' ('Poor Paddy, is it not Sunday morning with thee?') she said, but he did not pay her any attention and went on with his tune, saying, 'Fow royd dy lhie, Mall, ny verym yn ghrian soilshean trooid ny hasnaghyn ayd gollrish oashyr ribbit!' ('Away to bed with thee, Moll, or I will make the sun shine through thy ribs like they were a ribbed stocking!') He mastered the tune named, Bollan Bane, and it is still played today.

AWM-MBM xxii | AWM-MBM 76–77 | WWG-MS2 310–311

The cap of Nan y Caillagh

Public ram | Steep, rough and uneven ground, a committed walk | SC 3519 8939 | 54.273500, -4.532561 | Slieau Dhoo is the hill directly above Glen Dhoo and Ballaugh. It is best accessed via one of the footpaths marked on the OS map.

Older Ballaugh people as late as the 1930s would say that when cloud or mist covered Slieau Dhoo, the hill was wearing the cap of Nan y Caillagh. This caillagh was considered 'a powerful witch,' but no further details or specific stories of her are recorded.

DC-MI 227 | MD-WCEV 56 | PIOMNHAS 4.3.469

Carn Vael

Public ram | Steep, rough and uneven ground, a committed walk | SC 3422 8968 | 54.275818, -4.547641 | Carn Vael is a cairn is at the top of Glion ny Maarlys. It is on the track leading up from the Baltic Road in Kirk Michael, on the left-hand side of the track, less than 100 metres from where it meets with the track from Slieau Curn.

It is said that the parish takes its name from the giant named Michael who is buried here at Carn Vael (Michael's Cairn). When the giant was first buried here, the cairn erected over his body was twelve feet high and thirty-five feet wide.

This is also a site involved in the collection of the fairy tune, Bollan Bane. A man was walking on the hills near here when he heard the fairies playing a tune. The man was wearing some bollan bane at the time and so felt confident to stay and listen in closer to the tune as the plant was protecting him against their influence. After listening a while, he had the tune committed to memory and so set off towards home, but by the time he had got here to Carn Vael, he had forgotten it. So he returned the mile or so back to learn the tune again before finally returning home. By the time he was home in Orrisdale it was Sunday morning and his wife, Molly, scolded him for being out all night, but she quietened her complaint when he played her the tune. Known by the name, Bollan Bane, the tune is still played today.

WHG-MNM vi–vii | WWG-MS1 424–425 | WWG-MS2 311–312

Capturing the fairy tune, Druidale

Public ram | Rough and uneven ground | SC 3551 8810 | 54.262026, -4.526963 | A place on the Druidale river close to Montpellier Wood on the road between Ballaugh Glen and Sartfell Road. The river is crossed at the small bridge by the stone-walled parking area below Montpellier house.

A man named Bill Pherick was returning home late one night over the hills towards Ballaugh and as he crossed the Druidale river at a thorn-tree near here, he heard the fairies singing. He listened in and committed the tune to memory but then forgot it after setting off. He returned three times to try to learn the tune and he finally got it on the third attempt, just as the sun came up and the fairies disappeared. He got home whistling it and the tune, Bollane Bane, has been played ever since.

WWG-MS2 309–310 | YLM 2.195

Jack the Giant Killer

Public ram | Steep, rough and uneven ground | SC 3493 8814 | 54.262218, -4.535856 | The glen on the eastern side of Slieau Freoghane. This is the extension of Druidale, up beyond the Montpellier Wood, on the Druidale Road between Ballaugh Glen and Sartfell Road.

A young lad named Jack used to live here in this secluded glen and as he grew, he became braver and more uncontrollable. He was never to be seen without his stick, with which he went around beating animals and people indiscriminately. Because of this he became known as 'Jack the Giant Killer.'

One day he set off to find the Purr Mooar, an enormous and terrible wild boar which was terrorising that part of the Island, causing people to avoid Druidale and the Rheast at all costs. When Jack found the Purr Mooar in the Druidale river, they began to fight and although the boar gored him, Jack finally managed to kill the beast with a decisive blow to its head. Injured as he was, Jack had to drag himself home and he was never without a crutch for the rest of his life. Everyone was very happy about this as they no longer had to fear the Purr Mooar, or Jack the Giant Killer.

AWM-FIOM 65–66 | AWM-MN 121 | JJK-PN 448

Orrisdale

Public | Public road without a pavement | SC 3250 9299 | 54.304918, -4.575810 | Orrisdale is a small village north-west of Bishopscourt. It is easiest accessed via Orrisdale Road, which leaves the main road seawards north of Bishopscourt.

The devil and John Crellin

A farmer was returning home to Orrisdale late one night across the fields near Bishopscourt when he met the devil. Thinking quickly, the man said aloud a verse of a well-known hymn, to which the devil hissed and went away. The man then watched as the devil headed off with his bag towards Orrisdale, evidently in the hope of having better luck here. It is not known what the devil then achieved at Orrisdale, but it was assumed that he did not have much success as the formidable figure of John Christian Crellin, formerly of the 6th Dragoons, was living here at the time.

YLM 2.194–195

The fairies interrupting the bread delivery

One day in the winter of 1898/1899 the people of Orrisdale received no bread from the baker. When they asked about this the next day, the baker's delivery boy explained that his horse had seen the fairies in the dark while on the way to the village and so he had been forced to turn back instead of delivering the bread.

YLM 3.10.482

Onchan

Though small, Onchan's store of folklore is an important one. Clustered around Onchan village itself is a Death Coach, a poltergeist-like appearance of the fairies and a pile of sheep carcasses piled up at the vicar's door. Further afield, other highlights include a Fairy Bridge on the T.T. Course, vanishing fairy fishermen and the ghostly sounds of murder.

1. The ghost of the Brown Bobby
2. Easter Monday Sails
3. The fairy fishers
4. The Fairy Bridge, Glencrutchery
5. The White Lady
6. Fairies object to milling at night
7. The Onchan Death Coach
8. The betrothal cross
9. A vicar with the evil eye
10. The ghostly sounds of murder
11. The ghost of Molly Quirk's Glen
12. The woman with a candle
-    Ballig Well [private land]
13. The Hillberry Fairy Mound
14. The phynnodderee of Lanjaghyn

The ghost of the Brown Bobby

Public | Pavement beside a public road | SC 3752 7549 | 54.149421, -4.489259 | The Brown Bobby petrol station in Douglas stands on the site of the original Brown Bobby public house, at the corner of Peel Road and Circular Road.

In the nineteenth century a man was murdered here at the Brown Bobby inn, but the perpetrator was never brought to trial. The dead man's spirit continued to haunt this spot for a long time afterwards, making it sometimes very difficult to induce horses to pass along this stretch of the road.

This was also the limit to which the dead were carried from within Douglas, as it was here that they were transferred to a hearse and taken on to Braddan for internment.

JJK-PN 218 | KF-MR 13–14 | ML 2.3.19 | WWG-MS3 388

Easter Monday Sails

Private land – view only | Visible around Douglas Bay | Conister Rock is the island in Douglas Bay, on which the Tower of Refuge stands.

A popular Easter Monday activity used to be 'Easter Monday Sails,' when people would go out sailing in the bays or harbours around the Island. In Douglas it was said that bad luck would come to lovers who did not sail out to or around Conister Rock on Easter Monday.

LRM 32–35 | WWG-MS3 269–270

The fairy fishers

Public | Steep, rough and uneven ground, steps | SC 4047 7765 | 54.169813, -4.445375 | A small beach below King Edward Road, accessible via a path leading off from the northern end of Sea Cliff Road.

A man was close to here one morning before sunrise when he heard a noise from the shore below. He went down and found a great crowd of fishermen pulling their boats in. He joined in and helped them until the boats were all ashore. After they had thanked him profusely, the man asked how their fishing had gone, to which they said that their catch was poor but that of 'the worldly fleet' was very good. Just then, the day broke and the fishermen and their boats all disappeared, leaving the man alone on the shore.

YLM 3.4.158

The Fairy Bridge at Glencrutchery

Public | Paved road, not normally open to traffic | SC 3894 7795 | 54.171970, -4.468910 | Governor's Bridge, on the loop of road now only used for the T.T. Races. This stretch of road runs from Glencrutchery Road, opposite the top of Victoria Road, round to the roundabout at the base of Governor's Road.

This bridge used to be known as 'the Fairy Bridge.' This association with the fairies is likely to have meant that people would have avoided it at night whenever possible.

Perhaps related to this, the sound of a coach and horses can be heard passing over the bridge at night. This is the invisible appearance of a Death Coach travelling between the churches of Onchan and Braddan. It relates to a man named Finloe Oates who lived at Bibaloe but died at the feet of a woman named Barbara Moore after he had cursed her for rejecting him.

HIJ-JG 22 | N-IOME-26011895 | WL-DPG 58 | WWG-MS1 344–345

The White Lady

Public | Rough and uneven ground beside a pavement | SC 3859 7782 | 54.170667, -4.474249 | A remarkable white boulder on a mound jutting out into the road on First Avenue, a little over 100 metres from Glencrutchery Road.

This remarkable white stone is known as 'the White Lady.' It is not known how this stone got its name, but a story of a lhiannan-shee or a female spirit turned to stone might once have been known here. When the former field was developed into what is here today, the stone was left untouched as it was held that misfortune would follow if it was disturbed in any way.

AJAF-ASG 194 | NM-OSV 2 | YLM 2.4

Fairies object to milling at night

Private land – view only | Visible from a pavement beside a road | SC 3994 7790 | 54.171839, -4.453549 | The site of the mill is today occupied by the houses of 90 and 92 Royal Avenue, which runs south from the main road through Onchan village.

When the mill stood here there was once so much work to be done that the two brothers who ran it decided to work the mill at night. After one such night of work, the brothers checked the building before retiring to bed and upon opening the door to one room they saw a broom shoot from one side of the room to smack against the wall on the opposite side. They suspected a practical joke and checked the whole building with their dog but found no one. When they reported this mystery to their mother, she recognised it as the work of the fairies and so recommended they close the mill for three days in order to avoid further disturbances. They did this and when they re-started the mill the strange happenings did not recur.

WWG-MS2 232

The Onchan Death Coach

Public | Public road with a pavement | SC 3993 7823 | 54.174830, -4.453870 | The main road through Onchan village.

An invisible horse-drawn carriage can sometimes be heard at night riding through Onchan village. Another account of the coach has it visible, with headless horses, but utterly silent.

Some accounts explain this as the ghostly Death Coach of a man named Spurrier, who was murdered by the notorious poisoner, Dr Palmer, in the mid-nineteenth century for the £1,000 he carried in his pocket. However, older accounts attribute the coach to a man named Finloe Oates who fell down dead at a woman's feet after he had cursed her for rejecting him. An even older account explains the sound as being that of the fairies out on a hunt.

ANL-LR 44–45 | EK-CC 364 | WH-DIM 108–109 #50 | WWG-MS1 344–345 | WWG-MS2 85–86

The betrothal cross

Open during daylight hours | Some uneven ground | SC 4005 7814 | 54.174047, -4.452039 | Cross no. 85, housed inside the Onchan parish church of St Peter's on Church Road.

This cross used to be known as the Troth Cross (Betrothal Cross). Engaged couples would place their hands on the head of the cross and pledge their dedication to one another, thereby ensuring a long and happy life together blessed with many children.

WWG-MS3 281

A vicar with the evil eye

Private land – view only | Visible from pavement beside a road | SC 4006 7819 | 54.174538, -4.451949 | The Onchan vicarage is opposite the churchyard of St Peter's, on Church Road.

In 1672 a Kirk Braddan farmer became concerned about his sheep when he saw the Onchan vicar, Thomas Thwaites, watching very closely as he rounded them up. When a number of his sheep died shortly afterwards, the farmer was sure that this was because the vicar had put the evil eye on them. In response, the farmer piled the carcasses of the sheep here in the porch of the rectory. Unsurprisingly, the Church paid little attention to the farmer's justification for his actions and sentenced him to imprisonment in the Bishop's prison as well as sitting on the 'stool of correction' at Douglas market.

DC-MI 21

The ghostly sounds of murder

Public | Public road with limited pavement | SC 4049 7876 | 54.179757, -4.445663 | The hill north of the White Bridge, beyond the houses at the northern end of Onchan village.

Late at night you can sometimes hear the sounds of a person who was murdered here. Nothing is seen but the blows of the attacker, the groans of the victim and the galloping away of the murderer on a horse can still be heard.

WWG-MS2 86

The ghost of Molly Quirk's Glen

Public | Rough and uneven ground | SC 4031 7887 | 54.180641, -4.448519 | Molly Quirk's Glen is on the western side of the White Bridge, beyond the houses at the northern end of Onchan village.

Molly Quirk's Glen got its name from the woman whose ghost still haunts the area. During her lifetime she gained a reputation for having a large amount of savings, for which she was eventually murdered when walking through this glen. Her ghost is still sometimes to be seen walking here.

FLS B/42 | NM-OSV 11

The woman with a candle

Public | Rough and uneven ground, steps | SC 4031 7942 | 54.185652, -4.448688 | The public footpath between the farms of Ballakilmartin and Ballig. The footpath can be accessed via the Ballakilmartin track, which heads west on Whitebridge Hill, 500 metres up from the bridge itself. Alternatively, the path can be reached from the track marked with a footpath sign from Little Mill Road.

The ghostly figure of a woman in a nightgown has been seen at night walking along this path holding a lighted candle. She is said to be the spirit of a woman who hanged herself in the nearby glen.

FLS B/42

Ballig Well

Private | On the private land of Ballig farm.

Although just over a mile from the sea, the water in this well rises and falls with the tide. A cure for sore eyes can be obtained from taking its water if the well is visited at daybreak on Easter morning.

Up until at least the 1880s, offerings of food and milk for the fairies used to be left in the niches in the wall on the way down to the water.

MD-EVAF 19–20 | WWG-MS1 23

The Hillberry Fairy Mound

Public | Public road without a pavement | SC 3902 7989 | 54.189453, -4.468797 | A stretch of Ballacottier Road close to the Mountain Road. The mound itself is on private land roughly 400 metres east of Hillberry Corner.

The ancient burial mound not far from the road here is known to be a favourite spot for the fairies. Because of this, people used to avoid coming near here or along this road at night.

YLM 2.5

The phynnodderee of Lanjaghyn

Private land – view only | Visible from rough and uneven footpath | SC 3772 8125 | 54.201208, -4.489357 | A private farm less than a mile west of Creg ny Baa. A public footpath leads through the farm's land, accessible from either the Mountain Road south of Creg ny Baa or the road which comes up from Abbeylands.

The phynnodderee used to be well known to help the farmer here at Lanjaghan, such as by thrashing corn or bringing in the sheep ahead of a storm. It was when trying to bring in the sheep one time that the phynnodderee mistook a hare for a loaghtan lamb and had to chase it around Snaefell three times before he caught it.

Even in the 1870s this association was so well known that when tempers were raised the farmer here would be taunted for his relationship with the 'hairy one.'

However, the phynnodderee was eventually driven off when the farmer tried to thank him for his work with a gift of clothes. The phynnodderee took such offence at this that he said in anger that, 'Though this place is thine, the great Glen Rushen is not,' and he was never seen here again.

HIJ-JG 91 | HIJ-JG 120 | JR-MFS 2.286

Patrick

Patrick is undoubtedly one of the Island's key folklore parishes and it boasts some of the most famous of all Manx folklore sites. Slieau Whallian, Niarbyl and Lag ny Keeilley are well known but there is a surprising depth and richness in their tales of witches, mermaids, fairies and ghosts. The parish is also perhaps the best-known home of the phynnodderee, and it boasts one of the Island's most important and interesting holy wells in Chibbyr Pherick.

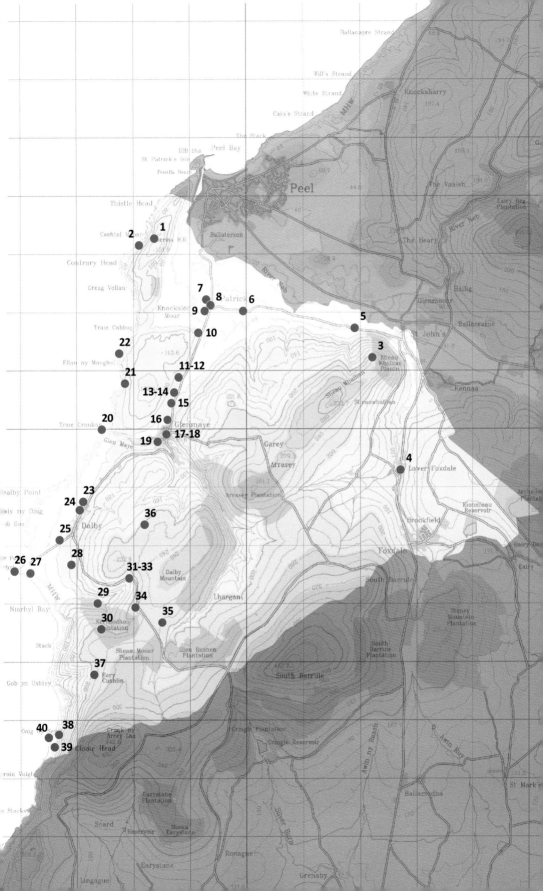

The Buggane of Peel Hill

PROW | Steep, rough and uneven ground | SC 2345 8326 | 54.214558, -4.709114 | The flat top of Peel Hill, close to Corrin's Tower.

In 1874 a young man was up close to Corrin's Tower when he saw a buggane coming up the slope from the shore. The young man reported that the buggane had 'the head, ears, and neck of a donkey, the body like that of a sheep, and that it was as big as a two-year-old heifer.' The creature came up to the top of the hill, followed the young man a short distance along the top and then returned back down the slope again. The story was related in the newspaper at the time, stating that many in the west firmly believed in the truth of the young man's story.

N-IOMT-07021874

Chibbyr Pherick

PROW | Steep, rough and uneven ground, footpath beside a cliff edge | SC 2317 8314 | 54.213372, -4.713223 | Chibbyr Pherick is a well on the seaward side of Peel Hill, below Corrin's Tower. From Peel, take any of the paths up the hill to the ridge close to the telephone mast, then take the path branching off right, continuing out through the stone wall and along the exposed broogh. The well is about 750 metres beyond the wall, on the landward side of the path, set back in a dip. The sea beast is the large rocky outcrop in the sea below the well, obvious with its ridged back, easiest seen from back along the path towards Peel.

Chibbyr Pherick originated with St Patrick, who was the first to bring Christianity to the Isle of Man. When he rode here on horseback over the sea from Ireland, Manannan saw him coming and covered the Island in mist, leaving St Patrick lost at sea with a sea beast closing in to devour him. The saint then heard a curlew calling, 'Come you, come you, come you!' to its young on the rocks close by, a goat crying 'Beware, beware, beware!' on the side of the hill through the mist, and the cockerel calling 'Come to us, come, come!' At this, St Patrick realised where he was and leapt up on his horse to land safely on the back of Peel Hill. Where his horse's silver-shod hoof first touched the land, this holy well sprang forth, which came to be known as Chibbyr Pherick. After this, St Patrick turned the sea beast to stone and banished Manannan from the Island. St Patrick then repaid the animals which had called to him; the curlew was rewarded with the honour of no one being able to find its nest, the goat with no one seeing the birth of its young, and the cockerel with crying at dawn at that same hour forever more.

Chibbyr Pherick used to be one of the Isle of Man's most famous holy wells and it was visited from far and wide for its cures. The offerings of these people taking its water led to the well becoming known as Chibbyr yn Argid (Silver Well). Another alternative name for Chibbyr Pherick has been Chibbyr Sheeant (Holy Well). As late as the 1870s offerings were being left here by some not for St Patrick but for the fairies. Alternative accounts have the water being good as a protection from the work of the fairies. The water here is also capable of granting wishes. If you drink it before sunrise on Old Laa Boaldyn (12 May) whilst making a wish, it will come to be granted before the next twelve months are through.

AJAF-ASG 197–198 | AWM-MN 131 | AWM-MN 144 | EK-CC 93 | HIJ-JG 172–173 | JJK-PN 362 | JT-HSA 2.41 | JT-HSA 2.121 | MD-EVAF 15 | SH-HSDV 102 | SM-MFT 20–24 | SM-MFT 228 | WC-WCF 48 | WH-MM1 146 | WWG-MS1 52-53 | YLM 3.4.137

Slieau Whallian

Public | Steep, rough and uneven ground | SC 2728 8121 | 54.197477, -4.649162 | Slieau Whallian is the prominent hill to the south over St John's. It can be accessed from the Slieau Whallian Road, which leaves the Patrick Road immediately after Delaney's Bridge in St John's.

Slieau Whallian is haunted by the spirit of a person who died here and their cries can still be heard on the hillside.

The most common story is that it was a witch who was executed by being rolled down the hill in a barrel inlaid with spikes. Before the plantation was established, there was a strip down the hill where the grass never grew, marking the path down which the witch rolled.

A different story has a man named Thomas Carran being falsely accused of witchcraft. Before his execution, he vowed that his innocence would be proven after his death if a thorn tree were to grow where the barrel first began down the slope. It was not long after the execution that a thorn tree indeed began to grow as predicted, thus proving Carran's innocence.

A variation on this has the falsely accused man proven innocent by his prediction of a thorn bush growing at his head where he was buried and a spring at his feet. To this was added his promise to return to haunt the neighbourhood with his cries to terrify and punish his false accusers. Another version has the man's spirit manifesting as a buggane after his execution and wailing on the hillside.

The apparent witch's crime is best known today as beginning with her prediction of a disaster for the Peel fishing fleet. However, the men ignored her warning and every ship of the fleet was lost, at which they turned on the woman and claimed that she had directly caused the disaster.

A less well-known alternative has her correctly accused of witchcraft because she was caught in the act of trying to kill someone. A father, jealous of his friend's son's success in qualifying as a vicar, called upon the witch to bring about the young man's death. She put pins in a roll of butter and set it before the fire, but as the butter melted the witch realised that the spell was not working to kill the rival son as someone was close by acting against the charm. A maid was then discovered hiding in the room and her cries brought the other servants, who laid hold of the witch. After a trial, the witch was taken to the top of Slieau Whallian and there given a last request before her execution. She asked for three unused pewter plates, which she put one at each side of her like wings and one behind her like a tail. She then began to rise up into the air, but unbeknownst to her one of the plates had been used before, so her flight failed and she fell back to earth. She was then rolled down the hill in the spiked barrel, but amazingly emerged unscathed. After this she was sent to Castletown and executed by burning.

A version of the story unrelated to witches has a woman named Molly McNana wrongly accused of murder and executed in the spiked barrel, but not before she promised to show her innocence by moaning on the hillside every night after her death.

AWM-FIOM 61 | AWM-FIOM 91 | AWM-MN 127 | BN-MS3 131–133 | EK-CC 357–377 | HIJ-JG 129–130 | GW-AIOM 159 | JT-HSA 2.167 | N-IOME-03091898 | RJK-SIOM 2 | SM-MFT 153–157 | WWG-MS1 456–457 | YLM 1.9.290

Hamilton rising from the grave

Public | Pavement beside a road | SC 2771 7928 | 54.180294, -4.641577 | Hamilton Bridge is at the lowest point of the main road through Lower Foxdale. Stone tablets with 'Hamilton' still legible on them are on either side of the bridge.

Before the man who built this bridge was born, the woman who was to become his mother was found to be dead. She was given a funeral and was buried, but that night some men went to dig her up to steal her rings. However, they were shocked when they opened the coffin and found her miraculously alive. She went on to have twins, one of whom was the Hamilton who built this bridge in 1769.

HIJ-JG 163

The Neb tarroo ushtey

Public | Pavement beside a road | SC 2698 8172 | 54.201952, -4.65418 | On the road between St John's and Patrick village, where the River Neb runs alongside the road for about 300 metres before branching off northwards when close to St John's.

A man was walking home late one night from Douglas towards Glen Maye, here where the road runs alongside the river, when he came across a giant bull standing in the road before him. Fearlessly, he hit it with his stick and the beast proved itself to be a tarroo ushtey as it went off to the river and disappeared.

SM-MFT 5–6

The tiny woman as a spool

Public | Narrow pavement beside a road | SC 2503 8201 | 54.203892, -4.684132 | The Parson's Bridge is believed to be that on the road between Patrick village and St John's, by Ballamoar and Ballacosnahan. The bridge is identifiable by the stone wall that runs beside the road just before the tight corner.

A man was walking home late one night from Douglas towards Glen Maye, and here at the Parson's Bridge he came across 'a little thing just like a spinning wheel' with 'a little, little body sitting where the spool is.' The man hit the little person hard with his stick and the person replied, 'Ny jean shen arragh!' ('Don't do that again!'). The man walked on regardless and did not meet the figure again.

Such a figure travelling while sitting on a spool has been identified as Ben Veg Carraghan, a ghostly figure better known at Carraghan in Braddan.

SM-MFT 5–6 | WWG-MS1 218

Trolly Pot

Private | A series of deep pools in a small gorge on private land in the river of Barnell Glen.

The name of these pools in this small gorge, 'Trolly Pot,' is thought to possibly derive from the Norse word 'pot,' for a rock hole in a river wherein water swirls, and 'troll.' No specific stories of trolls are known here but presumably they were thought to live in the gloom of the dark narrow cleft, which one writer has spoken of as suggesting 'lurking demons and other malign influences.'

WWG-MS1 459–460 | WWG-MS3 233–234

The dark cloud accompanying a ghost

Public | Pavement beside a road| SC 2439 8220 | 54.205342, -4.694086 | The gates to Knockaloe are at Patrick village, on the main road south from Peel towards Glen Maye.

On a clear moonlit night in the winter of 1902 a preacher was going towards Peel from Patrick chapel. However, shortly after setting off, the night suddenly grew dark around him. He then saw the ghostly figure of a woman who had died many years before walking beside him, keeping with him step for step as it grew increasingly dark around them. However, when they came to the Knockaloe gates and the cottage where the woman used to live, the man passed out of the darkness into the clear moonlight and the woman's ghost disappeared. The preacher met a man a little further on and confirmed that no cloud had been seen in the sky that could have accounted for the darkness the preacher had experienced.

YLM 4.159–160

Kirk Patrick

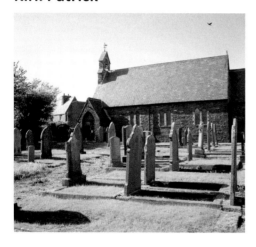

Public, open during daylight hours | Some uneven ground | SC 2443 8212 | 54.204635, -4.693342 | Kirk Patrick is the church in the centre of Patrick village, with its main entrance on the St John's Road.

The three lights

One moonlit night a woman in Patrick village looked out of her window and saw three lights like stars shoot up in succession from the churchyard. The next morning, she heard of the death of a young child in a house nearby. When he was buried shortly afterwards it was in the exact spot from which the lights had shot up.

WWG-MS1 483

Phantom funerals

Phantom funerals have been experienced a number of times in the road outside Kirk Patrick. Different people have been walking along in the empty road when they suddenly began to be jostled and shoved. It was as if they were in a crowd of people, even though no one could be seen.

N-IOME-01101898

Paul Creer and the 'scooyrit' bird

Private land – view only | Visible from pavement beside a road | SC 2435 8203 | 54.203838, -4.694523 | The former Methodist chapel is now a private residence at the southern end of Patrick village.

A man worse for drink was walking home from Peel towards Glen Maye and when he got to the Raggatt a little bird began to cry out his name, 'Paul Creer, Paul Creer! Scooyrit, scooyrit!' ('Drunk, drunk!'). The bird followed him crying out its message all the way here to Patrick, when Creer finally lost his temper, picked up a stone and threw it at the bird. However, the stone missed the bird entirely and smashed through the chapel window, interrupting a prayer meeting. The congregation was aghast at this and initially thought that it could be the devil himself, but when they came out to see who was responsible, they saw Creer continuing on his way, with the bird fluttering along beside him still calling out 'Scooyrit, scooyrit!' all the while.

VAMD 'Scoorit' | WWG-MS3 306–307

The Creggans

Private land – view only | Visible from a pavement beside a road | SC 2421 8164 | 54.200270, -4.696432 | The Creggans is the hill south of Patrick village. The main road runs over the shoulder of the Creggans after passing the St John's Road. Gob ny Creg is over the road at the eastern end of the hill.

The buggane of Gob ny Creg

A buggane used to be known to live here at Gob ny Creg. No specific stories are passed down to us of the buggane's activities, but this area would presumably have been avoided at night wherever possible.

WWG-MS1 493

The preacher and the cabbyl ushtey

After leading a prayer meeting in Peel, a Wesleyan local preacher retrieved his old white mare from the dark stall and set off towards his home on the far side of Glen Maye. However, at the Creggans the horse began to be uncharacteristically restless, growing more wild until it plunged through the bushes towards the sea. After failing to restrain the animal, the preacher feared for his life and called out, 'Lord, help me!' At this, the mare violently started and the preacher fell off safely onto the grass, just before the horse plunged over the rocks and down towards the sea below. Much disturbed by the experience, the preacher walked home, only to find his horse safely in the stable, where it had been all along as his groom had forgotten to take it to town. The preacher then saw that the horse he had ridden had really been the devil, out to be rid of him and his preaching. Later commentators, however, have identified it as a cabbyl ushtey.

MT 17-20 | WWG-MS1 492

Gordon House

Private land – view only | Visible from a pavement beside a road | SC 2387 8088 | 54.193320, -4.701202 | Gordon House stands over the western side of the main road between Patrick and Gordon.

Around 350 years ago the heir of the farm, Henry Radcliffe, married an Irish woman while on a running trade expedition to Ireland and returned with her here to Gordon House. However, shortly after, in 1677, he died at sea and left his wife at the mercy of his family. Because of their callous hatred of her Catholicism, they threw her out to live in a one-room hut towards the sea, known as Yn Thie Paabish (The Papist House). However, as she set off there that first time, she took to her knees in the field overlooking Gordon House and put up a prayer that the house would never be passed to an heir and that it would be divided against itself.

Both prophesies came true by the start of the twentieth century, at which point nobody had inherited the house, and a lawsuit within the family had the house divided between the two parts of the family, with a wall being constructed up the middle of the house, from the front door to the back.

FLS T/5D | N-IOME-14101953 | YLM 4.154–155

Lag Evil

Private land – view only | Visible from a pavement beside a road | SC 2388 8088 | 54.193303, -4.701134 | The remarkable dip in the private hillside behind Ballacallin, Gordon, visible from the Patrick to Glen Maye road.

One suggestion of where the name, Lag Evil, comes from is that it derives from Aoibheal, the queen of the fairies in Munster, Ireland. This association with the fairies is supported by the fact that Lag Evil features in a traditional Manx song which has the fairies rest here when on a trip around the Island. After setting off from Peel and visiting Ramsey, Douglas, Castletown, Port St Mary and Port Erin, the band of fairies stopped here to enjoy a haggis cooked for them by the woman in Gordon.

Perhaps linked to this Lag Evil's reputation as being a place where 'queer things' happen, such as lights being seen and then disappearing, or strange sounds being heard.

FLS CE/C | WWG-MS1 489–491 | WWG-MS3 214

The phynnodderee of Gordon

Private land – view only | Visible from a pavement beside a road | SC 2379 8060 | 54.190814, -4.702301 | The private farm of Gordon is to the east of the road between Peel and Glen Maye, up the hill a short distance north of Gordon village.

Gordon is perhaps the best known of all the places where the phynnodderee worked, and one account notes that he lived in the wood by the farmhouse when he was working here. The reclusive hairy giant of a creature would come to the farm at night to cut, grind, flail and thresh the corn. On one occasion he brought in the stooks at the harvest in one night just before the rain came. He was not the brightest of workers though, as was shown when he gathered in a hare after chasing it around Slieau Whallian three times, having mistaken it for a loaghtan lamb and put it with the rest of the flock.

The phynnodderee did not ask for payment of any kind and so Radcliffe, the farmer here, thought he would show his thanks by having some clothes made for him. But when the phynnodderee found the breeches, jacket, waistcoat and cap, he said:

> 'Coat for the back is sickness for the back!
> Vest for the middle is bad for the middle!
> Breeches for the breech is a curse for the breech!
> Cap for the head is injurious for the head!
> If thou own big Gordon farm, boy –
> If thine this little glen east, and thine this little glen west,
> Not thine the merry Glen of Rushen yet, boy!'

With this the phynnodderee flung away the gifts and went off to live up in Glen Rushen instead.

HIJ-JG 91 | SM-MFT 52–57 | WWG-MS1 490–491

Gef at Gordon

Private land – view only | Visible from a road | SC 2375 8053 | 54.190174, -4.702909 | The field behind the former chapel, the only building on the seaward side of the road at Gordon, the short run of terraced houses north of Glen Maye.

Gef, the Dalby Spook, better known internationally as 'the talking mongoose,' was seen by only a few people outside of the family at Doarlish Cashen. One of these people, a boy named Will Cubbon, saw Gef in this field. The boy reported that Gef was little, with 'a flat face, yellow and a big bushy tail at him,' and he dashed away out of sight much quicker than a rabbit would.

CJ-GTM 227

The horse with a man's face

Public | A pavement beside a road | SC 2371 8045 | 54.189437, -4.703367 | Gordon is the area around the short run of terraced houses on the east side of the Peel road just north of Glen Maye.

In 1922 a woman was cycling from Peel to Dalby before dark. At the cottages here at Gordon, something made her look behind her and she saw in the distance a pale grey horse with a man's head and face. She began to pedal hard up the hill to get away from it but it was going faster and gaining on her. At the top of the hill, on the edge of Glen Maye, she suddenly felt that the thing was gone and she turned around to see that it was no longer there. The thing was silent throughout, making no sound with its hooves even as it chased her.

Separately, a ghost was known to haunt Gordon in the mid-nineteenth century. However, no details of the ghost were recorded as the informant was a teetotaller who dismissed the sightings as merely the result of drunkenness.

FP-P2 127 | N-PCG-02021901 | WWG-MS2 250

Raby Keeill

Private | The keeill and associated sites are on the private land of Raby, a farm sat back on the seaward side of the Peel road just north of Glen Maye.

The screeching stones

In the nineteenth century the farmer at Raby used two horses to drag away some stones from the keeill site so that he could use them in a wall that he was building. However, when the stones were in their new location, they could get no rest at Raby for all the mysterious crying and screeching which was to be heard around the farm. Other things also then began to go wrong around the farm, including the death of cattle. So the farmer decided to move the stones back, but he could not shift them as they were now too heavy for any of his horses to move. He sought the advice of a southside woman and she told him to use seven young horses that had never been harnessed before. This he did and they easily dragged the stones back to the keeill site. The strange goings on around the farm stopped immediately.

N-IOME-24091898

The Cursing Stone

Close to the keeill is a raised mound on the top of which is a large round stone with a circular hollow in the centre. This is believed to be a cursing stone. When someone wanted to wish ill on a person, they would twist their thumb around anticlockwise in the hollow and speak a 'prayer of cursing' on the person.

Also close to the keeill is a well once believed to have curative properties.

VAMD 'Cursing stone' | JMM 4.59.123 | MNHL MS01086c | WWG-MS1 488

The cabbyl ushtey of Raby

Public | A pavement beside a road | SC 2368 8016 | 54.186778, -4.703766 | The hill just north of Glen Maye, leading up from Raby to the village, on the main road from Peel.

A man was walking home alone late one night towards Glen Maye when he saw a horse standing amongst the trees here at the bottom of the hill up to Glen Maye. Thinking he was in luck, the man leapt on its back and they set off at a gallop. However, as they passed under low branches, the man leant forward and saw that the horse had human ears, which identified it as a cabbyl ushtey. Realising that he was in great danger, the man leapt off, just as the horse veered off the road and jumped the hedge to make for the river. The man would surely have drowned if he had not jumped off when he did.

It is perhaps the same cabbyl ushtey which another man met at the gates of Raby, also at the bottom of the hill here. The beautiful grey horse was already bridled and saddled, so he assumed his sweetheart had left it there for him and he jumped on. However, the horse immediately bolted off the road, over hedges and ditches as it raced down the hill towards the glen. Realising the danger he was in, the man leapt from the horse's back and sustained terrible injuries from the fall. Although he was never to walk again, he had avoided certain death, as the creature then leapt over the sheer cliff edge into the river in the glen below.

EK-CC 352–353 | WWG-MS1 484

The ghostly hands

Private land – view only | Visible from a pavement beside a road | SC 2365 7990 | 54.184475, -4.703979 | The small cottage at the corner of Glen Rushen Road, at the top of the hill in Glen Maye village.

A room in this cottage is haunted by a spirit of disembodied hands floating around one of the rooms. This is the apparition of a labourer who struck his head on a stone one day at work and later, in a fit of madness, strangled his wife as she was sitting on the sofa. This was a story well known in the 1920s, at which point the ghostly hands were seen by people who peered in through the window of the cottage.

ML 2.3.16

The fairies kidnap a man

Private land – view only | Visible from pavement beside a road | SC 2358 7982 | 54.183772, -4.704989 | Glen Maye is south of Peel, between Patrick and Dalby. Perhaps the most likely location for this story is the terrace on the main road just up from the Shore Road car park.

Two men from Glen Maye once arranged to go together to the fishing in Peel. One was to whistle and knock at the other's door as he passed in the morning. Early the next day, the whistle and knock was heard but the man went to his door and found no one there. Assuming that his friend had gone on already, the man swiftly went on up the road to catch up with him. However, not long after this there was another whistle and knock at the door and the man's wife went to find the friend there waiting at the door. He knew nothing of the earlier calling and so he ran on up the road to look for his friend, but he was not to be found, then or after.

It later became known that the man had been taken by the fairies, as his cries were to be heard in the lower part of Glen Maye when the boats were putting out to Peel.

WWG-MS3 364–365

Spooyt Vooar, Glen Maye

Public | Steep, rough and uneven ground, steps | SC 2347 7977 | 54.18326, -4.706782 | Spooyt Vooar is the waterfall at the top of the public glen of Glen Maye, a short distance down the footpath from the car park at the top of Shore Road.

The buggane of Glen Maye

There was a woman living close to Glen Maye who was so scandalously lazy that the buggane came and snatched her up from her house just as she was beginning to bake one night. Carrying her on his shoulder, the buggane rushed to Glen Maye where he swung her up by her apron ready to toss her into Spooyt Vooar. However, the woman cleverly cut the apron strings and fell to safety as the buggane was caught off-balance and fell into Spooyt Vooar himself. As he was falling, he roared loudly:

'Rumbyl, rumbyl, sambyl, I thought I had a lazy dirt,
And I have but the edge of her skirt.'

That was the last that was ever seen of the buggane.

An earlier version of this tale has the 'Buggane y Spoot' ('Buggane of the Waterfall') trick the woman out of her home by calling that the cattle had got into the haggart. It was when she unlocked the door and rushed out that he grabbed her and set off for the waterfall. The conclusion of this version reports that the buggane's blood was found on the rocks around the waterfall in the morning, showing where he had hit them during his fall.

N-PCG-06041901 | SM-MFT 7–12 | WWG-MS1 487

The headless black calf

A girl was once out on the road by the glen one dark evening when she saw a headless black calf with a chain hanging about it. The thing leapt across the lane and then down into the deep place below the waterfall, with the chain rattling as it went. The fright was such that the girl never did much good ever again. This headless calf appearance is the usual form that the buggane that lives here takes.

ML 2.3.16 | WWG-MS1 487 | WWG-MS2 215

Glen Maye shore

Public | Steep, rough and uneven ground | SC 2251 7997 | 54.184744, -4.721474 | Glen Maye shore lies at the bottom of Glen Maye. It is accessible on foot, along the public footpath down the glen beyond the end of Shore Road.

The fairy battle

The fairies who live at the top of Glen Rushen used to go out fishing from Glen Maye shore, using the boats which they stored in the caves here. On one occasion a man happened to be on the brooghs over the shore as the fairies arrived and found a group of Irish fairies landing in their boats. The two groups then set to battle, wounding and killing one another with fists and stones. At last, another group of Manx fairies rode down onto the beach lead by a figure on a white horse. These riders drove the Irish back with sticks until they were forced back into their boats and away. However, in the process, the rider on the white horse fell off into the sea, crying out, 'Yee mie!' (Good God!) and drowned. The fairy's words had been what the man on the brooghs had been wanting to say but had found himself unable to do so. It was later realised that the fairy who drowned was a person who had been taken by the fairies earlier when he had been drowning at sea. After this battle at Glen Maye shore, he was never seen again.

WWG-MS3 363–364

The glashtin of Glen Maye

A man came across a glashtin in Glen Maye but he mistook it for a normal horse and so he climbed up onto its back. Immediately the glashtin dashed down the glen until it reached the shore and plunged into the sea with the doomed man still upon its back and unable to escape. The man's body was never seen again but his ghost still haunts the glen below the waterfall.

This was not the only time the glashtin was observed, as others saw it standing placidly at the roadside hoping for someone foolish enough to climb up on its back. It was often heard in the middle of the night crashing into the water below Spooyt Vooar from the cliffs above.

EK-CC 352 | HIJ-JG 152

The giense in Ooig Vooar

Inaccessible | Ooig Vooar is a cave on Raby shore, below the Raad ny Foillan. It is not safely accessible.

A fishing boat was passing by Raby shore one fine evening when they heard beautiful fiddling and singing coming from inside Ooig Vooar. The crew stopped and came in close to listen until eventually voices from within called for the men to join them. The fishermen did not dare go in but one called for his favourite tune, 'The Wind that Shakes the Barley,' which was then played by those inside the cave.

WWG-MS1 446

The preacher and the cabbyl ushtey

Private – view only | Visible from steep, rough and uneven ground, steps, a committed walk | SC 2282 8129 | 54.196666, -4.717593 | The brough north of the small footbridge along the Raad ny Foillan, between Knockaloe and Glen Maye, below Ballacallin.

A Wesleyan preacher got on what he thought was his mare after a prayer meeting in Peel. However, at the Creggans the horse crashed through the hedge and raced towards the brooghs. Just by the cliffs here the preacher cried out, 'Lord, help me!' At this, he was thrown off to safety just before the creature leaped off the broogh and into the sea. The preacher understood the horse to be the devil in disguise, but others took it to be a cabbyl ushtey.

MT 17–21 | WWG-MS1 492

Old Ballelby house

Private land – view only | Visible from a layby on the public road| SC 2217 7873 | 54.173432, -4.726004 | Ballelby is the first farm on the seaward side of the main road north of the church at Dalby. The site of the former farmhouse is the square of trees visible below the small layby, 100 metres north of today's farm.

The site of the former Ballelby farmhouse has a reputation for being 'a fairy place' and somewhere to stay clear of. The sound of humming can sometimes be heard here, like from the big wheel used in making fishing nets, as used to be done here when the old house was still standing.

In the early part of the twentieth century the space was an orchard and, although the apples were collected here during the day, the children were sternly forbidden from coming here in the dark. Their father had experienced something strange here but he never told anyone about it. In the 1970s farm workers would never go by here after dark, instead returning to the farmhouse through the fields rather than pass along the track running along the edge of these trees.

FLS K/115 | WWG-MS1 473–474

Chibbyr ny Creg

Private | Chibbyr ny Creg is a well formed from a rock basin on private land, close the shore below Ballelby, north of Glen Maye.

People used to come here to Chibbyr ny Creg as its water has curative properties. They would wash their eyes in its water seeking to improve or preserve their sight.

WWG-MS1 29–30

Caillagh y Drommag

Private land – view only | Visible from a public road | SC 22109 78609 | 54.172352, -4.726850 | Ballelby Glen is on the south side of Ballelby, the first farm on the seaward side of the main road north of Dalby village. The area of the private glen associated with the Caillagh is likely to be above the main road.

The famous 'psychical researcher,' Nandor Fodor, visited the Isle of Man in 1937 to seek out Gef, the Dalby Spook. His diary notes that Ballalby Glen was the home of Caillagh y Drommag. Nothing further was noted of this figure, other than that she was a misshapen, shrunken old woman. However, in being a caillagh, it is likely she was a witch-like figure who would pose a threat to anyone who came across her in the lonely hills.

CJ-GTM 221

The Child's Grave

Private | On private land in Ballelby Glen, north of Dalby village.

This small rectangle of stone slabs protruding up from the ground is known as a child's grave. The children of the neighbourhood used to be forbidden to touch these stones or any of the others nearby. It is not recorded what, if anything, was expected to happen if they disobeyed this decree.

FLS K/115

The Arkan Sonney of Niarbyl

Public | Public road | SC 2177 7809 | 54.1675775, -4.7317515 | Bayr Corrag is a former track which came off the road between Dalby village and Niarbyl. It used to leave the road at a point opposite the first purpose-built passing point closest to Dalby. It is marked today only by the hedge and line of trees heading away behind on the north-west side of the road.

It was near the junction of Bayr Corrag in the 1870s that a young girl saw an Arkan Sonney, a pig that brings great luck to anyone who sees it. However, the girl only realised what it really was when she called her uncle back to try and help her catch the beautiful little white pig, but by the time he arrived it had disappeared.

WWG-MS1 444

Niarbyl

Public | Rough and uneven ground, tidal | SC 2096 7755 | 54.162458, -4.743772 | Niarbyl is on the coast below Dalby. From the village, a road is signposted to Niarbyl. Park at the cafe and walk down to the shore. Although 'Niarbyl' is today commonly used to refer to the whole shore here, it more correctly applies only to the tail of rock stretching out into the sea.

The Dalby Boatman

On summer evenings long ago an old man with long white hair would row until close to Niarbyl. Here he would lean on his oars and sing a song, before going off again into the distance and out of sight. The people of Dalby would come and listen to the man but he was too far out for them to hear his words. All they could hear was the tune, which they learnt and passed down through the generations to us today. Nothing more was found out about this mysterious man, where he came from or where he went to.

A later account from the same original source for the story has the boatman coming from the west, perhaps as a visitor from Tír na nÓg, the idyllic land of eternal youth known from Irish folklore.

MD-AG | MJ 1.51 | WWG-MS1 435

The dooinney marrey and the crab

A man named Juan was fishing for crabs among the rocks here when a dooinney marrey came up out of the sea to ask for a crab. Juan asked what he would receive in exchange and the dooinney marrey promised to tell his fortune. Juan threw him a crab and the dooinney marrey called out before diving back into the sea, 'Choud as vees oo bio er y thalloo, cha bee oo dy bragh baiht er y cheayn.' ('As long as you live on the land, you will never be drowned at sea.')

Another version of this tale has it as a ben varrey (a mermaid), and the man's name as Joe Clinton.

SM-MFT 221 | VAMD 'Partan' | WC-WCF 31 | YLM 4.155

Friends with a mermaid

An old man in the 1890s reported that he used to meet with a mermaid near here. She would come to visit him and 'sang to him most beautiful.' However, she later took to another man and married him instead.

YLM 1.9.290

The limping man's spirit

A man was fishing here one day at the Niarbyl when some neighbours thought they saw him limping badly into his house and so they called in to ask how he was. They were surprised to find only his niece there, and shocked when they together came back outside to see the man down at Niarbyl fishing. It was another two hours before the old man returned home, at which point he was limping more than usual. He explained that he had slipped, hurt his leg and had considered returning home, but had instead decided to stay on to fish some more. It can be assumed that it was at that moment when he thought of returning home that the neighbours had seen his spirit limping into his house.

ML 2.3.19

Ooig ny Meill

Public | Slippery and uneven ground, tidal | SC 2124 7753 | 54.162331, -4.739581 | Ooig ny Meill is a cave just south of Niarbyl, around the headland south of the small fisherman's hut. Accessible only at low tide, this large cave is distinctive for having three entrances, facing west, north and south.

One night in the 1850s or 60s a young man was on the shore by here when he heard music and saw a glimmering light from within Ooig ny Meill. Bravely he went into the cave but he found no one there at all. However, by the light on the moon he saw tiny footprints in the white sand. Looking closer, he saw that they were from tiny clogs the size of his thumb, which came in from the western entrance and went around the large rock in the middle of the cave.

It was on this rock that the Shenn Ven Ooig ny Meill (Old Woman of Meill Cave) would be found looking out westwards. No further details of this figure or what she did are known.

SM-MFT 97–100 | MJ 5.282

Ballacooil

Private land – view only | Visible from public road without a pavement | SC 2198 7765 | 54.163675, -4.728325 | A private house south of Dalby, 300 metres down the first seaward road off the main road after leaving the village.

The Old Christmas

A woman named Peggy Shimmin used to live here at Ballacooil. She knew that the Old Christmas (5 January) was the true Christmas and that no work should be done until it was past. However, one year she had some spinning to be done and so she pretended to herself that it was only a superstition. After her husband had gone to bed she called on Margad, her young maid, to join her at the work. Although Margad was terribly afraid, she obeyed Peggy and they set to spinning at their wheels on the kitchen floor. Just before midnight the flax which Peggy was drawing from the distaff grew blacker and blacker. Peggy was horrified that this was a sign and so she ordered the work to stop and the wheels were put away. Peggy retired to bed very frightened but Margad went outside to see if the stories of Old Christmas were true. She was amazed to see the myrrh plant bloom, the bullocks go down on their knees, and the bees come out to fly about their hive. All of this showed beyond doubt that the Old Christmas was indeed the true Christmas.

SM-MFT 159–162

The turning stone of Ballacooil

A large block of stone with a smaller one facing it used to stand here at the entrance to Ballacooil. This larger stone was said to turn around three times when it heard the cock crow.

WWG-MS1 472–473

The scaa olk of the Kellya

Public | Steep, rough and uneven ground | SC 2244 7700 | 54.158033, -4.720791 | The Kellya is a tholtan just off the public footpath in Kerrowdhoo plantation. From the bottom of the plantation, follow the path past the Dalby Community Woodland Scheme site, cross the stream and continue up the path a short distance to where the remains of the Kellya are visible on the left. Alternatively, the site can be reached from the top of the plantation, from along the track to Fary Cushlin.

In the second half of the nineteenth century this house was terrorised by a poltergeist. There was flying crockery, furniture shifting around on its own and unaccountable noises. The man who lived in the house, Tom Kellya, tried to halt it by means of iron or steel crosses over the door and windows, but that only made matters worse when the spirit became further infuriated as it could not get out and so raced around smashing things until daybreak. Kellya then went to consult a woman well known for her knowledge of such things and she identified the problem as a scaa olk, the malevolent spirit of a living person, in this case haunting the place in an attempt to gain possession of his bag or chest of money. At her suggestion, when the scaa olk came again the following night as he lay in bed, Tom thrust out a sharp piece of steel behind him three times without turning his head. All went quiet, and in the morning it was discovered that a man living nearby had died in the night. No more disturbances were experienced here at the Kellya after that.

WWG-MS1 465–468

The curative well of Kerrowdhoo

Public | Steep, rough and uneven ground, effectively inaccessible | SC 2251 7655 | 54.154042, -4.719566 | A well deep in the Kerrowdhoo plantation, which is extremely difficult to reach due to the gorse and other vegetation. From the track to Eary Cushlin, enter the plantation via the gate closer to the Eary Cushlin end and head down the track. After about 250 metres, turn left along the remains of an old hedge. The well is today merely a patch of damp on the downhill side of this hedge, just over 100 metres on, at the point where it meets another former hedge coming down from uphill.

People used to come from great distances to obtain water from this well as it had the power to cure various ailments, including bad eyes.

WWG-MS1 81–82

The Fairy Glen

Private land – view only | Visible from a public road without a pavement | SC 2297 7743 | 54.162031, -4.712937 | The Fairy Glen is below Droghad Ruy, the bridge the road passes over at the sharp narrow bend of the road on the climb up from Dalby towards the turning for Eary Cushlin.

This northern branch of the Lag Mooar is known as the Fairy Glen. No specific tales relating to this glen are known but the name suggests that it used to be known as a place for the fairies.

WWG-MS1 464 | WWG-MS2 221

The running man falling apart

Public | A public road with limited narrow pavement | SC 2289 7748 | 54.162494, -4.714304 | The Droghad Ruy is the small bridge on the steep narrow road from Dalby up towards the turning for Eary Cushlin. It is discernible by the stone wall that borders the road on both sides where the road narrows to its thinnest and turns sharply over it.

In the 1910s a woman was gathering blackberries here one afternoon when a mist suddenly came down over the whole area. She looked up and saw what appeared to be a man running down the ravine towards the road but he 'looked as if he was coming loose, all falling to pieces.' She took fright and ran some distance away to the nearest house.

WWG-MS1 461–462

The souls of the damned

Private land – view only | Visible from a public road without a pavement | SC 2304 7736 | 54.161412, -4.711925 | Although the house is no longer here, the site of the Narruy is discernible from its track. On the road from Dalby to the turning for Eary Cushlin, the site is uphill from the thin and tight bend at Droghad Ruy and the gate on the uphill side. The old track to the Narruy can be made out vaguely in the overgrown strip of rough land between two streams on the hillside above the road. The house formerly stood at the top of this track, roughly 100 metres above the main road.

A man was walking up the hill from Dalby to his home in Glen Rushen one evening when he felt an invisible something close to him pushing him into the hedge. The man turned in here to the Narruy to take refuge in the house, hoping that the thing would have gone away when he emerged. However, two hours later, when he returned to the road, the force was still there and, beyond the Mountain Gate, close to the Sound Road, he began to make out figures and faces in the mist. One he recognised as a recently deceased man who had misspent his life, but the traveller was even more frightened by those he did not recognise, as he saw that they 'had come from a no good place.' Seeing the danger he was in, the man stopped, drew a circle on the road with his knife and stepped inside. He then watched as the figures outside went around him but could not come into the circle. The man remained like this until the morning, when the sun came up and he was able to continue on to his destination at the top of Glen Rushen.

WWG-MS1 462–463

The Death Coach of the Dalby Road

Public | Public road without a pavement | SC 2310 7693 | 54.157574, -4.710766 | The Mountain Pillars used to stand on the main road between Dalby and the Round Table, about 200 metres north-west of the turning to Eary Cushlin. The pillars were the divide between farmland and moorland, standing by the gated track on the upland side of the road.

One summer night two ladies were sat in the grass beside the road here when they saw a Death Coach go by. It was a black spectral funeral coach with waving plumes and a procession of many ghostly figures fading into the darkness behind.

This is also the area of the road where the man protected himself from the souls of the damned after resting briefly further down the hill at the Narruy.

WWG-MS1 344 | WWG-MS1 462–463

The phynnodderee's wife's rock

Private land – view only | Visible from a rough and uneven footpath | SC 2359 7667 | 54.155415, -4.703133 | Cleigh Feeiney is a tholtan beside the river in Glen Rushen, with a large rock perched on a hedge close by on the other side of the river. The tholtan and the rock are on private land but they can be seen from the Bayr ny Skeddan, which leaves the main road 200 metres south-east of the turning for Eary Cushlin. The rock can be seen when looking back from about halfway to the plantation, and the tholtan is through the trees on the other side of the river.

When the phynnodderee left Gordon after taking offence at the offer of clothes, he came to live in Glen Rushen. He did work for Juan Mooar Cleary, who lived here at Cleigh Feeiney, cutting the meadow, cutting turf and seeing to the sheep.

One winter night there was a great snowstorm and the phynnodderee came to Juan to tell him that he had already got in the sheep, including one young loaghtan that he had to chase around South Barrule twice before he could catch it. In the morning Juan discovered a hare amongst the sheep, which the phynnodderee had obviously foolishly mistaken for a loaghtan.

Another time the phynnodderee and his wife fell to arguing when they were up on the top of South Barrule making a big pot of porridge. Tempers rose until she eventually took flight. When she got as far as here by Cleigh Feeiney, the phynnodderee threw an enormous boulder at her from up on South Barrule and it hit her on the heel. The rock is still here, with her blood staining it still. Also here are the many smaller rocks nearby which the phynnodderee threw at his wife as she stooped to put a rag on her heel. After this, the phynnodderee's wife ran off down the Lag and took two leaps across the sea to Ireland, where she was safe from her husband at last.

SM-MFT 55–57 | HIJ-JG 93

The home of the Dalby Spook

Public | Steep, rough and uneven ground, steps, a committed walk | SC 2326 7836 | 54.170480, -4.709038 | Although the house no longer stands, the site of Doarlish Cashen is easiest reached from the car park at the turning for Eary Cushlin. From the car park, walk down the main road towards Dalby for about 200 metres. Turn off right onto the Sound Road, the loose stone track which runs up and down hill, before eventually going over a stile and turning uphill along an old dirt track. At the top, follow the footpath sign left through a gate and down the narrow, rutted track. When the track opens up into a rough field to your left, the site of Doarlish Cashen is to the right of the path before you, where the wall leaves the path and dissolves into the field. The modern fence passes through the site of the house.

Known in the Isle of Man as 'The Dalby Spook,' the 'earthbound spirit' that once was resident at Doarlish Cashen is better known all over the world as Gef the Talking Mongoose. This strange creature talked to the Irving family who lived here from behind the walls for a period of years, starting in 1931 before petering out by the 1940s. As well as talking, Gef would sing, swear, make threats, sometimes spit or throw things at the family as well as showing itself to have a clairvoyant knowledge of things in places a considerable distance from this lonely hillside. A number of people saw the animal fleetingly, and many more heard it, with some even having conversations with Gef. No conclusive explanation of this strange phenomenon was ever reached, but some link it to strange occurrences in the house before and after the years of Gef's appearances and seemingly independent of him.

CJ-GTM

The invisible push

Private land | A private field by the top of Ballelby Glen. The field is visible on the north side of the glen, from the site of Doarlish Cashen. The old hedge has been completely removed, but it was roughly in the middle of today's large field.

A funerary urn with black ashes inside was once dug up in this field and reburied nearby in the hedge. A long while afterwards, a man was hunting with his dog here when he thought he saw a rabbit bolt into the hedge. The man began pulling away the stones and soil to get to it but he felt himself suddenly pushed back by an invisible force. He tried a second time but he felt the push again, whereupon he took fright and ran home. A white stone was placed to mark the location in the hedge after that but it has now been removed entirely, along with the rest of the hedge.

WWG-MS1 455

Eary Cushlin

Private land – view only | Visible from a rough and uneven track | SC 2237 7577 | 54.146920, -4.721160 | Eary Cushlin is a remote house overlooking the coast north of Cronk ny Arrey Laa. It is accessed via a signposted track heading south-west from the level part of the main road between Dalby and the Round Table.

When Eary Cushlin lay unoccupied in the 1930s it was held to be haunted and people would not go near the building after dark. This view was shared by Gef, the Dalby Spook, who reported that the place was haunted and referred to it as 'the Land of Mist.' At another time Gef also used this curious phrase to speak of where he was to go after death.

CJ-GTM 221–223

Chibbyr Vashtee

Public ram | Steep, rough and uneven ground, a committed walk | SC 2176 7475 | 54.137573, -4.729956 | Chibbyr Vashtee is a well beside the path close to Lag ny Keeilley. From the car park close to Eary Cushlin, take the track past the house and continue along the path heading south-west along the brough for 1.2 miles. The chibbyr is 150 metres before Lag ny Keeilley on the landside of the track. It is sometimes overgrown and difficult to spot.

When the ancient Norse Kings of the Isle of Man became too old to rule, they were brought to this spot to be beheaded and then laid to rest at Lag ny Keeilley, leaving the throne free for the next in line to begin their reign.

The well was held in high regard as a healing well into the twentieth century, with at least one case of its water being collected and taken away for someone suffering from tuberculosis.

AJAF-ASG 201 | PIOMNHAS 1.7.297 | PMCK-MAS 1.25 | WWG-MS1 73

Lag ny Keeilley

Public ram | Steep, rough and uneven ground, a committed walk | SC 2169 7454 | 54.135637, -4.730912 | Lag ny Keeilley is a keeill on the hillside of Cronk ny Arrey Laa overlooking the sea. From the car park close to Eary Cushlin, take the track past the house and continue along the path heading south-west along the broogh for 1.3 miles. The keeill is at the termination of the path, on a small plateau, the entrance to which is between two stone cairns.

The child without a name

A woman at Eary Cushlin gave birth to an unwanted child who died shortly after being born. The mother took the baby and buried it secretly here at Lag ny Keeilley. After this the fishermen out in the bay at night began to see a light and hear crying as if from a lost little child on the shore, after which they would see the light run up the broogh to the keeill. The men began to take fright and resisted going out in the boats at night, so an old man named Illiam Quirk went out in a boat to try to discover more. When he saw the light and heard the crying, he went in closer and heard the child crying, 'She lhiannoo beg dyn ennym mee!' ('I am a little child without a name!'). Illiam removed his hat, stood up in the boat and threw some water towards the light, crying out, 'If thou are a boy, I chrizzen thee in the name of the Father, Son, and Holy Ghost, Juan! If thou are a girl, I chrizzen thee in the name of the Father, Son, and Holy Ghost, Joanney!' The crying stopped and the light went out instantly, and neither were seen or heard again.

The earlier version of this tale has the child born out of wedlock and the child 'done away with' in order to 'hide her shame.'

SM-MFT 36–39 | WC-WCF 5

The fairies' party at Lag ny Keeilley

Less than a couple of hours before sunrise one night in the 1890s, a man was alone on the deck of a fishing boat sailing north from Bradda Head when he saw lights go up from the shore to Lag ny Keeilley, one at a time, each about thirty-five metres apart. This went on until there were about fifty of these lights at the keeill. The beat of a drum then began and wonderful music could be heard, at which the lights began to move. The fisherman called his crewmates to the deck, and all of them heard and saw the same thing, confirming to each other the belief that it was the fairies. The moving lights and music went on until morning when the lights disappeared one by one and the music died away into the distance.

Strange lights can still be seen here at night moving about the broogh, especially in bad weather. Other accounts have it as a single bright light frequently seen at midnight. Some link these lights to the internments at the keeill.

KR-MNQ 150 | MJ 5.286 | WWG-MS1 73 | WWG-MS1 429

The Irish grave-robbers

In around 1850 a man named Phil Moore was living at Eary Cushlin when two Irishmen came asking to be shown to the place 'where the Irish kings were buried.' He led them along the path towards the keeill and on the way he accepted their offer of a drink from what they had in their knapsacks. After this he became drowsy and fell asleep by the keeill, only rousing to see them digging in the graveyard around the keeill and filling their rucksacks with what they found there. Upon seeing him awakening, the men gave him some more drink and he fell asleep for the rest of the afternoon, though not before sleepily seeing the men make off with full knapsacks.

This is likely to be connected to St Patrick having seen this place and decreed that this should be the resting place of 'kings and princes.' King Orry and his line of the Kings of Man and the Isles are said to be buried here. Perhaps independently to of this, the Irish used to come here to be buried as they would thereby reach heaven quicker.

AWM-MN 116 | HIJ-JG 94 | PIOMNHAS 4.2.205 | WWG-MS1 73 | WWG-MS1 428–431

The dead mermaid
After a shipwreck near here some men were on the shore looking for valuables amongst the wreckage brought in on the tide but they were surprised to find a dead mermaid. They carried her up the slope and buried her here at the keeill.

KR-MNQ 208 | WWG-MS1 429

Ooig ny Seyir

Inaccessible | A cave at the northern end of the shore below Lag ny Keeilley. It is not safely accessible.

This cave has the name, Ooig ny Seyir (Cave of the Carpenter), because of the fairy carpenters who work here. Woodchips are sometimes seen floating in the water by here and their hammering was frequently heard by passing sailors. If this hammering is heard in May, it is a sign of a good season to come at the fishing, as the fairies will be at work making barrels to salt the herrings which will soon be caught.

Alternative reports of the fairy carpenters here have them working on furniture, boats for their fishing fleet, or even at coffins for humans soon to die.

JJK-PN 48 | KR-MNQ 218 | PIOMNHAS 1.9.561 | MJ 5.285–286 | WC-WCF 18 | WWG-MS3 361-362

Rushen

Rushen is the Isle of Man's richest parish for folklore, boasting everything from fearsome bugganes to captured mermaids. The Fairy Hill has one of the best known of all tales of the fairies, but there is hardly a patch of the parish which is not alive with tales of figures like the lhiannan-shee, ghosts, giants, the devil and others. This is in great part thanks to the work of Karl Roeder and Edward Faragher, whose collecting in the 1880s-1900s provides us with most of the amazingly detailed tales to be found here.

1. Cronk ny Arrey Laa
2. The glowing rock of the Sloc
3. The landslide which sunk the Sunday fishers
4. The man who went blind from digging up a graveyard
5. The standing stone built into the chapel
6. Ballakilpheric
7. The tarroo ushtey of Ballakilpherick
8. Tom the Dipper's candle
9. Fairy music in the kitchen
10. Kirk Christ Rushen
11. The old vicarage of Kirk Christ Rushen
12. Ballachurry
13. The Fairy Hill
14. The Surby lhiannan-shee
15. Fleshwick
16. St Patrick's landing at Raclay
17. Bradda Head
18. The buggane of Spaldrick Dip
19. St Catherine's Well
20. Mermaids at Port Erin

21. The ferocious pig of Ballafurt Road
22. Struan Snail
23. Harry Ballahane's lhiannan-shee
24. The lhiannan-shee of Glendown
25. The beast emerging from the sea
26. The lhiannan-shee of Kentraugh Bridge
27. Shore Road
28. The Smelt
29. The Four Roads
30. By Port St Mary Railway Station
31. The Giant's Quoiting Stone
32. Ballacreggan Corner
33. Plantation Hill Road
- The Giant's Quoiting Stone of Cronk Skibbylt [private land]
34. The giant hare of Port St Mary harbour
35. Lime Street
36. The Kallow Point caillagh
37. Lag y Voddey
38. Perwick

39. The fairies' mooring place
40. Glenchass
41. Cronk Glenchass
42. The Howe
43. Buitched to not find a way out of a field
- Corvalley [private land]
44. Poyll Vill
45. Two fairies in the quarry
46. The women listening at the door at Hop tu Naa
47. The tall lady who could not cross the stream
48. The captured mermaid
49. The Chasms
50. The Sugarloaf
51. The mermaid of Cass Struan
52. Spanish Head
53. Finn MacCooil and the giant
54. The underground passage to the land of Manannan
55. Ghaw ny Spyrryd
56. The Sound
57. Kitterland
58. The mermaid's garden

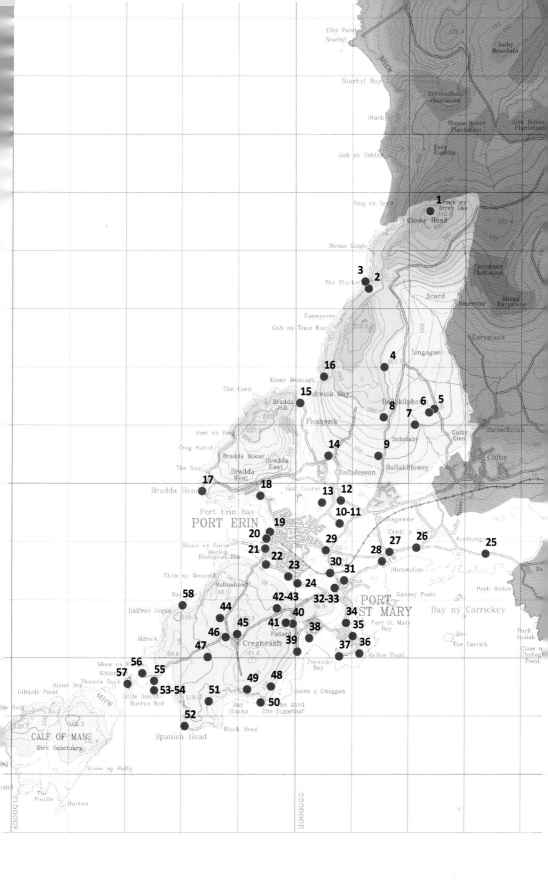

Cronk ny Arrey Laa

Public ram | Steep, rough and uneven ground | SC 2244 7467 | 54.137086, -4.719427 | Cronk ny Arrey Laa is a hill on the edge of Rushen and Patrick parishes, standing over the west coast.

The Caillagh ny Fai'ag lives here at Cronk ny Arrey Laa. This old woman is central to determining the weather for the coming season by whether it is wet or dry at Laa'l Breeshey (1 February). If it is wet, then the caillagh cannot gather sticks and so the weather will be fine in the future. Alternatively, if the weather is fine on Laa'l Breeshey, it will be poor in the future.

Perhaps independent of this, Cronk ny Arrey Laa is the home of the White Lady of the Cronk. Only one story of this caillagh is known to have been recorded, when she emerged from the form of a cloud towards a man digging turf on Cronk Fedjag close by, solidifying into a hag 'with teeth as long as his forearm.' However, the man called out, 'What in God's name is this?' and the White Lady of the Cronk faded back into being a cloud.

It is also said that the cairn at the hill's peak here is the resting place of the ancient Kings of Man.

JT-HSA 1.265 | RJK-SIOM 115 | WWG-MS1 350–351 | WWG-MS1 450–451

The glowing rock of the Sloc

Public ram | Dangerously steep, rough and uneven ground close to a cliff edge | SC 2132 7345 | 54.125727, -4.735847 | The Cabbyl is a large boulder connected to a wall of quartz halfway down the steep slope from the Sloc towards the sea. It is on the slope, on the south side of the stream, beyond a broken wire fence. There is no defined path that runs to the rock and the slope is very steep and dangerous. It is not safely accessible.

This enormous white rock has the strange property of sometimes lighting up from within at around dusk. Lights have also been seen by fishermen wandering about the cliffs here, especially in bad weather.

WWG-MS1 509

The landslide that sunk the Sunday fishers

Public ram | Visible from rough and uneven ground close to a cliff edge | SC 2135 7337 | 54.125016, -4.735395 | Garroo Clagh is a coastal headland of fallen rocks south of the Sloc. It is not accessible, but it is visible from the rocky brooghs of the Sloc itself.

The large fishing fleet of Dalby put out for their fishing on a Sunday evening but before long a storm came up and the ships took shelter by coming in close to the rocks here. However, a great landslide happened, forming the Garroo Clagh and causing the boats to be swamped in the swell until they were all sunk. Since that time the fishermen of Dalby would never fish on a Sunday.

WC-WCF 29–30 | WWG-MS1 243

The man who went blind from digging up a graveyard

Private land – view only | Visible from a rough and uneven footpath | SC 2164 7200 | 54.112813, -4.730070 | Today named Upper Kirkle, this private farm is on the slopes of Lhiattee ny Beinnee. It is west of the main road, with its farm track just south of the turning for Ballakilpheric Road.

A burial site used to stand on the land of Kirkle and it had lain untouched for a long time until the 35-year-old farmer here decided to dig it up with a pick so that the land could be cultivated. His father warned him that bad would come of it but he persisted in digging out the stones and bones. It was not long after he had completed this desecration of the site that he fell blind.

JRB-AS6 52 | KR-MNQ 161

The standing stone built into the chapel

Private land – view only | Visible from a public road | SC 2250 7127 | 54.106555, -4.716478 | Ballakilpheric Chapel is at the roadside in Ballakilpheric, a village north of Colby, halfway along Ballakilpheric Road, between Colby and Lhingague.

The large stone placed at the corner of the chapel is from the original keeill dedicated to St Patrick which gave Ballakilpheric its name. This Keeill Pherick was built at the direction of St Patrick himself, who asked for it when he first landed from Ireland and climbed Lhiattee ny Beinnee for a good view of the Island before identifying this as the ideal spot for the Island's first chapel. Incorporated into the doorway of the keeill were two large stones, which were possibly previously pre-Christian standing stones. These remained with the rest of the keeill remains in the field to the north of the chapel until they were cleared away in the 1850s. One of these stones was then set at the corner of the chapel here where it remains today.

JRB-AS6 48–49 | MD-EVAF 16 | WC-IH 15 | YLM 3.11.504

Ballakilpheric

Private land – view only | Visible from a public road without a footpath | SC 2243 7123 | 54.106248, -4.717605 | Ballakilpheric is a village north of Colby, halfway along Ballakilpheric Road between Colby and Lhingague. The farm of Ballakilpheric itself is less than 100 metres down the road to the west of Ballakilpheric Chapel. The farmhouse is opposite to the entrance to the farm.

Two ghost lambs

One winter a woman who lived near here had two twin children who died at the age when they were beginning to walk. After the children had been buried, the woman at Ballakilpheric heard a knock at her door one night. She opened up and was surprised to find two lambs stood there acting as if they were trying to look under the steps at the door. In the morning the woman looked under these steps and found the pair of scissors which had been lost sometime before. She believed that the twins had hidden them, but had returned in the form of the lambs to tell her where to find them.

KR-MNQ 171

Attacked in bed for cursing a foul smell

Four men set out from Fleshwick to fish at sea but bad weather forced them to put in at Niarbyl and walk home to Ballakilpheric. When close to Cronk ny Arrey Laa they saw a small light above them on the hill and they passed through a 'horrid suffocating smell.' One of the men, named Quayle, cursed the smell but the others thought it wiser to pay it no mind. When Quayle reached his cottage here at Ballakilpheric, he got into bed in the loft and extinguished the light. He immediately heard the window open and a great deal of whispering as a group of fairies jumped down from the window and surrounded the bed. They lifted up the sheets and blew a freezing air over every part of his body until he felt himself near to death. It was only with an enormous effort that Quayle was able to break free and tumble out of his bed and down to his mother who was sleeping below.

YLM 3.4.173–174

The tarroo ushtey of Ballakilpherick

Private – view only | Visible from rough and uneven ground, steps | SC 2218 7101 | 54.104121, -4.721214 | The river below Burnbrae, a house south-east of Ballakilpheric. Take the road behind Ballakilpheric Chapel, past the farm of Ballakilpheric itself, and take the public footpath by Burnbrae. The path weaves around the house and over the river.

When this was still farmland, a tarroo ushtey used to be seen here with sparkling eyes and short ears, but otherwise similar to normal cattle. It would emerge from the river to mix and attempt to mate with the cattle. On one occasion when a man came across it here, he rendered the beast powerless to attack when he 'switched his stick back at him' as a charm.

KR-MNQ 102 | YLM 3.4.138

Tom the Dipper's candle

Public | Rough and uneven ground at the roadside, steps | SC 2163 7113 | 54.105033, -4.729723 | The site of Tom the Dipper's house is north of Port Erin on Ballakillowey Road. A picnic area with a good view east loops off the road about a mile north of Port Erin, and the site of Tom the Dipper's house is marked by a sign 100 metres further up the road on the opposite side.

A well-known poet and character of the nineteenth century was Tom 'the Dipper' Shimmin, who built his own house here with his wife in the 1870s, when in his 70s. One night he was here talking and smoking with friends when they were amazed to watch as the flame of their candle rose up 30cm or so above the wick. The flame remained suspended there a short while and then returned to its natural place on the candle. The people there explained this strange occurrence as the work of a buggane in some form.

JQ-KP2 17

Fairy music in the kitchen

Private land – view only | Visible from a public road without a pavement | SC 2155 7046 | 54.098983, -4.730625 | Ballakillowey is a farm on the west side of Ballakillowey Road. The private road to the farm is half a mile up from the large roundabout between Port Erin and Colby.

The tenant at Ballakillowey used to hear the fairies making music in the kitchen below them when they were up to bed. One of the instruments they played was the trumpet.

WWG-MS2 231

Kirk Christ Rushen

Open during daylight hours | Some uneven ground | SC 2087 6931 | 54.088423, -4.740297 | The church of Kirk Christ Rushen is halfway along Church Road, which comes off from the main road between Port Erin and Port St Mary at the Four Roads.

Phantom funerals

Phantom funerals have been experienced by people on the road here by the church. They are stopped or pushed back by some invisible force, which occupies the road for a period before disappearing and allowing the people to pass by unhindered again. This is most commonly explained as the passing of a phantom funeral, with the ghostly carriage and mourners occupying the road. However, another explanation used to account for this experience is that it is from the passing of the Death Coach known to run from Ballagawne to the church here.

WWG-MS2 52–53

Oural Losht

The Manx term, Oural Losht, refers to a burnt sacrifice. One of these took place here in 1719 when a farmer's wife looked to change their bad luck by burning a calf in the entranceway to the churchyard. Apparently, the offering was successful, as their cattle multiplied from then on, but this was only used as further proof of wrongdoing at the ecclesiastical trial for diabolical practices which followed.

DC-MI 26–27

Travellers lost in the churchyard

Two men set out from Ballafesson to visit a woman in Ballasalla. However, despite knowing the way well, they found themselves in unfamiliar country not long after setting out. They went over a hedge and were surprised to get down into snow, as there was no snow in the Isle of Man at that time. They went on and came to a house well-lit with lights which they had never seen before, but as they opened the garden gate to the house, all its lights went out. The men wandered on for an indefinite time until they eventually realised that they were in the churchyard here at Kirk Christ Rushen, not very far from where they had started. They returned home and did not dare to try the journey the following night.

WWG-MS3 405-406

Sanctuary from the fairies

After a silver cup was taken one night from the fairies' feast within the Fairy Hill, the man escaped the vengeful fairies by running down the stream and clambering over the wall and into the sanctuary of the church grounds here. The silver cup was then given to the church, where it was used as a communion cup for many years.

GW-AIOM 139 | HIJ-JG 80 | JT-HSA 2.154 | SM-MFT 28–35 | WWG-MS1 514–518 | YLM 2.48

The buried bull's heart

A man named Billy Hom Collister set out to get vengeance on the woman who rejected him in love. He came here to Kirk Christ Rushen with two friends as accomplices secretly one night, and buried a bull's heart in a small coffin-like box in the churchyard. The full Christian burial service was performed over the grave, including the sprinkling of soil over the box. However, for the name of the deceased, Billy Hom said the name of the woman who had rejected his love. The woman, who had just got married, to another man then began to waste away and was soon dead. Years later, after his own death, the ghost of Billy Hom was often seen walking about his home at Corvalley.

BN-MS1 4–15 | WWG-MS3 339–340

Trapping a ghost out of its grave

A blacksmith from Port St Mary was asked to put an iron cross over a grave here at Kirk Rushen so that the ghost of the person buried here would be stopped from coming out. However, the ghost was already out when the blacksmith lay down the cross and so the spirit was prevented from returning into the grave. The ghost was angry at this and shouted at the blacksmith, 'Trog shen!' ('Lift that!'). The blacksmith did as he was commanded, but he was affected by that meeting for the rest of his life and he never did much good again.

YLM 3.4.158

The old vicarage of Kirk Christ Rushen

Private land – view only | Visible from a public road with a pavement | SC 2085 6928 | 54.088160, -4.740531 | The old vicarage is directly beside the church of Kirk Christ Rushen, which is halfway along Church Road, which comes off from the main road between Port Erin and Port St Mary at the Four Roads.

The white lady of Kirk Christ vicarage

Two men were walking by here one night when they came across a woman stood at the front door of the vicarage. When they went closer to her, she gripped the man closest to her and the two men had to struggle fiercely to get him free again. He looked visibly years older after the experience and he bore the marks of her fingers on his arm for the rest of his life.

WWG-MS3 358

Urine protection from the fairies

One version of the silver cup story of the Fairy Hill has the manservant of the vicarage, a man named Donaghue Lowey, entered the Fairy Hill one night and was witness to a great fairy feast. Before escaping with a silver drinking cup. To avoid the vengeance of the fairies, Lowey ran into the cowhouse here at the vicarage and used a spade to fling the cows' mooin (urine) all around the entrance and the wall. This formed an effective barrier over which the fairies could not cross, ensuring his safety until morning.

YLM 2.48 | YLM 3.4.145

Ballachurry

Private land – view only | Visible from a public road with a pavement | SC 2087 6969 | 54.091838, -4.740495 | The large private farmhouse of Ballachurry is on Ballafesson Road, to the north-east of Port Erin. It is amongst the trees on the north side of the road, a short distance from the Ballakillowey roundabout on the main road towards Colby.

The tall man of Ballachurry

A man named Tom Craine was going home at midnight to Colby from Bradda Mines when a little dog appeared from the shadows and followed at his heels for some way before it ran on ahead out of sight. The man was shocked when he saw it again a little further on as the dog had grown to be as large as a goat and was still growing. It had grown as large as a donkey before it galloped on again out of sight along the road by Ballachurry. When the man came to the Ballachurry gates there was no beast, but only a very tall thin man leaning with his arms folded on the top of the gate. This tall man walked away towards to the house, but upon reaching the door, he turned and came back towards the road. By the moonlight, Tom saw the tall man's strange old form of dress, with knee breeches and a ruffle around his neck, but it was the tall man's white and dreadful face which was most horrifying and Tom ran off towards Colby. However, on the road he met two friends, and together they decided to go back and take another look. Sure enough, they met the man, as tall as two normal men, walking away towards the house. But upon his turning, the men saw something that gave them such a shock that they ran home terrified and they could never be brought to speak of what they saw to anyone.

SM-MFT 101–103

The witch in the form of a hare

A greyhound chased a hare to Ballachurry and bit it on the thigh, before it slipped away through the gate to the house here. The people with the dog then went inside and found the old woman who lived at Ballachurry with blood running down her thigh from just the place where the dog had bit the hare. This was not doubted as proof that the woman was a witch who could turn herself into the form of a hare.

YLM 3.4.164

The ghost of Ballachurry

Ballachurry has a reputation for being haunted. One story of this was when some men were sat in the kitchen with the young women of the house one evening when suddenly the locked back door opened and a very big man unknown to them came in and walked upstairs, where he made a great noise in the rooms above. The young people were very alarmed but none of them dared to go upstairs and instead they simply moved away into another room.

KR-MNQ 152

The buggane watching at the window

A buggane used to be often seen between Ballachurry and Ballagawne. It was sometimes seen in the form of a black pig but it followed a woman and her boy home when in the form of a man with officer's clothes. When the two had got home and were in bed, the boy was towards the wall and the woman looked round to see the buggane at the window. She shifted the boy to the floor side of the bed and the buggane disappeared. When she put the boy to the wall side again, the buggane was back at the window in an instant, so she shifted the boy back to the outside and the buggane did not appear at the window again.

KR-MNQ 16

The dead's secret and the drunk

The dead can sometimes tell secrets to living people to help them. This person cannot then pass the secret on or else they would both lose out on the benefit it brings and call upon themselves the wrath of the dead spirit. Once, a person who had received such a secret was so drunk one night that he was rolling in the roadway here near Ballachurry, singing, 'We won't go home till morning.' Two friends found him like this and thought it was their opportunity to uncover his secret. They asked him directly what the ghost had said to him, but at this he sobered instantly and fell silent. This did not last very long though as he was soon singing again. They asked him again and the same thing happened. When they asked him a third time, he picked himself up without a word and walked steadily away.

WWG-MS2 83–84

The Fairy Hill

Private land – view only | Visible from rough and uneven footpath | SC 2054 6967 | 54.091541, -4.745537 | The Fairy Hill, also known as 'Cronk Howe Mooar,' is on the edge of Rowany Golf Course, to the north-east of Port Erin. Although visible from the main road, the site is best seen from the footpath which comes off Balllafesson Road at a stream just north-east of the golf course.

Fairies

The Fairy Hill is renowned as a fairy place. Fairies have frequently been seen on top, or setting off on their hunts from here, riding out with their whips cracking loudly. Fairies are also known to live inside and some accounts even report that it is the palace of 'the fairy king.'

People used to avoid the hill wherever possible, especially at night. On one occasion a boy ignored this and played near there but ever after his mouth was twisted to one side and he did not grow any more.

One of the most popular of all stories of the fairies relates to a silver cup obtained from within the Fairy Hill. The best-known version of this is of a man named Colcheragh who found his cows becoming poorly and so suspected the influence of the fairies. He stayed up late and saw the fairies coming into his barn and riding off on the cows, so Colcheragh leapt on his horse and followed them, right into the Fairy Hill. A great dance was going on inside, which Colcheragh watched until they all moved to eat at the tables. One of the fairies, who seemed familiar to Colcheragh, secretively moved closer and warned Colcheragh not to drink the wine or else he would end up as one of the fairies as he had. So, when the silver cup was passed around for him to drink, Colcheragh instead threw the wine on the lights and made a dash for the door. Knowing the fairies could not get him in water, Colcheragh fled down the stream until he reached the churchyard, where he was on hallowed ground and safe at last.

Other versions of the story have the man's name as Donnaghue, Donagher or Dunnagha Lowey, who merely found the entrance to the Fairy Hill and entered out of curiosity. Instead of the churchyard, the man found safety in the vicarage cowhouse, but only after he spread cow urine around the doorway so that the fairies could not get in.

In all versions, the silver cup was presented to Kirk Christ Rushen, where it was used for many years as the communion cup.

GW-AIOM 139 | HIJ-JG 80 | JT-HSA 2.154 | SM-MFT 28–35 | WWG-MS1 514–518 | YLM 2.48 | YLM 3.4.145 | YLM 3.4.161

Hom Mooar

One of the many names recorded for this hill is Cronk Hom Mooar (Big Tom's Hill). Hom Mooar was the famous fairy fiddler who would lure people into the hill with his beautiful music, after which they would seldom be seen again. Some accounts have Hom Mooar as a glashtyn or cabbyl ushtey, though appearing in a human form to play his music. Hom Mooar was also sometimes said to have lured people to their doom in other places, though his home was here at Cronk Hom Mooar.

JT-HSA 2.154 | WWG-MS1 284–285 | WWG-MS1 514–518 | YLM 3.4.144

Phantom funerals

Phantom funerals have often been seen leading to the Fairy Hill. This was once so well attested that, by the 1690s, even the Lieutenant Governor came to hear of it.

AWM-FIOM 162 | WS-AIOM 20 | YLM 3.4.145

The resting place of King Reginald

It was also commonly known that Fairy Hill is the burial mound of Reginald Olafsson, the King of Man slain by Knight Ivar on 30 May 1249. Some accounts have it that this is also the site of Reginald's murder and that he was buried where he fell. One account even reports that the mound was built by Reginald's wife, who carried the earth here in her apron to build the mound over her husband.

AJAF-ASG 215–217 | DR-TIOM 74–75 | GW-AIOM 139 | HAB-HIOM 221–222 | HIJ-JG xxiv | JF-TIOM 250 | WS-AIOM 20 | YLM 3.4.144–145

The Surby lhiannan-shee

Public | Public road | SC 2065 7047 | 54.098807, -4.744406 | Surby is a small village north of Port Erin, along the road towards Fleshwick. The small green is at heart of the village, on the north side of the road.

A man from Surby went out to meet his wife one night but he came across a lhiannan-shee and thought it was her and so spoke to her. This empowered the ghostly figure to follow him wherever he went and she began to plague him without break until he successfully managed to throw her off by some charm.

Perhaps related to this tale, a lhiannan-shee was also seen chasing a man in Surby in the appearance of his own wife.

KR-MNQ 100 | YLM 3.4.162

Fleshwick

Public | Rough and uneven ground, close to parking | SC 2015 7138 | 54.106792, -4.752517 | Fleshwick is a bay over a mile north of Port Erin. It is reached via the Surby Road from Ballafesson, north of Port Erin.

The mermaid of Fleshwick

A man once caught a mermaid here on the shore at Fleshwick but he agreed to let her go when she promised that she would ensure that no woman in his family would ever die in childbirth. She remained true to her promise as one of the descendants, an MHK in the 1920s, was able to confirm many years after this took place.

WWG-MS1 507

The pearl

A boat was fishing one night from Fleshwick out in the Big Bay, between Fleshwick and Niarbyl, when the men carelessly let the net go to the bottom of the seabed. It was then a very difficult job for the whole crew to pull it up again as they could only manage about a metre at a time before needing a rest. However, when they eventually got the net to the surface, they were aghast to find there a pearl so bright that it lit up the cliffs all around them, even brighter than the full moon. But the men took fright at the amazing thing and so dropped their nets again, letting the pearl slip back under the waves. Some of the men in the boat were to lose their minds from that sight of the pearl, but that did not stop others from searching for it. But no matter how often people have searched for it in the bay here, the pearl has never been recovered.

EF-MSR 130–131 | YLM 3.4.155–156

St Patrick's landing at Raclay

Public | Visible from rough and uneven ground | Raclay is the cliff over the next bay to the north of Fleshwick, north of Port Erin. It is best viewed at low tide from the left side of Fleshwick. Raclay itself is not possible to be visited safely.

It was St Patrick who first brought Christianity to the Isle of Man and he continued to make many visits to the Island. On one such visit, the saint got lost in the mist and put up a prayer for help. A curlew then came flying through the mist, calling out as it went, and led the boat to the shore. The saint landed safely here at Raclay, where he blessed the curlew and promised that its nest would be hidden from humans from then on. It was from here that the saint then climbed the hill and determined that a keeill should be built at the place that became known as Ballakilpheric.

JJK-PN 51 | MD-EVAF 16 | PIOMNHAS 4.2.205 | WC-IH 15

Bradda Head

Public | Steep, rough and uneven ground | SC 1843 6986 | 54.092499, -4.777831 | Bradda Head is the headland to the north of Port Erin. Milner's Tower is on its brow.

Carried away by the fairies

A man was walking home towards Fleshwick when he came to a deep bog in the road and so climbed the hedge to avoid it. However, as he went over the hedge, he felt himself going at a great speed, hardly knowing where he was as his feet barely touched the ground for the speed he was running. He went on like this over the fields until eventually he came to the very top of Milner's Tower. Here he stopped as he was at last left alone by the fairies.

YLM 3.4.153

Led astray to Bradda Head

A man living at Fleshwick went out to urinate before bed late one winter's night but after doing so he could not find his own house again. He walked and walked in search of it, travelling through the night without crossing any hedges or finding anything by which to recognise where he was. However, as daylight came, he finally knew where he was, as he saw that he had somehow come to be on the top of Bradda Head.

YLM 3.4.152

The buggane of Spaldrick Dip

Public | Public road with a pavement | SC 1947 6977 | 54.092083, -4.761990 | Spaldrick Dip is on the main road north of Port Erin Promenade. It is on the road, Bradda East, at the footpath leaving the road opposite to Bradda Glen Close.

A buggane lives in the small glen here at Spaldrick Dip and it was known to occasionally come out and chase people along the road. Its home was originally the curragh field behind but that has long since been converted into a part of the golf course, so modern accounts of the buggane report it as now living in the small glen here.

This buggane was probably responsible for what was experienced by a man who was coming along the road at one o'clock in the morning when he heard a terrifying sudden noise in the road here. It was like the rattling of chains with 'such harassing and tearing away.' The man took fright at this and shouted out, 'Lord, bless me, what's that?' After saying these words, no harm came to him.

YLM 3.4.142 | YLM 3.4.160

St Catherine's Well

Public | Public road | SC 1961 6913 | 54.0863884, -4.7594672 | St Catherine's Well is at the shore in Port Erin. It is marked by an ornate stone structure in the seaside wall towards the northern end of Shore Road.

Although today it appears to be little more than a drinking fountain, St Catherine's Well is a holy well whose water has the miraculous power to heal the sick. This is especially so if visited at Laa Luanys, at the start of August, when its water is even more effective in curing ailments.

In the 1880s this well was singled out as one of the six most significant holy wells in the Isle of Man, and even in the 1970s its waters were reported to 'work wonders.' However, today the water from the fountain is piped from the mains, leaving the water from the well itself to empty out into the sand.

AJAF-ASG 213–214 | EK-CC 93 | JJK-PN 22 | JQ-KYP1 2 | JRB-AS6 55 | JT-HSA 2.121 | WH-MM1 146 | WWG-MS1 60

Mermaids at Port Erin

Public | Sand, tidal | SC 1956 6905 | 54.085667, -4.760167 | Port Erin is the most southerly major town on the west coast of the Isle of Man.

Before the 1650s mermaids and mermen were regular night-time visitors to Manx shores. They combed their hair and played amongst themselves, but they would dive back into the water if any human ever came near. However, some people lay out a net on the shore here at Port Erin and hid some distance away to watch as a mermaid came ashore and became caught in the net. The people picked her up and carried her to a house where they attempted to care for her kindly, but without success, as she refused any food or drink and did not speak at all. After three days of this they grew worried of what might happen if they allowed the mermaid to waste away in their care and so they opened the door to allow her to escape. She got up on her tail and 'glided with incredible swiftness' to the shore and plunged back into the sea. Upon the questioning of her friends, she reported that she had seen 'nothing very wonderful' on the land, 'but they are so ignorant as to throw away the water in which they have boiled their eggs.'

Another time, some people by the name of Kelly found a mermaid stranded by the tide here on the shore. They kindly returned her to the sea, whereupon she blessed them so that none of the Kelly women would ever suffer long labours at childbirth. This proved to be true for generations afterwards.

AWM-FIOM 67–68 | GW-DIM 54–55 | HIJ-JG 44–45 | JT-HSA 2.145–146 | WWG-MS1 507–508 | YLM 3.4.160

The ferocious pig of Ballafurt Road

Public |Public road with a pavement | SC 1956 6888 | 54.084113, -4.760102 | Ballafurt Road leaves the shore at Port Erin and rises steeply up the hill turning southwards.

Some fishermen were on their way to Port Erin shore to dig for sand eels when they saw a little white pig here on Ballafurt Road. It went into the hedge and one of the men put his knife in the hedge after it in an attempt to stab it. This angered the pig, who came back out onto the road as it grew as large as a bull and started to attack them. The men were forced to use their knives to defend themselves until they got to one of their homes and burst inside to safety.

KR-MNQ 183

Struan Snail

Public | Public road with a pavement | SC 1956 6859 | 54.081541, -4.759890 | Struan Snail is a collection of houses on St Mary's Road on the south side of Port Erin. St Mary's Road runs from the Howe Road (initially as Truggan Road) to Ballafurt Road. Struan Snail is the area around the bend in the road at the entrance to the tennis courts, 150 metres from Ballafurt Road.

The lhiannan-shee of Struan Snail

A lhiannan-shee used to be seen here in the form of a white woman. This visible figure is perhaps related to the lhiannan-shee who lived with a man here. People passing by the man's house would hear her and the man talking together and to their children, but neither the woman nor the children could be seen. The man would always know if people were listening, as the lhiannan-shee would tell him.

KR-MNQ 100 | YLM 3.4.161–162

The returned spirit of a man at sea

One sunny day a man was at a house on business here in Struan Snail. As he was leaving the house, he was surprised to meet the young man who lived there, who he had thought was off fishing in Crookhaven. The man was obviously fresh back, in his sailor's clothes and his bag on his shoulder, but the young man made no reply to the visitor's greeting as he went on round to the back door of the house. The visitor went off but returned soon after to catch up with the fisherman, but the family knew nothing of his return and they reported that they had seen nothing of him. It was then realised that what had been seen was the man's spirit separate to his body, returned home perhaps at a point when he was wishing especially strongly to be at home.

KR-MNQ-77 83

The rushing pig

Three men finally escaped a strange rushing pig by jumping over the hedge here at Struan Snail. (See Ballacreggan Corner).

KR-MNQ 185

Harry Ballahane's lhiannan-shee

Private land – view only | Visible from public road with limited pavement | SC 1995 6838 | 54.079757, -4.753735 | The old Ballahane farmhouse is now a renamed private house close to the south-eastern edge of Port Erin, on Truggan Road.

A man named Harry used to live here at Ballahane, where he was constantly accompanied by a lhiannan-shee who was invisible to anyone other than him. He was known to throw her some of his porridge, or else divide off some of his food for her at meals.

BN-MS2 'The Little White Lady' | WWG-MS3 357

The lhiannan-shee of Glendown

Private land – view only | Visible from public road without a pavement | SC 2012 6828 | 54.078956, -4.751193 | Glendown is the most easterly farm on Truggan Road, close to the south-eastern edge of Port Erin. The old Glendown farmhouse stands over the road from the farm and today bears a different name.

The man who used to live here at Glendown was haunted by a lhiannan-shee. This was a female spirit who attached herself to a man and never left his side again. It was well known that the lhiannan-shee lived with the man here at Glendown.

KR-MNQ 100

The beast emerging from the sea

Public | Pavement beside a road | SC 2345 6879 | 54.084701, -4.700601 | The main road between Castletown and Port St Mary which passes the farm, Strandhall, on the east side of Bay ny Carrickey.

A young man from Ballafesson was walking home from Castletown one night when 'some big black thing' came out of the sea and crossed the road just in front of him somewhere here near Strandhall. This buggane then continued to terrorise the man in various ways all the way to his home at Ballafesson.

WWG-MS3 376

The lhiannan-shee of Kentraugh Bridge

Public | Pavement beside a road | SC 2223 6889 | 54.085105, -4.719348 | Kentraugh Bridge crosses the Colby River at the northern end of Bay ny Carrickey. The shore road goes over it close to the Shore Hotel, by Kentraugh Mill Road.

A man named Maddrell was walking home from Castletown towards Fistard at around midnight when a young woman walked up beside him here by Kentraugh Bridge. The man asked her questions, but she only looked at him and did not say a word as she continued alongside him. When they reached Ballacreggan Corner and she followed him as he turned down towards Port St Mary, he knew that she must be a lhiannan-shee and so he threatened her by saying, 'If you don't tell me what you are, I'll make a sacrifice of you, by God.' At this, the woman grinned up into his face and disappeared.

KR-MNQ 100 | YLM 3.4.162

Shore Road

Public | Wide pavement beside a road | SC 2176 6881 | 54.084288, -4.726478 | Shore Road runs along Bay ny Carrickey, north-east of Port St Mary. The brewery used to stand at the junction of Shore Road and Mount Gawne Road.

The buggane of the old brewery

A strange beast in the form of a bear haunts this area around where the old brewery used to stand. It is the deformed ghost of a man named Gawne, who was such a sinner that after his death even his horses refused to take his body to the churchyard for the funeral. So it was that he was doomed to haunt the area here in the form of 'an enormous bear-like monster.'

One particular sighting of it was by the couple who lived in the Brewery House. They heard a strange sound outside, like a wave tumbling onto the shore, and together they summoned the courage to open the door and look out. There they saw the bear-like beast, almost as large as an elephant, making a rumbling sound as it went along the road towards Kentraugh.

WWG-MS3 394 | YLM 3.4.151–152

The talking horses

Two men were coming back from Douglas when they came across two horses in the road. These horses would not let the men pass and so they decided to climb up on their backs and ride them. Within a few minutes of setting off they were here at the shore of Bay ny Carrickey, where one of the horses spoke, asking the men the curious question of what their wives said when they sneezed. One of the men replied, 'Ride on, devil!' at which the horses ran down onto the shore and towards the sea. One of the men then called out 'God bless us!' and the horses immediately vanished, leaving the two men sitting alone on the shore.

YLM 3.4.142

The Smelt

Public | Sand, tidal | SC 2147 6863 | 54.082512, -4.730681 | The Smelt is at the junction of Beach Road and the shore, at the south-western end of Bay ny Carrickey, the first bay north-east of Port St Mary.

The buggane of the Smelt

A buggane used to be well known to be found here at the Smelt. Some believed it to be the ghost of a person murdered here, but others thought it was a member of the Gawne family who was doomed to haunt the area after their death.

One story of this buggane was when it was seen at the roadside by a man who was walking past the Smelt. The man was too frightened to pass the beast and did not know what to do, but the buggane spoke to him, saying, 'Ny cur boirey orryms, as cha derrym biorey orts' ('Don't bother me and I won't bother you').

Another time, a woman was walking here when she saw the buggane standing on a stile at the roadside. Thinking quickly, she said the Lord's Prayer and the buggane disappeared.

KR-MNQ 11 | WWG-MS3 376

The darkness of the Smelt

A man was making his way home from Port St Mary to Cregneash but he got into some darkness just as he came to his house. He could not see where he was going and wandered around blindly for some time. Eventually he emerged from the darkness again and was shocked to find himself up against the mill door here at the Smelt. He had lost his cap on his wandering but, upon reaching his home again, he found it just outside his own door, where he had obviously lost it in the darkness.

KR-MNQ 151

The Four Roads

Public | Pavement beside a road | SC 2061 6885 | 54.084198, -4.743961 | The Four Roads is the crossroads between Port Erin and Port St Mary marked with a roundabout.

The big stack of fire

Some men were heading home from Port St Mary one Saturday night at about one o'clock in the morning when they saw 'a great big stack of fire' coming in from the sea. It moved inland and on towards the Four Roads, where a group of men were drunkenly fighting. The stack of fire then disappeared, and the row between the men instantly ceased.

KR-MNQ 137

The giant's stone

As well as the giant's quoiting stones at Ballacreggan and Cronk Skibbylt, a third stone used to stand here by the Four Roads. They were thrown by three giants on South Barrule, who were competing to see who was the strongest. The giant who threw the stone here was proven to be the weakest.

YLM 3.4.160

By Port St Mary Railway Station

Public | Pavement beside a road | SC 2069 6845 | 54.080682, -4.742580 | Port St Mary Railway Station is on the road between the Four Roads and Port St Mary, by the Railway Station Hotel.

The two calves

In the days before the railway was built, a man was walking here not long before dawn when he saw two strange creatures like calves in the road. Recognising them as not fully normal, the man climbed over the hedge and made his way across the field towards Plantation Road. But when he got there, the calves were there already in the road in front of him. The man went across another field but met them again, so he hid in the yard of a nearby hotel. From there he watched the cows go on towards the Port, as he waited until the sun came up before moving on.

KR-MNQ 182

The untouchable thing in the road

Before the railway was built a man was walking along the road here one night when he came across a black thing in the road. He tried to kick it but he could not touch it. It then began to grow until it was as large as a horse. The man drew his knife and cautiously stepped away backwards until he reached a house near Ballacreggan and burst inside to safety. He stayed there until morning before venturing outside again.

KR-MNQ 179

The Giant's Quoiting Stone

Private land – view only | Visible from a pavement beside a road | SC 2090 6830 | 54.079421, -4.739216 | The Giant's Quoiting Stone is a large standing stone in the field north of Ballacreggan Corner, the crossroads at the edge of Port St Mary.

Two giants were once at Meayll Hill and wanted to discover who was the strongest. They each picked up a high rock and threw it as far as they could. One reached as far as Cronk Skibbylt, but the winner threw this one here.

Another version of this story has it as three giants on South Barrule, with this as the intermediate throw. The winner reached Cronk Skibbylt, but the loser only reached the Four Roads.

DR-TIOM 74 | GW-AIOM 139 | HIJ-JG 87 | HIJ-JG 149 | JGC-HPECL 144 | JT-HSA 1.266 | JT-HSA 2.174 | SH-HSDV 118 | YLM 3.4.160

Ballacreggan Corner

Public | Pavement beside a road | SC 2080 6823 | 54.078715, -4.740694 | Ballacreggan Corner is the crossroads at the edge of Port St Mary, towards Port Erin.

The rushing pig

Three men were out walking one Sunday night when they came across a very large pig in a great hurry at the crossroads at Ballacreggan Corner. At every corner after that they met this big pig rushing past at full speed. This happened at Surby, Bradda and Port Erin but at Struan Snail the pig began to follow them. The men took fright and jumped over the hedge. The pig did not leave the road to come after them but it remained standing there at the hedge watching them. The men did not return to the road but went home over the fields and thankfully did not see any more of the strange creature.

KR-MNQ 185

The vanishing lhiannan-shee

A man named Maddrell was walking home from Castletown and at around midnight a young woman walked up beside him as he reached Kentraugh Bridge. The man asked her questions, but she only looked at him without saying a word as she continued to walk alongside him. At Ballacreggan Corner she turned and walked with him down the road a short way towards Port St Mary. This made him sure that she was a lhiannan-shee and so he threatened her by saying, 'If you don't tell me what you are, I'll make a sacrifice of you, by God.' At this the woman grinned up into his face and disappeared.

YLM 3.4.162

Plantation Hill Road

Public | Pavement beside a road | SC 2077 6820 | 54.078438, -4.741156 | Plantation Road leads from Ballacreggan Corner, the crossroads on the edge of Port St Mary, up towards the Howe.

The monstrous greyhound

A young man was walking towards Plantation Road at around eleven at night when he saw 'a great monster' in the bright moonlight. It was a bit like a greyhound but very high. It crossed the road before the man and into a field, passing through a closed gate as if it were not there. The man believed that the beast was some form of fairy.

KR-MNQ 186

The Ballacreggan buggane

A woman was walking home one night and between the railway station and Ballacreggan she came across 'a great monster' in the road making a terrible noise. She bravely went past it and continued on, but at the bottom of the hill here she heard a great noise behind her. She turned and saw the thing coming after her. It had no shape or form, but it was like a turf stack. It followed her up to the top of Plantation Hill, but it did not go any further.

KR-MNQ 180

The witchman in the form of a hare

A farmer by Bay ny Carrickey was suffering with poorly cattle and often losing them to sickness. Suspicion fell on a hare which was frequently seen around the cattle, but the farmer was never able to shoot it. Early one Sunday morning the farmer's son and manservant were returning home from seeing some young women when they came across this hare. They set two swift dogs after it and followed on behind as it took off up the hill. Near the top, the hare leapt over a hedge and the dogs went after it barking, but when the young men caught up with them over the wall, they found a man there fending the dogs off with a stone in each of his hands. He claimed he was off to see his daughter in Fistard, but the men knew that he must be the 'witchman' who had been coming to the farm in the form of the hare.

YLM 3.4.164

The Giant's Quoiting Stone of Cronk Skibbylt

Private | A large standing stone in a private garden of Cronk Road, the road running above Port St Mary from the top of Plantation Road down to Bay View Road.

This enormous standing stone is the partner of the one at Ballacreggan Corner and together they are the Giants Quoiting Stones. Two giants at Meayll Hill were competing to discover who was the strongest by who could throw an enormous rock the furthest. One reached as far as the field opposite Ballacreggan, but the other of the two only reached here on the side of Cronk Skibbylt.

Another version of this story has it as three giants on South Barrule, with this stone as the winning throw, since the others only landed at Ballacreggan Corner and the Four Roads.

DR-TIOM 74 | GW-AIOM 139 | HIJ-JG 87 | HIJ-JG 149 | JGC-HPECL 144 | JT-HSA 1.266 | JT-HSA 2.174 | SH-HSDV 118 | YLM 3.4.160

The giant hare of Port St Mary harbour

Public | Sand and uneven ground, tidal | SC 2098 6759 | 54.073034, -4.737662 | Port St Mary harbour is at the bottom of the town, below the Albert Hotel. The main sandy harbour and the small rocky beach to the north are divided off from each other by a wall.

Late one night two fishermen were going to their boat on the shore at the top of Port St Mary harbour. As it was low tide, the men were walking to it over the sand of the inner harbour when they saw a hare running about. One of the men suggested to the other that they catch it, but at this the hare started to come towards them, getting larger and larger with each jump. The hare was soon so big that the men took fright and ran to the nearest boat to lock themselves in the forecastle. The hare came on board and tried to get in with such violence that it seemed the boat would break. The men stood by with a hatchet and a poker ready to defend themselves but after three hours the thing finally gave up and went away at last.

KR-MNQ 181

Lime Street

Public | Pavement beside a road | SC 2107 6738 | 54.071224, -4.736124 | Lime Street runs south-east from the inner harbour past the Lifeboat Station towards the sea before turning to become Clifton Road.

The silent carriage

A carriage pulled by four black horses used to be seen after midnight riding along Lime Street. It could be seen going towards the Point in complete silence, without even the wheels or the horses making a sound.

Alternative versions of this describe a carriage pulled by a pair of grey horses which pass two or three times a year towards the breakwater, or that it can be heard but no driver is visible.

KR-MNQ 146

The rush of people in darkness

One night a fisherman went from his home on Lime Street to put a sight on his boat by the pier. He had not gone far when he came into complete darkness. He could not see a thing and he could feel nothing with his hands but it felt as if he was in a crowd being pushed back up the street. He continued like this until he was able to escape into a small opening between two houses. As soon as he was off Lime Street, he was immediately free of the crowd and of the darkness. He believed that this experience was an omen of death.

KR-MNQ 151

The Kallow Point caillagh

Public | Uneven ground | SC 2120 6708 | 54.068536, -4.733870 | Kallow Point is a distinctive flat outcrop of rock on the coast between the Outer Pier and the anchor and flags of the Mona's Queen Memorial at Port St Mary.

Although written similar to the surname, Callow, Kallow Point used to be pronounced 'Callie.' This has led some to believe that the name links to Caillagh ny Fai-ag, the old woman of the prophecy. She goes out hunting for sticks for her fire on Laa'l Breeshey (1 February) and if it is wet on that day, she cannot gather dry ones and so she will ensure good weather for the season to come, so that she can gather the sticks then. In reverse, if the weather is fine on Laa'l Breeshey, it will mean that the weather will be bad in the season ahead. Some have even seen the caillagh on this day, in the form of a bird flying with the sticks in her mouth.

WWG-MS1 351

Lag y Voddey

Public | Rough and uneven ground | SC 2085 6703 | 54.067988, -4.739262 | Lag y Voddey is the beach below the car park towards the end of Clifton Road, just over 100 metres beyond the Mona's Queen III Memorial.

Lag y Voddey means 'Hollow of the Dog,' which has led some to believe that it got its name from a moddey doo which used to haunt this area.

WWG-MS3 214

Perwick

Public | Rough and uneven ground, steps | SC 2033 6733 | 54.070447, -4.747365 | Perwick is a bay south-west of Port St Mary. It can be accessed from a footpath leading from Perwick Road or Fistard Road down to the shore.

The fairy fires of Perwick brooghs

The brooghs above Perwick have been seen on fire at night many times, only for no trace of it to be found in the morning. These mysterious fires were identified as being fairy fires.

KR-MNQ 136

The fairies pulling in their boats

A man landed his boat at Perwick but it was too heavy for him to be able to pull it above the high-water mark. So when the wind got up that night, he went back to check on the boat and he was surprised to hear voices on the shore as he approached. He arrived to see a great number of people hauling a boat up the shore and shouting to each other, 'Ooilley Cooidjagh!' ('All together'). He went towards them but they disappeared, only to appear a short distance away hauling in another boat. He did not go near them a second time as he recognised them as fairies.

KR-MNQ 140

The fairies' mooring place

Public | Slippery, rough and uneven ground, tidal | SC 2012 6710 | 54.068338, -4.750472 | Collooway is the next bay south from Perwick. Although it is accessible from Perwick at low tide, the rocks can be slippery and dangerous.

A group of children were here at Collooway one Sunday morning when they were surprised to come across a metal bolt and a mooring ring firmly attached to a rock which none of them had ever seen before. They returned to the same spot a few days later and found that it had gone, and there was no hole to be found in the rock where it had been. Their conclusion was that it had previously been accidentally left there by the fairies who had been using it to tie up their boats.

An alternative version of this tale has it as a well-known bolt and ring of which no one knew the origins. A group of men decided to root it out but failed that day. When they came back, there was no trace of the bolt and ring anywhere. They too concluded it had belonged to the fairies but they had taken it away when they discovered that it was being tampered with.

BN-MS3 111–115 | WWG-MS3 365

Glenchass

Public | Rough and uneven ground, steps | SC 2003 6759 | 54.072677, -4.752053 | Glenchass is below Port St Mary, running from close to the Howe on the main road to Cregneash, down to Perwick. The area of Glenchass includes both the houses of the road and the glen itself, along which a public footpath runs.

The fairy feast

An old sailor was awoken in his house here in Glenchass one night by sounds in the kitchen. He went to see what it was and found a great number of people sat in the light of many candles at a long bench cutting up a fine beef with cleavers and saws. Recognising them as fairies, the old man did not say a word but drew silently away and returned to bed. In the morning he was amazed to find that the fairies had left the house completely clean and tidy, without even a mark or stain of the food anywhere.

KR-MNQ 126

The fairies try to steal a person

An expectant mother was lying awake in bed one night here in Glenchass with her husband lying asleep next to her. She looked over and saw a good number of fairies with big heads and ears the size and shape of wine bottles looking into the room. They then began to come in and they started to make an effigy, causing her fear that they had come to take away either herself or the baby. She tried to wake her husband but it took some time, though he did finally wake. As soon as his voice was heard, the fairies ran out of the room and bumped down the stairs with their almost-complete effigy.

KR-MNQ 133

The tall white woman

A man was once in his fields at sunset here at Glenchass when he met a tall ghostly woman in white coming up by the hedge. He did not say a word to her, nor did she speak to him, but he was so affected by this experience that he never went into that field again after sunset.

KR-MNQ 143

The grinning hag

A man had been in a house until late here at Glenchass and then he set off home towards Fistard. In the field in front of the house he saw something black in the hedge. Thinking it was a piece of clothing, he went to remove it, but when he got close it reared up as an old woman before him. She came towards him 'grinning fearfully' and began to open her mouth wide enough to swallow him. At this he turned and ran home as fast as he could. It took six to seven months before he fully recovered from the experience.

KR-MNQ 145

Cronk Glenchass

Private land – view only | Visible from public road | SC 1995 6759 | 54.072695, -4.753319 | Cronk Glenchass is the hill standing over Glenchass, below Port St Mary. The hill is not publicly accessible.

The fairy stronghold

Cronk Glenchass is considered to be a 'fairy stronghold.' Indeed, in the 1890s some even thought that the fairies had departed from everywhere in the Island except for this hill.

Fairy hunts have been seen here at night. On one occasion a man watched as first the fairy hunting dogs came and took a drink from the stream as they passed, before the fairies themselves came along, on horses and on foot. They were wearing red hats but the man could not tell in that light whether their coats were green or black.

KR-MNQ 21 | KR-MNQ 127 | WWG-MS1 514

The invisible companion

A man was once walking over the Cronk when he saw a group of men standing at the foot of the hill. When they saw him, they all stopped their activity and watched as he approached. When he reached them, they reported that they had seen someone dressed all in white walking beside him on the hill. He did not believe them at first, as he had not seen or heard anyone, but the seriousness with which they told him of the figure convinced him that they had seen a ghostly figure invisible to him.

KR-MNQ 144

The Howe

Public | Pavement beside road | SC 1977 6781 | 54.074564, -4.756196 | The Howe is the small collection of houses clustered around the chapel on the Howe Road, between Port St Mary and Cregneash.

The devil angry at the revivalists

The Howe Chapel used to be a thriving place for revivalist meetings and it was after one of these that a woman left the chapel after midnight one evening. She was following behind a group of people ahead of her singing hymns when she heard a noise from behind the hedge like a horse galloping with iron chains clanking around its feet. The sound went on and approached the group ahead of her, but it then came back quickly towards her again. The hedge was lower there and she was able to see that the sound was from a monstrous giant bull, leaping in fury at their religious singing. The woman was in great fear at this but the thing went off when one of the men from the group came back to get her. The woman believed this beast was the devil.

KR-MNQ 184

The woman with long yellow hair

Two men were going home from the Howe Chapel one clear moonlit night when they came across a woman with long yellow hair down to her waist sitting by the roadside. When the men came to her, she got up and walked away. The men followed her at a short distance and watched as she turned in at a house and sat down beside some flowers by the window. But when the men came to the place, she had vanished. They searched for her in every possible place there, but she was not to be found.

YLM 3.4.156

The spectral procession

A retired Presbyterian Minister once saw a spectral funeral procession going along the road here at the Howe. Amongst the procession the Minister recognised someone he knew. A couple of weeks later, that man was dead.

WWG-MS2 51

The lost wife of the Howe

Shortly after a woman had given birth at her home here in the Howe she was taken by the fairies and in her place they left a dead carcass. The husband buried the body in belief that it was the woman's and sometime after he took a second wife. Later, he was out late one night when he met the first wife again and she explained to him what had happened. She told him that he could free her from the fairies if he cleared the barn completely of any straw and then took her hand as she rode through the barn in a few nights' time. After telling his second wife about the encounter, the man cleared the barn of all its straw. However, he was heartbroken when he stayed up to see the first wife ride through with the fairies but he was unable to keep a hold of her hand. She called out that his second wife had hidden a piece of straw under a barrel, making it impossible for her to escape from the fairies.

YLM 3.4.149

The three big men of the Howe

Some men were walking along the Howe Road after midnight one moonlit night when they met three big men wearing caps as wide as wheels. These big men made no sound as they walked by and passed the two men.

YLM 3.4.149

The fairy hunters

The fairies used to hunt around the Howe with their dogs yowling and whips cracking. On one occasion two young men were going home late from the Howe when 'an army of fairy men and horses' came up the road. The men climbed over the hedge and watched as they went past. The fairies all had red caps and coats on, and there were so many of them that it took a long time before the road was clear again.

Another time a woman named Creggin thought she heard her son amongst them, shouting 'Hout, hout!'

YLM 3.4.150 | YLM 3.4.160

A thousand singing girls

A man at the end of the nineteenth century would tell of an experience he had on this road when he was a boy. One night after midnight he was walking here towards the Chasms when he met a thousand or more little girls, none of whom carried a light despite the dark. Some of these girls sang a song with the words, 'We met to part no more, Mary Oir.'

YLM 3.4.150

Buitched to not find a way out of a field

Public | Rough and uneven ground, steps | SC 1976 6785 | 54.074981, -4.756355 | A small field behind the Howe Chapel. Take the narrow path just below the chapel and after about 30 metres the track goes over an old stone stile, entering the field. The stile which the woman had hoped to exit by was along the wall by the house.

A woman set off home after a late meeting at the Howe Chapel one fine and light wintery night. However, after climbing the stile and entering this small field, she could not find the other stile out of the field, and she was surprised to find the hedge too tall to climb over. She walked along the hedge looking for the stile but she could not find it or a place low enough to clamber over anywhere. After a long time searching, she grew tired and wanted to stop but she could not do so as there seemed to be something urging her on. She walked on constantly through the night until she could hardly drag her feet by the morning. However, at the first rays of the sunrise, she again found herself in this small field as she knew it, with the stile where it had always been and the hedge low enough to climb all the way around.

KR-MNQ 196

Corvalley

Private | Corvalley is a farm at the Howe, on the Howe Road between Port St Mary and Cregneash.

The ghost of Billy Hom Collister

The ghost of a man who killed a woman through witchcraft used to be seen wandering around his former home here at Corvalley. A man named Billy Hom Collister lived here and at midnight one night he went with two friends as accomplices to secretly bury a bull's heart in its own small coffin in the churchyard. This was as an act of witchcraft against the woman who had rejected his courting years earlier as the full Christian burial service was performed over the grave, with Billy Hom putting in her name where the dead person was to be spoken of. The charm proved successful as the woman, then newly married, wasted away and died shortly after this. Later, when Billy Hom himself died, his ghost was to be seen wandering around here at Corvalley, his former home.

BN-MS1 4–15 | WWG-MS3 339–340

Cassemish, Harry and the Irish giant

A man named Harry used to live here at Corvalley and was great friends with a man named Cassemish who lived close by at the Howe. Together these great strong Manx men often went to Ardglass in Ireland to enjoy the fishing, the company of the women there and the drink made of ale and milk, called shellebuck. However, a giant lived there and would trouble the locals, frightening off the women and taking their shellebuck. When the giant came out while Harry and Cassemish were there, the women ran away leaving just the two Manxmen to face him. Cassemish told Harry to fight him, but Harry told him to fight instead, so he did. The giant had the first blow, but Cassemish withstood it and then threw the giant to the ground, whereupon he and Harry set to beating the giant until he was dead. The Irish girls were delighted at this and they ensured that the men had as much shellebuck as they wanted. It is said that, even now, the people in that area of the country still especially like the Manx because of this.

EF-MSR 167–168 | YLM 3.4.164–165

Poyll Vill

Private – View only | Visible from rough and uneven ground, close to a road | SC 1876 6767 | 54.072981, -4.771532 | Poyll Vill is a former small lake on the Mull Road, close to Cregneash. The dried-up remains of Poyll Vill are a small semi-circular area of rushes and grass just on the Sound side of the road, about 30 metres from where the Mull Road leaves the Sound Road just beyond Cregneash.

Poyll Vill is well known for its association with the fairies and for the many strange things that have been experienced here.

A man was out to visit his sweetheart in Cregneash late one moonlit night and as he came up from Port Erin he came across a great crowd of people near here at Poyll Vill. The finely dressed men and women were dancing, jumping and playing games like 'kiss in the ring,' laughing and shouting merrily. The man stopped and watched this strange sight for a while but they paid him no attention and eventually he went on away towards the village.

Another man was coming up the same way from Port Erin when he came across a crowd in the road. They took hold of him and brought him here to Poyll Vill, where they met a very big man, who was annoyed at them for bringing him. The very big man told them to, 'Let the decent man go, right before the wind.' This they did and the man got away as fast as he could.

A different man was coming from Port Erin late at night and as he came by Poyll Vill a hand bell began to ring at a great rate just beside him. He stopped to see who it was but it fell silent and he could see no one. When he began moving again the bell started once more and went on all the way until he was at Cregneash. Sometimes the ringing was on his left side and sometimes on his right and he looked all about him but he never saw anyone or anything to explain it.

In around the 1830s a new boat was built in Port St Mary and brought up to a house near here, ready for launching at the Sound when the weather was fine. It lay there for over a week during which time people saw the boat on Poyll Vill every night as the fairies took it there for a sail.

One Pancake Day evening a woman was heading towards the Sound from Port Erin in order to make pancakes. As she got here to Poyll Vill, a darkness fell around her so that she could not see where she was going at all. She walked on, hoping to come out of it but she walked all night and never came to a hedge or a building at all. However, as daylight came the darkness dissolved around her and she found herself close to Ballahowe, on the cliff over Ghaw ny Mooar.

KR-MNQ 197–199

Two fairies in the quarry

Public | Paved parking area | SC 1908 6739 | 54.070579, -4.766501 | The quarry is today used as the car park for the Cregneash museum. It is before the village on the right-hand side of the road as you approach from Port St Mary.

A man from Cregneash came across two fairies in the quarry here. They were about two or three feet tall and dressed in red caps, and they ran away when they saw him looking at them. The man was very lucky to have seen them first, as they then could not do him any harm.

WWG-MS2 211–212

The women listening at the door at Hop tu Naa

Public, but there is admission charge to enter the site | Uneven ground | SC 1887 6734 | 54.070022, -4.769717 | Ned Beg's Cottage is the final thatched cottage in Cregneash village, on the left-hand side of the main road as you travel from Port St Mary towards the Sound.

Edward Faragher came upon some young women listening at his front door here on Hop tu Naa night. They each had a mouthful of water from a well that never runs dry, and they were listening in to hear the first name to be mentioned in the conversation of those inside. This was a divination practice where the first-heard name was also that of their future spouse. Although widely known, this is one of the very few instances of it being recorded in practice.

EF-MSR 148–151

The tall lady who could not cross the stream

Private land – view only | Visible from rough and uneven ground | SC 1855 6701 | 54.066962, -4.774287 | Part of a private field below Cregneash. From the village, take the farm trail track leading through the yard of Church Farm. Follow this path for about 500 metres until it begins to turn back towards Cregneash. Directly in front of you is a gate into a private field with a stream running along its left edge. The paths of farm vehicles lead to a gate just out of view on the left side of the field, leading to the small bridge over the stream referred to in this tale.

There used to be no road from Cregneash to the Sound, but only a path across the fields which came this way. A man was walking here towards the Sound one night when a very fine big lady stepped up to walk beside him. He took fright and began to run but she kept pace with him, no matter how fast he ran, even as he leapt over hedges. She did this all silently, making no sound even with her feet, but when he came to the stream here and jumped over, the woman was left behind as she was not able to cross it.

It was also in the fields between Cregneash and the Sound that two men were out hunting one night when they were shocked by their dogs coming back to them and refusing to leave their side. They then saw a white dog with 'a curly mane like a lion' appear and pass them by in the moonlight.

KR-MNQ 190 | YLM 3.4.151 | YLM 3.4.165–166

The captured mermaid

Private land – view only | Visible from Rough and uneven footpath | SC 1966 6652 | 54.062941, -4.757163 | Kione y Ghoggan is a headland between Port St Mary and the Chasms. From the Chasms, it is the first section of headland where Port St Mary is visible.

A young man once captured a mermaid in one of the caves or clefts here under the headland of Kione y Ghoggan. He took her home with him, but after a time he became tired of her and instead began to see a human woman. The mermaid then left him and returned to the sea here where she had first been captured. When the man returned and found the mermaid gone, he was overcome with remorse and so flung himself to his death from these same cliffs.

WWG-MS1 502–503

The Chasms

Public | Rough and uneven ground, dangerous hidden drops | SC 1926 6646 | 54.062261, -4.763203 | The Chasms are on the coast south of Cregneash. From the small car park at the end of the road leading south through Cregneash (at a right-angle to the main road from Port St Mary to the Sound), climb the stile and go down the steep hill to the building below. The Chasms are accessed through the gate in front of this building. The nature of this site makes it potentially very dangerous.

The sheep slaughtered in the Chasms

In around the 1800s a man lost one of his loaghtan sheep into the Chasms and he had himself lowered into the fissure in a basket in order to retrieve it. The depth of the descent was so great that every rope in Cregneash had to be tied end-to-end before the basket reached the bottom. Here the man could hear the sound of his sheep being slaughtered in a neighbouring part of the cavern by a group of boisterous people clattering their drinking cups with glee. Frightened of meeting the same fate as the sheep, the man returned to the basket and signalled to be hoisted up again. Just then the people down in the Chasms heard him and ran out to get him, but thankfully he was already hoisted out of their reach.

AWM-FIOM 74 | JT-HSA 2.164–165

The fairies cooking down the Chasms

Some men were walking here one fine Sunday morning when they heard a cock crowing down in part of the Chasms. The men could not see to the bottom of the fissure, but instead they rolled a stone down into where they had heard the crowing. Nothing more was heard, but a cloud of smoke rose up out of the shaft. They interpreted this as showing that they had dropped the rock into the fairies' broth pot and broken it into the fire down below, sending the puff of steam up towards them at the top.

KR-MNQ 176

The lights foretelling death

Late one night some fishermen saw a strange light on the side of Spanish Head. They watched it move along the cliff until it finally came to a stop at the Chasms. A few nights later they saw another light at Glen Wither, and again it moved along the cliffs to stop at the same point here at the Chasms. Sometime after this a man fell to his death at this exact point at the Chasms, proving the lights to have been a foretelling of his death.

KR-MNQ 150

The Sugarloaf

Inaccessible – view only | Visible from rough and uneven ground, close to cliff edge | SC 1948 6623 | 54.060268, -4.759734 | The Sugarloaf is a large stack of rock standing alone off the coast at the Chasms, south of Cregneash. It is visible off to the left from the cliffs of the Chasms. Access to and climbing of the Sugarloaf is subject to seasonal restrictions due to bird nesting.

The two ladies of the Sugarloaf

Very early one summer morning a man was pulling heather near the Chasms. Just as the sun was rising, he saw two finely dressed ladies coming up the slope from by the Sugarloaf. The women passed him without speaking and went about a little before going to the cliff and calmly walking over the edge. The man knew that no normal person could walk down the sheer cliff here and so he took fright and ran home. He was ill with the fright for some time after this.

These women are perhaps the same as were seen by two fishermen who were sailing home to Port St Mary from the Sound as the sun was going down behind the land. Just past the Sugarloaf they saw two ladies leisurely walking about on the perpendicular cliff face. The women, one of whom had a red dress on, gambolled around as easily as if they were in a field, running about for some time and remaining visible to the men even as they passed Perwick.

KR-MNQ 149

The lady in the boat

An old fisherman was on his way home alone to Port St Mary from the Calf of Man one evening as the sun was setting. There was little wind and the sail was flapping around, but as he passed the Sugarloaf the wind caught and spread the sail out to reveal a woman sitting looking out silently at the bow of his boat. The fisherman could not see her face and he was too frightened to speak to her but he watched as the breeze dropped again and the sail obscured her. When the wind took the sail again the woman was no longer there. The man did not go fishing alone near here ever again.

KR-MNQ 149

The merman of the Sugarloaf

A merman was once seen swimming between the Sugarloaf and the land here. He was referred to as the 'guilley beg' ('little boy') by the fishermen, who did not dare to refer to him as a merman when at sea. They would throw him a sandwich of oatbread and butter when sailing near here to win his favour.

EF-MSR 139–140

The mermaid of Cass Struan

Inaccessible – View only | Visible from rough and uneven ground | SC185662 | 54.060124, -4.773679 | The shore below Cass Struan, the stream which runs into the south-western end of Bay Stacka, between Black Head and the Chasms. A footpath passes over the stream, though the shore below is better seen from the Chasms.

Mermaids used to be common around the coast here and fishermen would regularly throw them oak-cakes with bread and butter. Later, mermaids began to be seen less frequently, though they were still to be occasionally glimpsed here, such as when two men saw a mermaid so close to them that they could see the web between her fingers. Another mermaid, with large breasts, was also seen on a rock here by a man and his two sisters, but she jumped into the sea as soon as she saw them.

EF-MSR 139–140 | YLM 3.4.159

Spanish Head

Public | Rough and uneven ground, close to cliff edge | SC 1814 6582 | 54.056107, -4.779846 | Spanish Head is the western end of the large headland between the Chasms and the Sound, accessible via the Raad ny Foillan.

Manannan's path off the Island

At the arrival of St Patrick on the Isle of Man, Manannan took the form of three legs and rolled from his home at the top of South Barrule down to Spanish Head. Here he rolled over the edge of the cliff so swiftly and quietly that none of the birds on the cliff face below were disturbed at all. Manannan then rolled over the sea to an Island off the Calf of Man, which he then caused to sink to the bottom of the sea. However, this island returns to the surface once every seven years, just before sunrise when Old Laa Boaldyn falls on a Sunday, so that Manannan can look upon the Isle of Man again. But at the first rays of the sun hitting on its hills, the island sinks again below the waves.

This is distinguished from a similar story of Manannan at Burroo Ned because here it is perhaps linked to something seen by a man some time before the 1880s. He was here early in the day when a three-legged figure with no head rolled past him towards the cliff edge and then off and away out of sight. Remarkably, the thing did not disturb any of the vast quantities of birds that were nesting among the rocks below.

SM-MFT 22–23 | WWG-MS1 388 | YLM 3.4.135

The tall man and mermaids

A man was here at Spanish Head just before daybreak checking on the snares he had set when he was shocked to see a man of nine feet tall walking up the cliff face. This tall man did not stop at all when he reached the top but went on and walked away.

The neighbourhood of Spanish Head has also been observed as once having been 'rich in traces of the mermaid.'

WWG-MS1 504 | YLM 3.4.158

Finn MacCooil and the giant

PROW | Rough and uneven ground, close to cliff edge | SC 1763 6644 | 54.061549, -4.788089 | Faint remains of three roundhouses on the end of Burroo Ned, the prominent headland to the north-east of the Sound. From the Sound car park, head south-east along the Raad ny Foillan in the direction of Port St Mary. After about 300 metres the path goes over a stile into an open field. Follow the edge of the field up the hill and over another stile onto the exposed end of the headland. On very rare occasions, the marks of three roundhouses dating to the Iron Age can be discerned here under the right weather conditions.

The great Finn MacCooil used to live in these houses here at Burroo Ned. When the giant of South Barrule heard of Finn's great strength, he came down to challenge him to a fight. Seeing the enormous giant coming, Finn went quickly into the house and had his mother tuck him into the cot like a baby. When the giant entered, the old lady explained that Finn was out and that the baby was Finn's child. The giant was very impressed that the baby of Finn would have such a beard as he had already. Finn then slipped out and met the giant again in the fields, where he pretended to be merely a cowherd. In this disguise, Finn fought with the giant over a cow until each grasped a horn and pulled it clean off the beast. The strength of even this lowly employee of Finn's impressed the giant immensely. The giant then went off through the fields as Finn went home and had his mother bake two cakes of oatmeal, one with the griddle hidden in the middle. Finn then went to the giant and finally identified himself and agreed to a fight, but only after he had rested. The giant agreed and accepted Finn's invitation to a meal, at which the giant was amazed to see Finn chewing his cake easily while he could not bite through his at all. After this they rested and in the morning the giant agreed to a swim before they fought, but upon hearing of Finn's plan to swim to Wales and back, he finally realised that it wiser to flee back up to South Barrule instead.

In an alternative version of this story, it is a buggane rather than a giant who comes from South Barrule to fight Finn.

EF-MSR 168–171 | KR-MNQ 230 | SM-MFT 45–49

The underground passage to the land of Manannan

Private land – view only | Visible from rough and uneven ground | SC 1758 6646| 54.061654, -4.788848 | The eastern face of Burroo Ned, the prominent headland to the north-east of the Sound. The eastern face is best visible from the small headland south of the Sound car park.

At the arrival of St Patrick in the Isle of Man, Manannan took the form of the Three Legs of Man and rolled from his home at the top of South Barrule down to Burroo Ned. From here he rolled over the edge and plunged into the sea below to leave the Island completely.

This is similar to a story at Spanish Head but here on the side of Burroo Ned there is said to be a concealed entrance to an underground passageway. This leads out under the sea all the way to the hidden kingdom of Manannan.

WWG-MS1 388 | WWG-MS1 504

Ghaw ny Spyrryd

Private land – view only | Visible from rough and uneven footpath | SC 1759 6659 | 54.062867, -4.788767 | Ghaw ny Spyrryd is a small gully on the Calf of Man side of Burroo Ned, the prominent headland to the north-east of the Sound. It is visible from the Raad ny Foillan after you walk past an exposed section of path and over a stile.

Ghaw ny Spyrryd means 'Creek of the Spirit' in Manx, and it was to this spirit, or spirits, that fishermen used to give offerings in the hope of ensuring good weather during the fishing season. Some believed that this spirit was a buggane, and at least one person would not pass along the cliffs here without throwing down some rum for the buggane and calling out, 'Gow shen, y veisht!' ('Take that, evil spirit!'). One account of the beast to be found here reports it as having a head like a big pot with three great horns. Its howls from within the creek are sometimes still to be heard.

AWM-MN 159 | JJK-PN 37 | N-IOME-05121914 | WWG-MS1 102

The Sound

Public | Paved ground by the car park | SC 1737 6671 | 54.063900, -4.792159 | The site of the Sound farm is today occupied by part of the Sound Cafe. It is located at the bottom of the Isle of Man, overlooking the Calf of Man.

The devil dancing to the fiddle

When an old man who played the fiddle lived here, the neighbours would often come round to dance to his playing. One evening he was alone and he played until it became dark, when suddenly the fire blazed up and he saw the devil or some of his imps dancing on the floor before him. He immediately threw away the fiddle and never played it again.

KR-MNQ 194

Hundreds of fairy dogs

One night the man living here at the Sound was outside when he heard a shrill whistle. He whistled back and, in a moment, there were hundreds of 'tiny little dogs' all around him, and their owners soon came after them on their hunt. The man got inside quickly and the fairies and their dogs went off towards Spanish Head.

Another version of this tale has only a dozen dogs and no hunters present.

KR-MNQ 190 | YLM 3.4.151

Kitterland

Inaccessible – view only | Visible from paved car park | Kitterland is the large Island in the channel between the Isle of Man and the Calf of Man. Access is restricted due to wildlife conservation.

In the days of Norse rule in the Isle of Man, a Baron named Kitter hunted all over the Island until every wild animal was killed. At this point Kitter then set off to hunt on the Calf of Man. Frightened that Kitter would also soon begin to kill their livestock, the Manx people turned to a witch named Ada for help. She went to Kitter's home on the top of South Barrule, where the baron had left his cook, Eaoch of the Loud Voice, in charge. But Ada used her craft to cause Eaoch to fall asleep, and the fat from the cooking pot bubbled over until the house was soon on fire. Eaoch then awoke and called out to Kitter on the Calf. Kitter heard Eaoch's loud call and immediately set off back towards the mainland in a small boat. However, Ada caused a storm and the small boat hit the island here and Kitter and his men were all drowned. The island has been known as Kitterland ever since.

AWM-FIOM-07 27–28 | HIJ-JG 156-158 | JT-HSA 2.177–178 | KR-MNQ 231 | SM-MFT 109–111

The mermaid's garden

Private land – view only | Visible from rough and uneven ground close to cliff edge | SC 1811 6789 | 54.074709, -4.781621 | Lhiondaig Pohllinag is at the bottom of the grassy slope at the western end of Bay Fine, about three quarters of a mile south of Port Erin along the Raad ny Foillan. Lhiondaig Pohlinag is west of the gully, Glen Wither, which runs down the broogh over Bay Fine. The site is private land and it is not safely accessible owing to the steepness of the slope.

The Manx name of this place, Lhiondaig Pohllinag, translates as 'Mermaid's Green.' Mermaids or mermen used to be seen here, basking themselves in the sun or sporting about.

KR-MNQ 209 | N-IOME-05121914

Santon

Although not copious, the folklore of Santon is varied and interesting. A fairy well, a giant's grave, ghosts, charms and witchcraft are all present, as well as the bridge with the Island's oldest and strongest claim to be a Fairy Bridge.

- The Fairy Well [private land]
1. Hanging hair from the steeple
2. Ballalona Bridge
3. Death after seeing a thing in the ditch
- The ghost smugglers [private land]

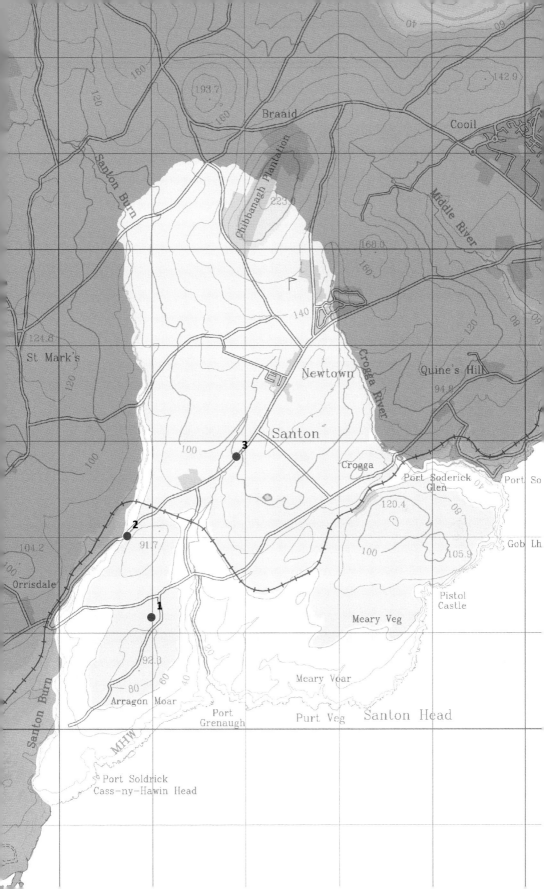

The Fairy Well

Private | A well on private land within Crogga Glen close to the railway line.

This well was known as 'the Fairy Well' and coins, pins or buttons were left here as offerings for the fairies into the second half of the nineteenth century, presumably left here by those who had taken its water. However, the building of the railway line so close to here caused the fairies to leave, as they went off to find somewhere more quiet and remote.

HIJ-JG 75–76 | HIJ-JG 88

Hanging hair from the steeple

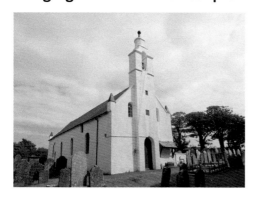

Open during daylight hours | Some uneven ground | SC 3106 7115 | 54.108437, -4.585639 | The Parish church of Kirk Santon is off the Old Castletown Road, which runs to the east side of today's main road between Douglas and Castletown. The turning towards the church is signposted just over three quarters of a mile from the steep hill that joins the main road to Ballasalla.

In 1690 a farmer somewhat naively asked the vicar's permission to carry out the charm he had received for 'the falling evil' which was afflicting his sister-in-law. A wise woman of Ballasalla had advised him to tie some of his sister's hair to the church steeple here, above the level of the bell, before sunrise on three Sundays. However, rather than grant permission, the vicar brought the man to ecclesiastical court for attempted witchcraft.

DC-MI 29

Ballalona Bridge

Public | Public road | SC 3062 7198 | 54.115716, -4.592874 | Ballalona Bridge crosses the Santon Burn at a bend in the main Douglas to Castletown road, about two miles away from Ballasalla, at the bottom of a small hill and 200 metres on the Douglas-side of the Fairy Bridge.

Ballalona Bridge has the Island's strongest claim to be a Fairy Bridge. Since at least the 1860s it has been known as a place associated with the fairies, with people therefore trying to avoid it at night however possible.

By the start of the twentieth century people would doff their hats here in deference to the fairies. The explanation given for this was that a long time ago a battle was fought near here between the north and the south. The fairies of Ballalona Bridge were disturbed by this and so they set to plaguing the northern Manx with annoyances until they lost the battle. Ever since then the southerners doffed their hats here in thanks for this and to let the fairies know that they are of the preferred southern side and so to foster good luck.

However, Ballalona's first association with the mysterious was not with the fairies but with the devil, as it was said in the 1810s that the devil was frequently to be found here. At this time, the bridge was better known as 'the Devil's Bridge,' and people were extremely resistant to go over it after dark.

JGC-HPECL 29 | HIJ-JG 74–75 | HAB-HIOM 215–216 | N-MS-26081865 | PIOMNHAS 4.1.51 | WL-DPG 82

Death after seeing a thing in the ditch

Private land – view only | Visible from pavement beside a road | SC 3193 7286 | 54.123999, -4.573345 | The former Brown Cow inn is today a private house on the east side of the dual carriageway roughly halfway along the main road between Douglas and Ballasalla.

A man from Ballaglass in Maughold set off on a journey before daybreak, but just as he came out of the farm gates his horse refused to go any further and he noticed something black in the ditch outside. However, the man gave little attention to this and forced his horse on, though the wisdom of this was called into question later when his horse fell dead here by the Brown Cow and the man himself went on to suffer from an illness for months afterwards.

WWG-MS3 386

The ghost smugglers

Private | Knock Froy is a private farm on the south-east side of the main Douglas to Ballasalla road. The private track to the farm is almost opposite the Mount Murray Back Road.

The ghosts of three men are sometimes seen here at Knock Froy. One account was of someone who first saw them when he was a boy in the 1940s, while helping his father at work in one of the farm buildings. They heard footsteps and the father went and opened the door. He saw the ghosts and so called over the boy, who saw the ghostly figures of three men walking away, wearing rough clothing, one with a sack slung over his shoulder, one with a cloth cap on and one with a peaked hat of some sort. His father explained that they were the ghosts of smugglers and that they would do him no harm. The boy was to go on to see them two more times before he moved away. Ghostly figures, though less distinct, have been seen by at least one subsequent tenant of the farm.

CV-OH-BK | CV-YT-BK2

Sources

Add   Additional material collected or observed directly by the authors.

AELM-MY   Le Mothe, A. E. *Manx Yarns. Witty, Wise, and Otherwise.* Douglas: The Manx Sun Ltd., 1905.

AIOMS   *Account of the Isle of Man in Song.* Trans. Jennifer Kewley Draskau. Centre for Manx Studies Monograph 5. Douglas: Centre for Manx Studies, 2006.

AJAF-ASG   Johnson, Andrew and Fox, Allison. *Archaeological Sites Guide of the Isle of Man up to AD 1500.* Douglas: Culture Vannin, 2017.

ANL-LR   Laughton, Alfred Nelson. *High-Bailiff Laughton's Reminiscences.* Douglas: S.K. Broadbent & Co. Ltd, 1916. Reprint. Douglas: Dickinson, Cruikshank & Co., 1999.

AWM-FIOM   Moore, A. W. *Folk-Lore of the Isle of Man.* Douglas: Brown & Son, 1891. Reprint. Wakefield: S. R. Publishers Ltd., 1971.

AWM-MN   Moore, A. W. *Manx Names or The Surnames and Place-Names of the Isle of Man.* Second ed., London: Elliot Stock, 1903.

AWM-MBM   Moore, A. W. *Manx Ballads & Music.* Douglas: G. & R. Johnson, 1896. Reprint. Felinfach: Llanerach Publishers, 1998.

                  'Introduction.' xiv–xxx.
                  'Yn Bollan Bane / The White Wort.' 76–76.

BGIM-01   *Brown's Guide to the Isle of Man.* Thirteenth ed., Douglas: James Brown & Son. n.d. [but 1894].

BN-MS   Nelson, Blanche. *Manx Tales etc.* Manx National Heritage Library, MS 432A.

                  'The landing of King Orry, or "The Raad Mooar Gorree."' 3–11.
                  'A roll down Penny-Pot, or "A thorn-tree will grow."' 131–133.
                  'The Bolt in the Rock, or Where did it go?' 111–115.
                  'The Flowering of the Myrrh.' 21–29.

CJ-GTM   Josiffe, Christopher. *Gef! The strange tale of an extra-special talking mongoose.* London: Strange Attractor Press, 2017.

CV-OH   Culture Vannin Oral History recordings. https://culturevannin.im/watchlisten/oralhistory

                  CV-OH-EC Cleator, Ernie. Interviewed by Katie Newton, 27 August 2018.
                  CV-OH-BK Kewley, Bob. Interviewed by Katie Newton, 25 July 2018.
                  CV-OH-JC Crellin, Johnny. Interviewed by Joanne Sayle, 28 February 2019.
                  CV-OH-SWQ Quane, Sidney & Wesley. Interviewed by Katie Newton, 9 March 2020.
                  CV-OH-BS Sopher, Brian. Interviewed by James Franklin, 15 May 2023.

CV-YT   Culture Vannin video recordings.

 CV-YT-BK1 Kewley, Bob. 'Believing in Fairies; Motorbike racers visiting the Fairy Bridge.' *YouTube*, uploaded by Culture Vannin, 24 May 2019, https://youtu.be/bWmrLkB9UQE

 CV-VT-BK2 Kewley, Bob. 'The Ghosts of Knock Froy, Isle of Man.' *YouTube*, uploaded by Culture Vannin, 24 May 2019, https://youtu.be/-MSaFOqi4M8

 CV-YT-JC Cannell, John. 'Ballacarnane Keeill & Graveyard.' *YouTube*, uploaded by Culture Vannin, 28 June 2019, https://youtu.be/ddpyZPaqBd4

DC-MI   Craine, David. *Manannan's Isle*. Douglas: The Manx Museum and National Trust, 1955.

 'Sorcery and Witchcraft.' 13–30.

 'Milntown.' 94–99.

 'The Dungeon of St. German's.' 129–148.

 'The Great Enquest.' 149–173.

 'Ballaugh.' 210–229.

 'Kirk Patrick of Jurby.' 230–247.

DR-TIOM   Robertson, David. *A Tour Through the Isle of Man*. London: 1794. Reprint. Newcastle Upon Tyne: Frank Graham, 1970.

EF-MSR   Faragher, Edward. *Manx Stories and Reminiscences of Ned Beg Hom Ruy*. Ed. George Broderick, Yn Cheshaght Ghailckagh, 1991.

 'Stories about the Fishing.' 129–131.

 'Merman, Mermaid, Buggane.' 139–140.

 'St Bridget's Eve at Earyween.' 147–148.

 'Hallowe'en.' 148–151.

 'Father Kelly.' 160–162.

 'Story of 'Cassemish' and Harry of Corvalley.' 167–168.

 'Finn Maccooil and the Giant.' 168–171.

 'Story of the Glashten that was Castrated.' 175–176.

EK-CC   Kermode, E. *Celtic Customs: Superstitions, Customs and Observations connected with the Manx Calendar*. 1885. Leeds: The Moxon Press Ltd., 1985.

EW-FFCC   Evans Wentz, W. Y. *The Fairy-Faith in Celtic Countries*. New York: Henry Frowde, 1911.

FG-AIOM   Grose, Francis. 'The Antiquities of the Isle of Man, 1773-83.' *The Old Historians of the Isle of Man*. Manx Society, vol. xviii. Douglas: Manx Society, 1871.

FLS	Folk Life Survey, Manx National Heritage

FLS B001/A Notes from Rev. Clarke's book (1904-19).

FLS B/042 H.M. Briggs, Ballakilmartin, Mrs McCutcheon, Ballakilmartin and Mr A. Moore, Begoade-Ballig. Collector: Margaret Killip (December 1971).

FLS C/016-A Mr T. Costain, Riverside Cottage, Colby. Collector: Mary Quilliam (12 October 1949).

FLS C/043-A Caesar Crellin, Andreas. Collector: MQ (October 1952).

FLS C/117 Tom Crennell, near Ballaslieu, Andreas. Collector: Margaret Killip (December 1957).

FLS C/135 Mr Curphey, Maughold. Collector: Margaret Killip (May 1961).

FLS C/204 Mr Louis Crellin, Girvan Cottage, Rheast, Peel. Collector: Margaret Killip (April 1967).

FLS CC/B Charles Corrin, Bemeccan, Seaview Road, Onchan. Collector: Mary Quilliam (22 June 1949).

FLS CE/C Eric Cregeen. 'Notebook No.1' (1954).

FLS G018/A Mrs Glass (26 June 1954).

FLS K/106 Fred Kaighen, Main Road, Kirk Michael. Collector: Margaret Killip (May 1967).

FLS K/115 Mrs Smith, Ballelby, Dalby. Collector: Margaret Killip (July 1970).

FLS KM/C Information about Laxey. Collector: Miss Mgt. Killip.

FLS STW/D Mr. Stowell, Glen Ruy. Collector: L.Q. & Miss Killip (26th January 1949).

FLS Q/32A John Quayle, Glen Ruy, Lonan. Collector: MQ and Miss C. Quilliam (November 1953).

FLS Q/041-B Mr J Quayle, Barregarrow Cottage, Barregarrow, Kirk Michael. Collector: Margaret Killip (n.d.).

FLS R/011-E Mr W. Robinson, Glen Mona, Maughold. Collector: Margaret Killip (November 1972).

FLS S/012-C Mrs Emma Cameron, 40 The Crofts, Castletown. Collector: Miss Zilla Sayle (December 1968).

FLS S/14-A Richard Shimmin, 3 Funchal Avenue, Formby. Copy of letter to Mona Breadner, Union Mills (29 September 1956).

FLS STW/C Mr Stowell, Glen Ruy. Collector: Margaret Killip & J.L.Q. (12 January 1949).

FLS T/5-D Mr A Wilfed Teare, Grianagh, Albany Road, Peel. Collector: Margaret Killip, (October 1958).

FLS W/003-A Mr Watterson, Grenaby Schoolhouse (6 March 1951).

FP-P1	Palmer, Fred. *Peel One: Peel Hill and Shore Road.* n.d.
FP-P2	Palmer, Fred. *Peel Two: Around Creg Malin.* 1984.
GB-CKMI	*Cronica Regum Mannie & Insularum: Chronicles of the Kings of Man and the Isles.* Trans. George Broderick. Third ed., Douglas: Manx National Heritage, 2004.

GB-HLSM   George Broderick. 'John Kneen (The Gaaue), Ballaugh.' *A Handbook of Late Spoken Manx. Vol. I. Grammar and Texts*. Tübingen: Max Niemeyer Verlag, 1984, 230–269 & 427–440.

GB-LWC   Borrow, George. *Life, Writings, and Correspondence of George Borrow, derived from official and other authentic sources.* Ed. William I. Knapp. Vol. 2. London: John Murray, 1899.

GQ-TMB   Quarrie, George. *The Melliah Boh! Velshu Thiggal Shen? and Beeg Dinner was' Scotch Peeble, Exthronnaery Mate,* &c. Barrow: Carruthers Bros., 1880.

GQ-LOF   Quayle, George. *Legends of a Lifetime: Aspects of Manx Life*. Second ed., Wigan: Douglas Printers, 1979.

GW-DIM   Waldron, George. *A Description of the Isle of Man*. 1731. Ed. William Harrison. Manx Society, vol. xi. Douglas: Manx Society, 1865.

GW-AIOM   Woods, George. *Account of the Past and Present of the Isle of Man.* London: Robert Baldwin, 1811.

HAB-HIOM   Bullock, H. A. *History of the Isle of Man.* London: Longman, Hurst, Rees, Orme, and Brown, 1816.

HIJ-JG   Jenkinson, Henry Irwin. *Jenkinson's Practical Guide to the Isle of Man.* Second ed., London: Edward Stanford, 1878.

HL-CL   Lee, Harriet. *Clara Lennox; or, The Distressed Widow. A novel founded on facts interspersed with an historical description of the Isle of Man.* Vol. 2, London: Harriet Lee, 1797.

HRO-VIMA   Oswald, H. R. *Vestigia Insulae Manniae Antiquiora, or A Dissertation on the Armorial Bearings of the Isle of Man, The Regalities and Prerogatives of its Ancient Kings, and the Original Usages, Customs, Privileges, Laws, and Constitutionall Government of the Manx People.* Manx Society, vol. v. Douglas: Manx Society, 1890.

JC-MR   Clague, Dr John. *Cooinaghtyn Manninagh: Manx Reminiscences.* Castletown: M. J. Backwell, 1911.

       'Yn Lioar-Imbee / The Calendar.' 40–45.

       'Laa Boaldyn / May Day.' 46–55.

       'Yn Ouyr / The Harvest.' 74–81.

       'Obbeeys / Superstitions and Sorcery.' 166–181.

JF-TIOM   Feltham, John. *A Tour through the Isle of Mann, in 1797 and 1798.* Bath: R. Cruttwell, 1798.

JGC-HPECL   Cumming, Rev. Joseph George. *The Isle of Man; Its history, physical, ecclesiastical, civil and legendary.* London: John Va Voorst, 1848.

JJK-PN   Kneen, J. J. *The Place-Names of the Isle of Man.* Douglas: Yn Cheshaght Ghailckagh, 1925. Reprint. Douglas: Yn Cheshaght Ghailckagh, 1973.

JK-MD   Kelly, John. *The Manx Dictionary.* Ed. William Gill. Manx Society, vol. xiii. Douglas: Manx Society, 1866.

JMM   *The Journal of the Manx Museum.*
'Bronze Age Tumuli.' i.16 (September 1928): 121–122.
'Discovery of a Pre-Historic Oak Vessel.' ii.29 (December 1931): 38–40.
'The British Association Visit. Sunday 20th September, 1936. The Keeills of Kirk Marown.' iii.49 (December 1936): 153.
'The Kewleys of Ballafreer: Remarkable Record of a Kirk Marown Family.' iii.49 (December 1936): 157–159.
David Craine. 'Sorcery and Witchcraft in the Isle of Man in the 17th and 18th Centuries.' iv.59 (June 1939): 122–124.

JQ-KP1   Quilliam, John. *Gems from Know Your Parish, No. 1.* Isle of Man: Castletown Press, 1979.

JQ-KP2   Quilliam, John. *Gems from Know Your Parish, No. 2.* Isle of Man: Castletown Press, 1979.

JR-MFS   Rhys, John. 'Manx Folk-Lore and Superstitions.' *Folk-Lore.* ii (1891): 284–313
Rhys, John. 'Manx Folk-Lore and Superstitions, Part 2.' *Folk-Lore.* iii (1892): 74–88

JT-HSA   Train, Joseph. *An Historical and Statistical Account of the Isle of Man.* Douglas: Mary A. Quiggin, 1845.

KF-MR   Forrest, Kathrine A. *Manx Recollections: Memorials of Eleanor Elliott.* Douglas: James Brown & Son, 1894.

KG-TMC   Kniveton, Gordon N. and Goldie, Mike. *Tholtans of the Manx Crofter.* Douglas: The Manx Experience, 1996.

KR-MNQ   Roeder, Karl. *Manx Notes & Queries.* Douglas: S. K. Broadbent, 1904. Reprint. *Ghosts, Bugganes & Fairy Pigs: Karl Roeder's Manx Notes & Queries.* Ed. Stephen Miller. Douglas: Culture Vannin, 2019.

LQ-GIOM   Quilliam, Leslie. *A Gazetteer of the Isle of Man.* Cashtal Books, 2004.

LRM   Anon. *Legends and Recollections of Mona. with Other Poems from a Family Portfolio,* Guernsey: H. Brouard, 1849.

LT-SCI   Teignmouth, Lord. *Sketches of the Coasts and Islands of Scotland and of the Isle of Man.* Volume 2. London: John W. Parker, 1836.

MD-AG   Mona Douglas RBV, Bernard Caine RBV and Charles Guard. 'Arrane Ghleby.' *The Mona Douglas Manx Ceili (1974),* Culture Vannin, 2009. https://culturevannin.bandcamp.com/track/arrane-ghelby

MD-CTM   Douglas, Mona. *Christian Tradition in Mannin.* Douglas: Times Longbooks, 1965.
'The Earliest Manx School.' 21–25.

MD-DT   Denham, Michael Aislabie. 'Popular Rhymes, Proverbs, Sayings, Prophesies, &c., peculiar to the Isle of Man and the Manks people.' *The Denham Tracts: A Collection of Folklore by Michael Aislabie Denham and reprinted from the original tracts and pamphlets printed by Mr. Denham between 1846 and 1859.* Vol. I. Ed. Dr James Hardy. London: The Folklore Society, 1892, 186–204.

MD-EVAF   Douglas, Mona. *This is Ellan Vannin Again: Folklore.* Douglas: Times Longbooks, 1966.

      'The legend of Mananan.' 9–12.
      'Saint Patrick of Mann.' 13–17.
      'Wonders of Mannin.' 18–21.
      'Some Lonan lore.' 26–30.
      'The herb and the word.' 31–34.
      'Struan y Granghie: The Lonan legend behind a Manx folk-song.' 71–75.

MD-WCEV   Douglas, Mona. *We call it Ellan Vannin.* Douglas: Times Longbooks, 1970.

      'Mananan, King of Mannan.' 17–21.
      'Gone to Ballaugh.' 53–56.

MJ   *Mannin Journal.*

      S.M. 'Arrane Ghelbee.' 1 (May 1913): 51.
      Moore, J. R. 'Folk-Lore Notes. The Well at West Baldwin.' 4 (November 1914): 253.
      Moore, J. R. 'The Shore of Baie Mooar.' 5 (May 1915): 280–287.
      Cushag. 'Folklore Notes. The Evil Eye.' 5 (May 1915): 294–295.
      Moore, J. R. 'Folklore Notes. Buggane Gob ny Scuit.' 5 (May 1915): 296–297.
      G.G. 'Old Peel.' 6 (November 1915): 318–329.
      Moore, J. R. 'Folk-Lore Notes. A Lonan Folk Tale. Ewan y Darragh: The Hermit of Struan y Granghie.' 6 (November 1915): 360–363.
      Quine, F. 'Folk-Lore Notes. The White Lady.' 6 (November 1915): 363.
      Cushag. 'Folk-Lore Notes. The Sherragh Vane.' 6 (November 1915): 364.
      Douglas, Mona. 'Folk-Lore Notes. Lezayre Notes.' 7 (May 1916): 416–418.

MK-FIOM   Killip, Margaret. *The Folklore of the Isle of Man.* London: B. T. Batsford Ltd., 1975.

ML   *Manx Life.*

      Quirk, W. T. 'This Haunted Isle.' ii.3 (November/December 72): 15–19.
      Douglas, Mona. 'Why hunt the wren, Robin-y-Bobbin?' ii.3 (November/December 72): 35–36.

MNHL   Manx National Heritage Library manuscripts.

> **MNHL 09702** Letter from Dr John Clague to Deemster Gill, 5 December 1894. Available in Stephen Miller. '"Kiark Catreeney Marroo" Catherine's Hen is Dead.' *Culture Vannin*, www.culturevannin.im/manxfolklore/laal-catreeney-503817
>
> **MNHL MD 522** (MS 06731) Letter from John Quine to A. M. Crellin, 20 February 1898
>
> **MNHL MS 01086c** Letter from Sophia Morrison to J. J. Kneen, Undated

MQ   *Manx Quarterly.*

> Othigill, Juan. 'A Rural Academy: Reminiscences of Lonan.' i.7 (November 1909): 616–617
>
> Othigill, Juan. 'Wishing Wells and Superstitions.' i.9 (October 1910): 766–767
>
> Pitts, Rev Herbert. 'The Cross of St Maughold.' iii.17 (October 1916): 84–86

MT   *Manx Tales by Various Authors.* Douglas: S. K. Broadbent, n.d. [but c.1899].

> Bill Billy. 'Riding the Devil.' 17–20.
>
> 'The Supernatural in the South of the Island.' 29–33.

N   Newspapers.

> **N-MA-13071826** 'Superstition.' *Manks Advertiser,* 13 July 1826.
>
> **N-MH-10011844** '"Witchcraft"!!!' *Mona's Herald*, 10 January 1844.
>
> **N-MH-02061847** 'Sketches by the Way-side.' *Mona's Herald*, 02 June 1847.
>
> **N-MS-02101847** 'More Witchcraft.' *Manx Sun*, 2 October 1847.
>
> **N-MH-20051863** 'The Resurrection Case in Malew.' *Mona's Herald*, 20 May 1863.
>
> **N-MS-26081865** 'Cambrian Archaeological Society.' *Manx Sun*, 26 August 1865.
>
> **N-IOMT-07021874** 'Peel and the West.' *Isle of Man Times*, 7 February 1874.
>
> **N-MH-08041875** 'The Isle of Man in 1874.' *Mona's Herald*, 08 April 1875.
>
> **N-MS-17031877** 'The Archaeological Commission.' *Manx Sun*, 17 March 1877.
>
> **N-IOMT-07061879** 'Our Churches, and Chapels, and Meeting – Houses in the Isle of Man.' *Isle of Man Times*, 7 June 1879.
>
> **N-IOMT-11091886** 'Douglas District.' *Isle of Man Examiner*, 11 September 1886.
>
> **N-MS-11021888** 'Old Customs, VI.' *Manx Sun*, 11 February 1888.
>
> **N-IOMT-31101888** 'Antique Mona: No. V. – Folk-Lore.' *Isle of Man Times,* 31 October 1888.
>
> **N-IOME-26011895** 'Miscellaneous Observations.' *Isle of Man Examiner*, 26 January 1895.
>
> **N-IOME-03091898** 'Manx Folklore.' *Isle of Man Examiner,* 03 September 1898.
>
> **N-IOME-24091898** 'Manx Folklore by A. W. Moore.' *Isle of Man Examiner,* 24 September 1898.

N **N-IOME-01101898** 'Manx Folklore by A. W. Moore.' *Isle of Man Examiner,* 01 October 1898.

N-IOME-08101898 'Manx Folklore by A. W. Moore.' *Isle of Man Examiner,* 08 October 1898.

N-RWT-03121898 'Manx Folklore.' *Ramsey Weekly Times*, 03 December 1898.

N-MH-02051900 'Fairy Stories and Folk-Lore of Manxland.' *Mona's Herald*, 02 May 1900.

N-PCG-02021901 'Manx Reminiscences by Mr T. Crellin.' *Peel City Guardian*, 02 February 1901.

N-IOME-02031901 'What Mr. Thos. Crellin Remembers.' *Isle of Man Examiner,* 02 March 1901.

N-PCG-06041901 'A Buggane Story.' *Peel City Guardian*, 06 April 1901.

N-MS-15031902 'Glewn Nee-a-Nee!' by George Quarrie, *Manx Sun,* 15 March 1902.

N-IOME-29051909 A. W. Moore. 'The November-May Year in Man.' *Isle of Man Examiner.* 29 May 1909.

N-IOME-11061910 'Wishing Wells and Superstitions.' *Isle of Man Examiner,* 11 June 1910.

N-IOME-05121914 'Rushen Place Names.' *Isle of Man Examiner,* 05 December 1914.

N-IOMT-03101936 'More Graves at Peel.' *Isle of Man Times,* 03 October 1936.

N-IOMT-10061939 'In Romantic Agneash.' *Isle of Man Times,* 10 June 1939.

N-IOME-15091939 'The Professor and the Phynnodderee - No.31.' *Isle of Man Examiner,* 15 September 1939.

N-RC-03081951 'Governor with the Antiquarians: Visit to Shellag.' *Ramsey Courier,* 03 August 1951.

N-IOME-24081951 'Letter Box.' *Isle of Man Examiner,* 24 August 1951.

N-IOME-21081953 'No Barley Grows Jere – By Order of St Patrick.' *Isle of Man Examiner,* 21 August 1953.

N-MH-20011953 'John Kneen's Note-Book.' *Mona's Herald,* 20 January 1953.

N-MH-27011953 'John Kneen's Note-Book.' *Mona's Herald,* 27 January 1953.

N-IOME-16101953 'Romantic Home of a Manx Merchant Prince.' *Isle of Man Examiner,* 16 October 1953.

N-RC-10111961 'Ballaugh Glen, Ravensdale and Glen Doo.' *Ramsey Courier,* 10 November 1961.

NM-OSV Mathieson, Neil. *Onchan, Isle of Man: The story of a Village.* Douglas: Island Development Co. Ltd. (n.d.).

OS OS Maps.

OS-25-VIII.7 OS Map, 1/2500, Sheet VIII. 7, Published 1869.

OS-25-XIII.11 OS Map, 1/2500, Sheet XIII.11, Published 1869.

PIOMNHAS *Proceedings of the Isle of Man Natural History and Antiquarian Society*

Kermode, P. M. C. 'Report of the Archaeological Section.' i.7 (December 1911): 267–269.

'First Report of the Archaeological Survey.' i.7 (December 1911): 277–300.

Morrison, S. 'Manx Dialect connected to the Fairies.' i.9 (August 1914): 561–562.

Kermode, P. M. C. 'Third Report of the Archaeological Survey Committee.' i.9 (August 1914): 605–631.

'Excursion to the Barony, Maughold. [Mr P. M. C. Kermode, Leader].' ii. 1 (February 1923): 15–16.

'Excursion to Marown. [Leader, Rev. A. E. Clarke, Vicar].' ii.1, (February 1923): 17–21.

'Excursion to Skyhill and Glen Auldyn. [Leader: Mr. P. M. C. Kermode].' ii.1 (February 1923): 22–28.

'Excursion to 'Manannan Country,' 20 August 1921.' ii.3 (4 October 1917 to 13 March 1923): 202–204.

'Excursion in the Parish of German, 29 June 1922.' ii.3 (4 October 1917 to 13 March 1923): 210–211.

Quine, Rev. Canon. 'Report of Archaeological section. 1924-25.' ii.4 (31 May 1923 to 30 April 1926): 526–532.

Cubbon, W. 'Notes on Marown Church. By William Cubbon.' iii.1 (28 May 1925 to 17 April 1926): 13–22.

Kneen, J. J. 'Manx fairs and festivals. Part I – Pagan.' iii.1 (28 May 1925 to 17 April 1926): 38–56.

Kneen, J. J. 'Manx fairs and festivals. Part II – Christian.' iii.1 (28 May 1925 to 17 April 1926): 56–82.

'Excursion to the Point of Ayre. G. J. H. Neely, Leader. 21 May 1927.' iii.3 (17 February 1927 to 12 April 1928): 197.

Cubbon, W. 'The Royal Way. W. Cubbon. Read at Keeill Abban, 28 July, 1927.' iii.3 (17 February 1927 to 12 April 1928): 217–222.

Shimmin, C. R. 'Peel Castle. C. R. Shimmin, H.K. 25 August 1927.' iii.3 (17 February 1927 to 12 April 1928): 229–231.

'Excursion to Knocksharry, Etc. Leader: C. H. Cowley. 13 September 1928.' iii.4 (12 April 1928 to 17 April 1930): 279–280.

Cowley, C. H. 'President's Address. C. H. Cowley. 18th April, 1929.' iii.4 (12 April 1928 to 17 April 1930): 346–352.

Cubbon, William. 'Discovery of Pre-Historic Oak Vessel. By, F.R.S.A.I. 21st February 1932' iii.5 (22 May 1930 to 31 March 1932): 526–532.

'Excursion to Santon. 29th June, 1933. Leader- Revd. E. H. Stenning, M.A.' iv.1 (19 May 1932 to 28 March 1935): 51–53.

'Excursion to Corvally District.' iv.2 (16 May 1935 to 25 March 1937): 131–136

Cowley, C. H. 'Excavations at Peel Castle, 1929.' iv.2 (16 May 1935 to 25 March 1937): 165–174.

PIOMNHAS Bruce, J. R. 'Excursion to South Barrule, August 20th, 1936.' iv.2 (16 May 1935 to 25 March 1937): 200–205.

'Excursion to Santan. June 17th, 1937. Leader: Mr. Richard Lace.' iv.3 (27 May 1937- 31 December 1939): 268–271.

Cowin, Hilda. 'The Parish of Lonan. December 6th, 1938. By Miss Hilda Cowin.' iv.3 (27 May 1937 – 31 December 1939): 325–335.

'Excursion to Agneash, 18th May, 1939. Leader: Mr James Mylchreest.' iv.3 (27 May 1937 – 31 December 1939): 368–369.

Craine, David. 'Some notes on the Parish of Ballaugh.' Iv.3 (1939): 469–470.

'Excursion to Santan, 19th June, 1941. Rev. E. H. Stenning.' iv.4 (March 1940 – March 1942): 579–581.

Craine, David. 'Kirk Patrick of Jurby.' v.1 (April 1942- March 1946): 28–47.

Craine, David. 'Milntown.' v.2 (April 1946 – March 1950): 63–69.

Cubbon, W. 'The Ceasars of Ballahick, Kirk Malew.' v.2 (April 1946 – March 1950): 70–72.

Cowley, J. W. 'Historic Features of St John's.' v.5 (April 1954 – March 1956): 524–531.

Garrad, Larch S. 'The Archaeology and Tradition of some Prehistoric and Early Christian Religious Practices in the Isle of Man.' x.1 (1992): 79–103.

PMCK-MAS Kermode, P. M. C. *The Manx Archaeological Survey. A Re-Issue of the First Five Reports (1909–1918). 1909–1935.* Douglas: Manx Museum and National Trust, 1968.

PMCK-MC Kermode, P. M. C. *Manx Crosses.* London: Bemrose & Sons Ltd., 1907. Reprint. Balgavies, Angus: The Pinkfoot Press, 1994.

RJK-SIOM Kelly, Robert James. *Sketches of the Isle of Man.* London: Simpkin, Marshall & Co., 1844.

RP-MA Patterson, Robert. *Manx Antiquities; or Remarks on the Present Condition of the Antiquarian Remains of the Isle of Man, especially those situated around its coast line.* St Andrews: Cupar-Fife, 1863.

SH-HSDV Haining, Samuel. *A Historical Sketch and Descriptive View of the Isle of Man.* Liverpool: Harris and Co., 1824.

SM-MFT Morrison, Sophia. *Manx Fairy Tales.* Second ed., Peel: L. Morrison, 1929. Reprint. Douglas: The Manx Experience, 1998.

TC-BMV Cowell, Thomas M. *Baldwin, My Valley: The Life and Times of Thomas M. Cowell.* Ed. Gordon N. Kniveton. Douglas: The Manx Experience, 1990.

TK-FJ Kelly, Thomas. *Thomas Kelly and Famaly's Journal.* Ed. Margery West. Douglas: Times Press and Anthony Gibbs & Phillips, 1965.

VAMD Moore, A. W., Morrison, Sophia and Goodwin, Edmund, eds. *A Vocabulary of the Anglo-Manx Dialect.* London: Oxford University Press, 1924. Reprint. St Judes: Yn Cheshaght Ghailckagh, 1991.

WC-IH   Cubbon, William. *Island Heritage: Dealing with some phases of Manx history*. Manchester: George Falkner & Sons Ltd., 1952.

WC-WCF   Cashen, William. William Cashen's *Folk-lore*. Ed. Sophia Morrison. Douglas: Manx Language Society, 1912.

WCR-KBM   Radcliffe, William and Constance. *Kirk Bride: A miscellany*. Douglas: Nelson Press Company Ltd., 1982.

WCR-MRP   Radcliffe, William and Constance. *Maughold and Ramsey Place-names*. Inverness, 1978.

WH-DIM   Harrison, William, ed. *A Description of the Isle of Man*. 1744. Manx Society, vol. xi. Douglas: Manx Society, 1865.

WH-MM1   Harrison, William. *Mona Miscellany: A selection of Proverbs, Sayings, Ballads, Customs, Superstitions, and Legends, Peculiar to the Isle of Man*. Manx Society, vol. xvi. Douglas: Manx Society, 1871.

WH-MM2   Harrison, William. *Mona Miscellany: A selection of Proverbs, Sayings, Ballads, Customs, Superstitions, and Legends, Peculiar to the Isle of Man, Second Series*. Manx Society, vol. xxi. Douglas: Manx Society, 1873.

WHG-MNM   Gill, W. H. *Manx National Music*. London: Boosey & Co. 1898.

WK-KP   Kennish, William. 'The Kione Prash or the Brazen Head of Lewaigue.' *Mannanan-Beg Mac-y-Leirr… and The Kione Prash or Brazen Head of Lewaigue*. Douglas: S. K. Broadbent & Co., n.d. Reprint. 'The Chione Prash or the Brazen Head, A Manx Legend.' Robert W. Stimpson ed., *William Kennish: Manninagh Dooie – True Manxman*. Douglas: Robert Stimpson, 2011, 399–413.

WK-MI   Kennish, William. *Mona's Isle and Other Poems*. London: J. Bradley & Simpkin, Marshall & Co., 1844. Reprint. Robert W. Stimpson ed. *William Kennish: Manninagh Dooie – True Manxman*. Douglas: Robert Stimpson, 2011.

'Mona's Isle. Canto II.' 507–527.
'Old May Eve.' 533–544.

WL-DPG   *Ward & Lock's Descriptive and Pictorial Guide to the Isle of Man*. London: Ward, Lock, and Co., 1883.

WS-AIOM   Sacheverell, William. *An Account of the Isle of Man*. Manx Society, vol. i. Douglas: Manx Society, 1859.

WWG-MS1   Gill, W. Walter. *A Manx Scrapbook*. London: Arrowsmith, 1929.

WWG-MS2   Gill, W. Walter. *A Second Manx Scrapbook*. London: Arrowsmith, 1932.

WWG-MS3   Gill, W. Walter. *A Third Manx Scrapbook*. London: Arrowsmith, 1963.

YLM   *Yn Lioar Manninagh.*

'The Monument known as King Orry's Grave compared with tumuli in Gloucestershire, A. W. Buckland M.A.I. (Read February 7, 1889).' i.2 (1889): 42–50.

'Excursion to Sulby Glen, August 28, 1889. Leader: F. S. Tellet, L.K.Q.C.P.I.' i.4 (1889): 95–96.

F.S.T. 'Place Names. Lezayre.' i.4 (1889): 99–103.

'Excursion to Druidale.' i.7 (1890): 123–125.

'Proceedings and Transactions. Folk Lore.' i.6 (1890): 169–172.

'Excursion to Kirk Bride, July 22nd, 1890. Leader: P. M. C. Kermode, F.S.A., Scot.' i.7 (1890): 181–182.

'Folklore.' i.7 (1890): 189–191.

'Folklore' i.8 (1891): 221–223.

Roeder, C. 'Folklore collected by Mr. C. R. Roeder, of Manchester.' i.9 (1892): 289–292.

'Excursion to Michael, September 1st, 1891. Leader: J. C. Crellin, M.A., M.H.K, &c.' i.10 (1892): 307–308.

Moore, A. W. 'The Cup of Ballafletcher.' i.10 (1892): 318–319.

Roeder, C. 'Manx Folklore, 1882 to 1885. Collected by C. Roeder, Manchester. (From Lezayre).' i.10 (1892): 323–328.

Harrison, Rev. S. N. 'On some antiquities at Kirk Maughold.' i.11 (1892): 382–387.

'Excursion to Marown, June 30, 1892. Leader: A. W. Moore, M.A., F.R.H.S., Etc.' ii (1901): 2–3.

'Excursion to Conchan, July 26, 1892. Leader: T. Kneen, M.H.K.' ii (1901): 4–5.

'An account of the Parish of Marown (1776.). Written by John Christian, Vicar, for Thomas Pennant, Antiquary. (From a MS. belonging to A. W. Moore, M.A.).' ii (1901): 29–31.

Kelly, Henry. 'Ballaqueeny Cronk, The Clagh-Ard or Crosh Ballaqueeny, and Cronk How Mooar.' ii (1901): 47–51.

'Excursion to Glen Aldyn, Thursday, October 5, 1893. Leader - Dr Tellet, F.E.G.S., President.' ii (1901): 86–88.

Kewley, Rev. J. 'Antiquities of the Parish of Arbory.' ii (1901): 103–106.

Bradbury, Dr 'Rhullick y Keeil Khallane, Lonan.' ii (1901): 115–116.

Crellin, A. M. 'Some antiquarian notes in the Parish of Kirk Michael.' ii (1901): 122–126.

Crellin, A. M. 'Report of the Folklore and Place-Name Section.' ii (1901): 194–197.

Roeder, C. 'Contributions to the Folk Lore of the Isle of Man. By C. Roeder, Manchester' iii.4 (1897): 129–191.

Crellin, A. M. 'Report of the Anthropological Section. Folk-Lore.' iii.6 (1898): 285–287

YLM

Moore, A. W. 'Folk-Medicine in the Isle of Man.' Iii.6 (1898): 303–314.

'Excursion to Poortown, St German's (14th September, 1897). Leader- Mr P. M. C. Kermode, F.S.A., Scot., &c.' iii.8 (1898): 318–319.

Crellin, A. M. 'Report of Anthropological Section. Folk Lore.' iii.8 (1898): 379–380

Quine, Rev. John. 'Notes on Moore's Surnames and Place Names in the Isle of Man.' iii.9 (1899): 444–451.

Crellin, A. M. 'Report of the Anthropological Section. Folk-Lore.' iii.10 (1899): 482–486

'Excursion to St Mark's and Ballasalla. July 20, 1899. Leaders - Rev. A. J. Holmes and Mr. G. Patterson.' iii.11 (1901): 502–503.

'Excursion to the Sloc. September 8, 1899. Leader- Rev. C. H. Leece, Vicar of Rushen.' iii.11 (1901): 504–506.

Morrison, S. 'Manx Folk-Lore Notes. By Miss S. Morrison.' iv (1910): 154–176.

Glossary

Battle of Skyhill   A battle of 1079, resulting in victory for the Viking invaders and Godred Crovan becoming king of the Isle of Man.

Ben varrey   A woman of the sea, a mermaid.

Binjean   Junket, a milk-based dessert made with rennet.

Blood-charmer   A person who can stop bleeding by a charm, normally spoken.

Broogh   The sloped side of a hill or the coastline.

Buggane   A monster of various or shifting forms.

Buitcheragh   Witchcraft. To be 'buitched' is to have witchcraft done to you.

Cabbal   Chapel. A term sometimes used for keeills.

Cabbyl ushtey   Water horse, a creature similar to a horse but which lives in water and comes out at night seeking to drown anyone foolish enough to climb onto its back.

Caillagh   An old woman to be found in lonely places, often with large teeth and seeking to eat people. Less frequently, a caillagh can be an old woman known for her way with charms or magic.

Cairn   A pile of stones either covering a burial site or acting as a landmark.

Cashtal   Castle, fort or other similar fortification.

Chibbyr   A well or spring.

Craythur   Creature.

Curragh   A wetland or bog.

Death Coach   A ghostly coach or carriage associated with a funeral or a death. It is normally seen or heard along a road leading to a church.

Dooinney oie   The Night Man, a reclusive and frequently ill-tempered figure known for his loud shouting at night, normally done to warn of imminent bad weather.

Dooinney marrey   A man of the sea, a merman.

Earthwork   An ancient structure made of earth.

Evil Eye   Bad luck or harm transferred by a look from an ill-wisher.

Fairies   Little people who share our Island. They can sometimes be encountered at night and normally in remote places engaged in activities such as hunting, fishing or feasting. They can be disruptive, dangerous or vindictive. The term 'fairy' is also sometimes used to refer to unknown otherworldly or unexplained things.

Foawr	Giant.
Glashtyn / glashtin / glashtan	Variously applied to figures resembling the phynnodderee or the cabbyl ushtey. The spelling is left as per the original source wherever possible, in recognition of the variant spellings and the creature being identified.
Gef	The Dalby Spook, better known internationally as 'the talking mongoose.' A creature or spirit capable of speech, telekinesis and other strange abilities. He lived alongside a family in a remote house in Patrick in the 1930s.
Hop tu Naa	31 October. A day of activities, customs and traditions marking the start of the winter half of the year.
Hunt the Wren	The tradition of parading a captured wren around the streets on 26 December. It continues today with singing and dancing but no birds are now harmed.
Illiam Dhone	William Christian (1608–1663). A well-known figure of Manx history, executed at Hango Hill for his actions during the Civil War.
Keeill	An early medieval Christian chapel.
Laa Boaldyn	1 May. A day of traditions and celebrations marking the start of summer.
Laa'l Catreeney	6 December. The feast day of St. Catherine, celebrated most remarkably in Arbory.
Lhiannan-shee	A female spirit most commonly to be found in remote or lonely places, who permanently attaches to a man who speaks to or engages with her in some way.
Loaghtan	A breed of sheep native to the Isle of Man, distinctive with its brown fleece and many horns.
Manannan	The Isle of Man's pre-Christian god and first ruler. Amongst his many wonderous activities, he is known for covering the Island with mist to hide it from potential invaders.
MHK	Member of the House of Keys, an elected member of the lower house of the Isle of Man's parliament.
Midden	Dung heap.
Moddey doo	Black dog, a mysterious, ominous or dangerous creature. (Plural: moddee doo).
Mooinjer veggey	The little people (or folk), a name for the fairies.
Oie Voaldyn	30 April. The final day of the winter half of the year. A day of trepidation and tradition, as a person's luck or prosperity is most open to outside influence at this time of year.
Ooig	Cave.

Phynnodderee   A large, hairy, strong and helpful creature wary of human contact. A number of variant spellings have been recorded.

Pinjean   A traditional Manx dessert of milk curdled with rennet.

Promontory fort   An ancient fortification on a headland.

Raad ny Foillan   The coastal footpath around the Isle of Man.

Rhullick   A medieval burial ground, frequently surrounding a keeill.

Scaa olk   A malevolent shadow, a hostile or disruptive spirit projected by a living person.

Spooyt   A spout of water, a waterfall.

Tarroo ushtey   Water bull, a beast which lives in water but is otherwise almost indistinguishable from a normal bull. It is much feared, though its threat is normally restricted to livestock. (Plural: terriu ushtey).

Tholtan   A ruined abandoned house.

Tramman   An elder tree.

Tumulus   A mound of earth and stones raised over a grave or graves.

Tynwald   The parliament of the Isle of Man.

White Lady   A ghostly female spirit with a white appearance.

Index

H

M

N

O

P

R

S

T

U

V

W